E-GOVERNMENT AND PUBLIC SECTOR PROCESS REBUILDING

T0138052

E-government and Public Sector Process Rebuilding

Dilettantes, Wheel Barrows, and Diamonds

by

Kim Viborg Andersen

Copenhagen Business School,
Denmark

KLUWER ACADEMIC PUBLISHERS
BOSTON / DORDRECHT / LONDON

ISBN 978-1-4419-5458-9   e-ISBN 978-1-4020-7995-5

ISBN 1-4020-7995-8 (e-book)

Published by Kluwer Academic Publishers,
P.O. Box 17, 3300 AA Dordrecht, The Netherlands.

Sold and distributed in North, Central and South America
by Kluwer Academic Publishers,
101 Philip Drive, Norwell, MA 02061, U.S.A.

In all other countries, sold and distributed
by Kluwer Academic Publishers,
P.O. Box 322, 3300 AH Dordrecht, The Netherlands.

Printed on acid-free paper

Contents

Contents

Preface

Writing a book on information systems (IS) in government turned out to be targeting the market at a time when the topic of e-government is sprouting. Clearly, I am happy to have launched a book that hopefully can help drive the e-government race in the right direction. Most e-government plans are at the surface stylish and confident in their capacity to transform their country, county, municipality, and city. Under the first layer of confidence, there is little information on where the right direction lead to, what resources it will take to get there, who is getting there, and what will be the impacts.

We present a series of studies and observations that governments at present are taking the wrong track if the benefits of e-government is to be any different from the benefits achieved from information technology (IT) so far. The PPR-approach we launch in this book is not a guarantee for reaching the right goals. The goals and aims of the IT applications need to be identified in the organization of the activities that starts and ends with the customers. This book provides guidelines and inspiration for how these can be approached.

"*E-government and Public Sector Process Rebuilding: Dilettantes, Wheelbarrows, and Diamonds*" is chosen as the title of this book to reflect three overall goals.

First, the aim is to give a *constructive input to rebuild and improve the processes* in which the public sector perform *activities and interact* with the citizens, companies, and the formal elected decision-makers. The ambition is not to attack the public sector per se or to argue that no public sector should exist. That would a wrong motivation to adopt this book and would contradict the objectives of the PPR-approach launched in this book.

Second, we want to *emphasize information systems as the vehicle* for change. The book covers a *range of applications and technologies other than internet technologies* to demonstrate the plethora of technologies that are part of PPR.

Third, the subtitle of the book reflects that there are serious capability challenges in the public sector inhibiting the transformation towards activity and customer centric applications. The *dilettantes* in the public sector are in need of upgrading, rethinking, and refocusing their use of IS. Part of this involves a revisit of the extensive use of *digital wheel barrows* to transmit data, and complement the transaction focus with IT-enabled analysis of the activities. Also, there is a need to recognize that IS are not only flashy and shining *diamonds* to be shown off on special occasions. IS are, as are most diamonds, produced to be part of a set of activities and are intended for replacement whenever the diamonds are no longer serving their intended purpose.

The book should as such be seen as an input to researchers and graduate and Ph.D. students. Equally important readership for this book is the practitioner group comprised of public servants, managers, policy makers, consultant, and IT-suppliers. Consequently the book is written in a style and format that should appeal to both groups. The book downplays the more rigorous part of the arguments, tables, and figures although there are still be a few places with rather complex data and tables.

This book has had a long birth and the publisher has been very patient waiting for the final manuscript. The research and writing up of the pieces has been going through a series of drafting, comments from colleagues, students, and governmental workers. Without their comments, I would not have been able to complete the book.

Chapter 3 of this book was developed from a joint research project with Professor James N. Danziger from University of California at Irvine. Although the chapter has been conceptualized, reiterated, and rephrased, the bulk of that chapter and the research conducted is a result of joint forces rather than the results of my work only.

I am in debt to Department of Informatics at the Copenhagen Business School who granted me the opportunity to complete this book and provided the physical facilities to enable me to do so. During 2003, whilst the final outline and research for this book was completed, I was happy to benefit from the friendly atmosphere at the Department of Economics, Statistics, and Information Systems (ESI), Örebro University in Sweden. I am also appreciative of the School of Information Systems at Deakin University in Australia who hosted me during January 2004 where the last elements of this book emerged.

The text has been carefully proofread by Angela Wyatt from New Zealand and Birgitte Bush from the Department of Informatics at the Copenhagen Business School. Last, but certainly not least, Vicki Antosz has done an outstanding job in formatting, entering, and keeping track of the versions and iterations of this book.

Any errors that remain are clearly on my behalf only.

March 2004
Kim Viborg Andersen

Chapter 1

PRESENTATION OF THE PPR-MODEL

1. INTRODUCTION

Reorganizing work processes using information systems (IS) has been a focal point for consultancy work in the private and the public sectors. Ongoing modernization of management in the public sector, gray-zone/ semi-public organizations, and virtual/ teleworking/ Internet use are some of the organizational features that form a dynamic triangle of technical, organizational and institutional changes. These have altered the face of the public sector and paved the road for what we in this book label "Public Sector Process Rebuilding Using Information Systems" and use the abbreviation PPR.

With governmental expenditures on IS still escalating annually, rather than diminishing, it is evident that government has been seeking a return on their efforts to implement new IS in their organizations. For government, the motives to invest in IS may include issues such as; does R&D expenditures lead to higher economic growth? Does computerization of the public offices lead to savings in manpower, better service, and more services? Does interaction with citizens and companies improve? It is apparent that the use of IS does not live up to expectations and is a continual source of vexation for the government.

One way to solve the puzzle of missing benefits from IS-investments is to *increase the number of variables* and *approaches* to find valid explanations for *why IS does not always match the intentions, expectations, and needs.* The interest in factors leading to a successful implementation has spanned from technical issues, environmental concerns, organizational factors, and political issues. Parallel with the increase in number of variables, a growing variety of research disciplines have been brought together to solve the puzzle of the missing impacts of IS.

Another approach to solve the missing value riddle is to *refine the measurements of what constitutes successful implementation arguing for a change in focus* from assumed impacts to the exploitation rather than just the use of IS (Willcocks et al. 1997). Following this line of argument, IS-management rather than the magnitude and altitude of IS application is the key to understand how internal and external work *processes at micro, meso and macro level* of government can be improved.

The third track we want to highlight is the issue of the use of IS in government. From one perspective, government represents an institutional user that can implement new IS in a top-down command style. A competing view is to either follow *actor-network approaches* (Akrich 1994; Bijker 1994) and/ or *user centric-approaches* thus shifting the focus to the affiliations, environments, interactions, and identities of the social actors in government (Lamb and Kling 2003). In a governmental setting, it is important to consider this approach since the borderline between government, business and civil society often is blurred.

The final route that we highlight is the *government versus governance approach.* By governance, we refer to the "interaction between the formal institutions and those in civil society...a process whereby elements in society wield power, authority and influence and enact policies and decisions concerning public life and social upliftment" (Council-for-Excellence-in-Government 2001). By government, we imply the organization in charge of governing a political unit. We can distinguish between the two modes by asking the questions "who is using the IS?" versus "how is government using IS?" Often, the intention is to improve government rather than governance by using IS.

The four avenues that government and researchers have followed in their (studies of) implementing IS (segmented versus multi- and interdisciplinary studies, adoption versus exploitation, institutional versus user centric approaches, government versus governance) form the foundation of our PPR-concept in the sense that each dimension includes issues of which an understanding is imperative in order to rebuild the processes. There are indeed *various obstacles for reorganizing government*, such as the extreme *openness of the public sector organizations.* For example, every piece of information has to be filed. All applications have to be treated equally. Also, public *organizations rarely change in any rapid nor top-down manner.* Rather, they change in an incremental manner and only partly top-down. Whilst this applies to a large part of the public sector, the increased use of teleworking, virtual organizations, and quangos/ semi-governmental organizations, make us more optimistic about the prospects of reorganizing the "business processes" in the public sector.

1.1 Why IS in Government?

Despite IS in government being a research issues for many years - with highlights such as the Reinforcement Hypothesis (Danziger et al. 1982), the Dutton & Kraemer study on Fiscal Impact Budgeting Systems (Dutton and Kraemer 1985), the Osborne and Gaebler book on reinventing government (Osborne and Gaebler 1992) and the book on Public Administration in the Information Age (Snellen and Donk 1998) – the field still lacks a coherent approach to theory and theory building. In fact it is very difficult to point to any major area or field of government utilizing IS theories or theory building (Weick 1989; Whetten 1989).

The PPR method presented in this book calls for more action research (Argyris et al. 1985) and equally welcome studies that discuss the ontological, epistemological, methodological, and axiological dimensions of the PPR-approach (Fitzgerald and Howcroft 1998).

Beyond the need to build a more coherent research community, there are three overall arguments for doing research on IS in government. First of all, there is a high level of *policy saliency* and funding of development. There is also a potential to successfully implement application in areas such as health care and develop new generations of vertical and horizontal infrastructure.

Second, there are solid *scale* arguments for doing research on IS in government. Government might be decentralized and segmented in silos, but at the application level most applications are identical or even shared across departments. With the diversified user environment, this provides unique opportunities to study variance in the implementation of applications.

The third argument for researching IS in government is that researchers might have easier *access to quantitative and qualitative data* sources as compared to those researchers who investigate the private sector. Although issues on privacy, confidentiality, etc. are research components in both the private and public sector, the public sector might be keener to open the gates for researchers.

2. REORGANIZING THE PROCESSES

The concept of reorganizing processes originates in the basic questions; Are we doing our business in the most optimal way? Are we doing our job well enough? Are we giving all we've got? (Osborne and Gaebler 1992). The last question is just as crucial for the public sector as for any other large

organization, although it may be disputable whether its members contemplate enough. For example, in the mid-1990s OECD emphasized the following significant areas in facilitating the exacting of maximum organizational benefits from IS (OECD 1995):
– enhancing management, planning and control of the IS functions
– using technology to redesign and improve administrative processes
– providing better access to quality information
– harnessing the potential of new technologies
– developing and applying standards
– attracting and retaining high-caliber IS professionals
– increasing research into the economic, social, legal and political
  implications of new IS opportunities; and
– assessing experiences

Although we find that "using technology to redesign and improve administration processes" is on the OECD list, we may ask whether IS can be used to radically transform public organizations? The arguments twist around questions such as: Can IS be used to enable organizational changes in an instrumentalistic manner? Can organizations be changed at all? Do they change? If so, what is the nature of these changes? And, is it an incremental or a rapid diffusion process?

Within the private sector, concepts of reorganization, redesigning and reengineering the processes have gained enormous popularity and —— some argue —— produced valuable impacts on the actual practices. Besides the initial articles and books (Davenport and Short 1990; Hammer 1990; Hammer and Champy 1993), numerous books have been published illustrating how IS has affected dramatic and radical changes in organizations (Davenport and Stoddard 1994). Although BPR has been applied in the public sector (MacIntosh 2003), the public administration research community did not applaud the reengineering concepts as breaking new ground. Rather, they jeered that BPR was at best old wine in new bottles. At worst, BPR applied in the public sector would lead to misjudgment and actions inconsistent with the 'spirit' of the public sector.

The BPR approach emphasizes that changes in processes should be dramatic rather than incremental. Also, the approach points to broad, cross-functional processes and, if needed, a radical change is required towards implementing such processes. This of course involves a high risk of failure as well. Is risk part of the rationale of the public sector? Traditionally speaking, the answer would be a quick, resounding NO, but in 1997 we were not so fast to claim that taking risks is uncharacteristic of the public sector.

First of all, one part of the BPR tradition emphasizes short term efficiency and long-term strategic advancement. However, as noted by Coombs and Hull, during the 1990s a "soft BPR" emerged, emphasizing human costs and benefits (Coombs and Hull 1996), and in 2002 one of the original authors of the BPR-approach introduced the X-engineering approach. The cross-engineering approach replaced the original focus of BPR on fundamental, radical, and dramatic processes, with a key focus on technology, connectivity, efficiency, and value for customers (Champy 2002). In this book we will argue that this shift makes part of the BPR-techniques more applicable to the public sector and helps to close the possible gap between private and public sector BPR-approaches.

Second, the face of the public sector is changing radically not only with rightsizing and downsizing, but also in organization and leadership. It is old news that public services do not inevitably have to be performed by the public sector employees. By all means, contract them out. Form quangos. Farm out, but keep a short leash on the administrative power. And don't forget to take steering and delegating seriously. These are just some of the central shifts in public sector management during the 1980s and mid-1990s that make it uncertain whether the public sector is overly risk wary.

Within the public sector, scholars affiliated with the *US National Academy of Public Administration* define reengineering as: "...a radical improvement approach that critically examines rethinks and redesigns mission product and service processes within a political environment. It achieves dramatic mission performance and gains from multiple customer and stakeholder perspectives. It is a key part of a process management approach to aim for an optimal performance that continually evaluates, adjusts, or removes processes."

Likewise, the BPR concept argues that "researchers...and managers.. must begin to think of process change as a mediating factor between the IT initiative and economic return" (ibid. cit., p. 46). Thus, IT is not seen as the sole factor that can lead to a miraculous outcome. Instead, process reengineering is. However, IT is given the role as the almighty enabler connecting individuals, work groups and departments: "to suggest that process designs be developed independently of IS or other enablers is to ignore valuable tools for shaping processes" . In Davenport's work, the impacts from IT on process innovation are grouped in nine categories: *automational* (eliminating human labor from a process), *informational* (capturing process information for the purposes of understanding), *sequential* (changing process sequence), *tracking* (closely monitoring process status and objects), *analytical* (improving analysis of information and decision-making), *geographical* (coordinating processes across distances), *integrative* (coordination between tasks and processes), *intellectual* (capturing and distributing intellectual assets), and *disintermediating* (eliminating intermediaries from a process).

Although these impacts differ slightly from the findings that our research has identified for the public sector, they form a solid basis for addressing the use of IS within the service development, fulfillment and logistical functions of the public sector. In Table 1.1, we have used Davenport's list and adjusted it according to the public sector functions.

Table 1-1. IT and Process Reengineering: Development, Fulfillment and Logistical Functions in the Public Sector

Service/ Product Development	Service/ Product Fulfillment	Logistical Functions
Automational, informational, and sequential processes	Product choice systems Integrate services One-stop service	Locational systems
Simulation systems	Microanalysis and forecasting	Recognition systems
Tracking systems	Voice communication effectiveness Remote access by the public to government information and services	Asset management systems
Decision analysis systems	Virtual compositions	Logistical planning systems
Interorganizational Communication systems (integrative and geographical)	Interorganizational communications	Telemetry
Intellectual assets	Textual composition Simplification or elimination of routine and repetitive tasks	Textual composition

Source: Developed after Davenport (1993), pp. 50-63

Table 1.1 captures three core functions of the public sector's work processes. The first core function is the *ongoing innovation of the products and services* delivered by the public sector. The second function is the *fulfillment of the services/ products to the users* of the public sector (politicians, citizens, companies, other public organizations, international organizations. The third function of the public sector's work processes is *"bookkeeping" and ongoing planning* in the public sector, here labeled logistical systems.

Within the social welfare administration, IS has been applied to increase the *ongoing innovation of work processes* in case-handling. Within this area, it is also IT that enables the public administration to track case status. It might imply that when Peggy Sue submits an application for housing and/ or for a subsidy to a public housing authority, a variety of actions will be triggered from several public agencies. The status of the application and the processing time will be important to Peggy Sue, and here IT-enabled tracking can help. At the same time, it may lead to an awareness of the work processes and their eventual reorganization.

IT is also a powerful tool in facilitating integrative organizations and engaging in dialogues with agencies and various administrative levels of government spread over *different geographical locations*. In this area of IT applications, we have also placed forecasting and models. The use of the Internet or Intranet can aid co-operation in designing new procedures avoiding long flights and wasteful commuting time. In addition, knowledge workers in the public sector often need to access the same kind of data to design new work procedures. IS can be used to rationalize the use of the *intellectual assets* in the organization by providing easy access to frequently used data. For example, easy access can be granted to the budget of the organization, the current account, documents describing work processes, etc.

IT can also be used to *reorganize the service fulfillment*. Meeting the citizens' needs is essential for the public sector. Yet, quite often the employee has to choose between several solutions to match the requirements specified by the citizen. Sophisticated product choice systems are ideal for optimizing the needs of the citizens, while simultaneously balancing the financial constraints of the public sector's activities. EDI and web-based e-procurement and the *one-stop services* for the citizens are examples of how IS reorganizes service fulfillment.

Likewise, voice communication is essential for responding quickly to the voice of users of the public services and the professional inter- and intraorganizational communication. Computer-based voice response mail and answering machines have been catching up in public offices. In the US, the use of touch-tone based services have been spreading guiding the user through a sequence of events to enable e-services. In other countries, as the Scandinavian countries, the voice response mail has not been at the edge, although in areas such as taxation they are still widespread in use.

The use of *logistical systems* is prevalent in planning functions. An example where IS can be applied for serving logistical functions, is within the health sector. Scheduling nurses' work week is a highly complicated matter, the optimizing of financial issues while considering labor market regulations, etc. Logistical planning systems can help keep a record of regulations, stock of workers, etc. Also, IS allows remote monitoring of items/ processes. For instance, cars passing through a toll booth on a Singapore toll road do not need to toss money in a receptor or in the hands of an attendant. Instead, smart cards with bar codes are read rapidly using telemetry. In addition, Singapore's central government is in charge of exchanging data on various import/ export issues, such as international trade bodies, traders, intermediaries, financial institutions, and port and airport authorities. Exchanging data involves for example collecting, manipulating and transmitting data. By implementing new IS and reorganizing the work processes in the Trade Development Board, the Singapore authorities were

able to handle more cases, reduce the staff, and increase efficiency as well
(Teo et al. 1997).

3.   INDICATORS OF CHANGE IN INSTITUTIONAL
SETTING FOR IS USE

During the 1980s and 1990s, governments have been committed to de-
bureaucratization and viewed privatization as a means to achieve this goal.
The governments in most first world countries have behaved in line with this
strategy. In fact, the concept of privatization has been used in different ways
in recent years. Privatization may imply the sale of assets, contracting out,
introduction of user charges, voucher schemes, deregulation and government
withdrawal from public obligations.

The main objective of the modernization programs has been to improve
public services for citizens and companies, to use resources more efficiently,
and to halt the public sector expansion. Also, we have seen numerously

Table 1-2. Trends in the Public Administration Reforms

Areas / Core of trend	Implications for public administration
Reinventing democracy	Treating citizens as customers and including them in the process of governance
Business Process Reengineering	Business Process Reengineering achieves more dramatic changes than traditional quality management techniques
Information Systems	The rapid advance of information systems is providing dramatically better ways of simplifying government and involving citizens
Alternative Mechanisms for Government	Quangos / Public Sector Private Partnerships
Outcomes and Performance	Identifying and measuring desired outcomes, reporting results, and holding government accountable for those results
Partnerships	New Intergovernmental, Public/ Private, and Labor/ Management partnerships
Cutting Red Tape	Developing strategies for results also requires that we reform human resource, budget, procurement and other rule-based systems by cutting red tape
Rightsizing / Downsizing	Governments are responding with rightsizing/ downsizing efforts drawn from these concepts
Community Based Strategies	Strategies must achieve better service outputs for resources expended
	Inclusion of citizens and capitalizing on their diversity are constants in achieving these strategies

Source: Developed from inspiration drawn from the OECD (1995)

budget reforms, the introduction of management techniques from the private sector, de-bureaucratization, decentralization, experiments with more independent local governments, and a more flexible job structure within the public sector.

Budget reforms simplified many of the financial procedures within public institutions during the 1980s. Instead of practicing some highly complex budgeting and accounting procedures, many public institutions became free to act within a given financial limit during the 1990s (Andersen et al. 1996).

Management techniques from the private sector are now more widely applied. Corporate management techniques are adopted, chief executives' skills are upgraded, and focus on actual output receives more emphasis. *De-bureaucratization* has legitimized the task of minimizing the number of public rules and regulations. This has been achieved by merging different public institutions, privatizing public tasks, and simplifying the remaining rules and regulations. However, the results have been viewed with some skepticism.

Decentralization has been a major component in the strategy to reorganize the public sector. Decision-making responsibility has been shifted downwards from the central government agencies to local government and public institutions. Within local governments, the politicians have gained more power due to the extended use of framework laws. However, they have to share this power with street level bureaucrats and professionals who allow users to exert more direct influence on the day-to-day operation of public institutions. Within public institutions, executive managers have in general been granted more freedom to formulate strategies for future development. A more *flexible job structure* in the public sector has been introduced. In fact, salaries have been allowed to vary according to individual skills *and* performance.

These changes were all part of a responsive state strategy aimed to increase the efficiency of the public sector. A marketization strategy chaperoned this responsive state strategy, which promised to intensify the use of market forces and competition within the public sector, e.g. with respect to the current telecommunication industry, bus-services, airports, and national railway companies. In most countries, we have witnessed an increase in quarrels over who shall produce, organize, and finance public services. The overall trend seems to be: the democratic principles of the public sector will be left to the politicians. *Outsourcing* of production and finance will stimulate the application of BPR in the public sector. As such, the public sector's view on service information has been substantially revised. An OECD study on public administration arrived at the following objectives for information service which were formulated by the public sector during the mid 1990s:
– increase democratic legitimacy

– enable clients to claim entitlements
– improve clients' opportunities to influence service content and participate in the provision of services
– manage the expectations of clients regarding service levels and service quality according to the resources available
– facilitate and create conditions for client choice
– enforce performance on the providers
– restore the confidence of clients in the public sector and its agencies

Thus, at the meso-political level IT is seen as a tool that might help "reinvent" democracy. This can be achieved by facilitating public contact and citizen's access to public held data, implementing one-stop shopping, interactive e-services, point-of-contact data entry, expert systems, information storage, and revenue generation. Although we have seen a shift in the political agenda towards increased commitment to the use of IS in the public sector, we are yet to see empirical studies demonstrating the areas, time and significance of impacts achieved.

3.1.1   Quangos and Outsourcing: Reorganizing the Incentives and Management

The most radical use of new organizational forms in the public sector is seen in the widespread use of quangos. In 1992, the quangos in the UK used about 30% of the total public budget involving about 5,500 organizations. A similar importance was endorsed in the more socialist countries, such as the Netherlands and Denmark.

Also, outsourcing of computing activities has escalated during the past 10 years. In a study of computing in Japanese local government, it was found that the number of "outsourced" personnel has increased by 126% during the period 1985-1995. During the same period, the total number of computing personnel grew by about 88%. The computing expenses for local government skyrocketed by about 175%. The high percentage of outsourced employees shows that the computer capability of the existing in-house staff lags far behind the increase in the need for computing skills (Andersen and Sekiguchi 1997; Sekiguchi and Andersen 1999).

3.1.2   Virtual Organizations, Teleworking, Internet: Reorganizing the Face of the Public Sector

Virtual organizations is a very popular term and has been connoted with some of the elements in rebuilding organizations. Although there are varying definitions of what virtual organizations are, we find three elements in most definitions: *networking* (e-mail, voice-mail, facsimile, EDI, etc.), *restructuring of the organization* (outsourcing jobs/ functions, downsizing,

transformation), and *team culture* (geographically and functional) (Dutton and Peltu 1996). The use of such a virtual construct is facing major challenges since:
– most users have rejected major innovations in telecommuting (or tele-access) so far
– managers are often unwilling to relinquish control and supervision
– trust and commitment can be undermined if IT is used as a substitute for person-to-person communication
– privacy of users and consumers is threatened potentially

Within the public sector, many teachers, researchers, etc. work from home in an arrangement that often comes close to what we label virtual organizations. Although this group is important and substantial by numbers, few IT applications have aimed at stimulating the process and reorganizing the work processes. When we look at the much larger faction in the public sector employing case-workers (social security, housing, etc.), even less has been accomplished.

In a recent experiment in The Danish National Board of Industrial Injuries, a semi-virtual public organization was established. The cases handled by the Board are typically individual work related injuries. The work process involves retrieval of data, reference to legal data/ reference materials, and co-working with other colleagues in the office. Most contacts outside the organization are made through traditional mail (incoming mail is scanned) and by phone. Within the organization, communication consists of face-to-face meetings, phone meetings, memos, and exchange of electronic documents.

In a semi-virtual construct, some employees worked from home two days a week. They were equipped with office furniture, a computer, an ISDN/ ADSL-link, a phone-link, and access to all data. A total of 40 employees were involved in the project, although only 10 worked from home. They were the average, typical college graduates, knowledge workers, perhaps educated in the law department or the social sciences. The goals of the experiment were to increase worker satisfaction, productivity, and worker involvement in the ongoing planning of the work processes. Please note that the goals here are different from the BPR-concept's goals.

Similarly, the use of the Internet allows remote work and contact with the public sector's partners and citizens/ politicians which is an element that is rebuilding the public organization. So far, the knowledge of the impacts of this development is very limited. However, our studies on the organizational changes associated with the use of Internet indicate that they are not driven from top-down or in dramatic patterns. Our studies also show, however, that most Internet applications in government do not allow two-way communication nor access to public employees. They are in-house applications.

4.   REBUILDING THE PROCESSES

Previously, we have pointed to an overall modernization of the public sector, including two interesting new organizational forms: quangos and a (semi-) virtual construct. We see this development as a sign of a public organization that is moving towards IT based public organization. This does not mean that politics is no longer an issue, nor that technocratic factors no longer influence the capability, or opportunities or that information systems or new organizational forms erode power and politics as an element of the public sector.

Thus, our concept of PPR aims to glean some useful parts of BPR and process innovation ideas, while being responsive to criticism of the concept's application in the public sector. We believe in the validity of the concept, as managers and employees in the public sector are facing escalating investments in IS, deregulation, contracting out, quangos, and increased customer orientation. Also, reshaping the public organization with teleworkers, etc. poses particular challenges to the use of IS in a successful manner. Although we believe in principle that government activities should be as limited as possible and should be contracted out as much as possible, the core of the public sector needs above all to be in optimal working order. The public organization of today and tomorrow will not be easier to manage than older forms of organizations. On top of that, if all existing work procedures are merely transferred to remote workers without reorganizing the work processes, little will be accomplished, and counter productive results may result.

Local and central government, semi-governmental, and other governmental areas may benefit from our concept. We must remember that political processes include a wide range of activities, such as regulation of student admission at universities, personnel employment, or setting the level for welfare services. These are critical elements of (implementing) general political decisions and extremely important to the content of public policy. The million dollar question is: can IT be applied here along with a reorganization of the processes? In other words, can we help graduates from vocational training schools get a job faster by using IT and can this be done without expanding the number of state tasks to a level exceeding even the former Eastern European communist countries' abilities? We believe the answer is yes.

In the public administration area, we face high institutional powers with respect to checks and balances, power distribution and professional training. During the 1980s and 1990s, the public administration has witnessed ongoing low-risk automation, but we believe that more high risk re-engineering and paradigm shifts will appear. Researchers at the US National

Academy of Public Administration have formulated six starting points for reengineering in the public administration. We have adopted their insights and adjusted their list of factors which are critical to a successful reengineering in the public sector.

Table 1-3. Critical Success Factors for Rebuilding the Public Sector Using Information Systems

Factor	Characteristics
Understand process reengineering	Understand political process fundamentals.
	Know what reengineering/ rebuilding is.
	Differentiate and integrate process improvement approaches.
Build a case	Have necessary and sufficient business (mission and political delivery) reasons for the rebuilding process.
	Have the organizational commitment and capacity to initiate and sustain the reorganization.
	Secure and sustain political support for the process.
Adopt a process management approach	Understand the organizational mandate and set mission strategic directions and goals cascading to process-specific goals and decision-making across and down the organization.
	Define, model, and prioritize processes important for mission performance. Do not start out with unimportant activities.
	Practice "hands on" senior management ownership of process improvement through personal responsibility, involvement, and decision-making.
	Adjust organizational structures to better support process management initiatives.
	Create an assessment program to evaluate process management.
Measure and track performance continuously	Create organizational understanding of the value of measurement and how it will be used.
	Tie performance management to customer and stakeholder current and future expectations.
Practice change management and provide central support	Develop human resources management strategies to support the rebuilding process.
	Build information resources management strategies and a technology framework to support process change.
	Create a central support group to assist and integrate rebuilding efforts and other improvement efforts across the organization.
	Create an overarching and project-specific internal and external communication and education program.
Manage projects for results	Have clear criteria to select what should be redesigned.
	Place the project at the right level with a defined rebuilding team purpose and goals.
	Use a well-trained, diversified, expert team and ensure that it works-well.
	Follow a structured, disciplined approach.

Note: Adjusted from Caudle (1995)

It is important to set specific goals, but equally important to rebuild the structures to support these goals along with implementations of the new IS. But it requires that we know the work processes. Although this is the case in a large part of the public sector, the flow of information, the share of information, and the manipulation of information are just some of the items where our knowledge is quite limited. However, without such knowledge prior to rebuilding the structures, the outcome will depend more on luck than professional responsibility, commitment, and involvement.

Also, the keywords "measurement" and "expectations" should be considered carefully. Within the public sector, it is difficult, but not impossible, to measure the processes (including the input and outcome of them). Likewise, the expectations from the "stakeholders" must be identified and tied to the performance management. This is naturally complicated by the change of a political cabinet after a national election and by the often rigid systems through which customers may impose their influence on the content of the public service. Nevertheless, our message here is that rebuilding the public organization is not successful if it only results in increased satisfaction for the employees, or information systems with a better user interface. The clue is that the expectations have to be acknowledged, and the important ones are not the employees' expectations regardless of whether they are short-term or long-term.

In addition, the rebuilding efforts are dependent on the support from the organizations' employees. Needless to say, incentives to change are more effective than threats. Management of the building efforts should include communication and educational programs within the organization as well as the use of external educational programs. However, it is not a wise strategy solely to rely on external consultants for education.

Finally, the results should be kept in focus and not lost in the process. Therefore, it is important from the beginning to have clear *criteria on what should be rebuilt and what should be left intact*. The same person or group must be responsible for its outcome and rewarded for its successes. Although this conflicts with the nature of process improvement to some degree, it is important that the successful individuals, groups, or organizations are rewarded to maintain the drive and incentive with a view to new innovations within the work processes. Having said this, we must point out that such rewards need not be of a financial character. They may involve other organizational rewards and pay systems.

5.   THE ORGANIZATION OF THE BOOK

The chapters in this book are written both for the academic audience and in a form geared to the training of public managers. In particular, the six actions we have formulated in the concluding chapter may appeal to practice, yet, encourage the reader to flip through the book and digest the actions only. To get the full benefit, the book needs to be read in its full length. It is the combination of the parts that constitute the PPR-approach as a stimulating tool changing the role of IS in the public sector.

We will start the tour of the PPR in chapter 2 (*Activity and Customer Centric Government*) by elaborating on the activity and customer centric view. The mapping of individual public employees to their individual users can help build a stronger and more valuable linkage between financing, organizing, and implementing of the public services. This could help reduce staff hours, consultancy payments, and efforts spent on self-invented, not documented, and seldom used IT-projects.

In chapter three (*The Domains And Directions Of IT Impacts*) we advance our knowledge about the impacts of IT. In many discussions of the impacts, there is still a tendency to emphasize either a utopian pattern based on an idealization of the positive benefits that IT will bring to citizens and politicians or an Orwellian vision in which the effects of IT are generally inequitable and dehumanizing. The chapter provides a systematic examination of the impacts of IT. The list of variables derived from the chapter is suggested to serve as an input for PPR-domain initiatives.

The forth chapter (*Digital Wheel Barrows, containers and waste dump sites*) complements chapter 2 and 3 in the sense that back-office integration of data has been a main road for IS-projects in the public sector. The attempts to create, receive, and mail documents in digital format within governmental offices, between offices, and to businesses, citizens, and politicians have been in focus for a vast number of IS-projects. In the chapter, we argue that government has indeed been able to increase digitalization and reduce the transaction costs. Following the *digital wheel barrow approach,* government has been on the right track by loading the digital document and transporting the data. Yet, the challenge is to enhance the use of data from a pure transactional purpose to a more analytical purpose, i.e. to analyze resource consumption, whether services could be organized differently, load of services, etc.

The fifth chapter (*E-government objectives means, and reach*) argues that government approaches are loaded with dynamite by an almost exclusive push of IS applications oriented towards internal process improvement. This path might bring positive benefits to internal capabilities and transactions with the customers, but is unlikely to bring attention to and solve the areas where the IT-impacts are negative – within the domains of values and orientation of decision-making processes.

The sixth chapter (*The Organizational membrane penetrated by mobile technologies*) focuses on the changed organizational form of the public sector enabled by the mobile technology. We label the new stage the organizational membrane. The mobile technologies may accompany the transformation from the known and predictable sources and directions of interaction to the fuzzy and unpredictable interaction patterns within, at, and outside the organizational construct.

In this chapter we point to four key challenges that government will face in exploiting the organizational membrane: 1) the need to develop platforms that support productive and efficient collaboration and enable self-development, experimentation and innovative behavior; 2) counterbalance the need for managerial control and action with the privacy rights for the individual workers and citizens related to transactions and storage of their files; 3) outline strategies for having workers at home, satellite office, or the physical workplace; and 4) support knowledge creation, replication, adaptation, and utilization.

In chapter seven (*E-Procurement: The Improvement of Supporting and Strategic Operations*) we address e-procurement as a key focus of e-government initiatives. This issue is given a high priority since it is believed that this area is *loaded with easy gains*. The rationality behind e-procurement is to streamline the handling of orders and invoices to reduce the re-keying time, and gain to a better overview of what has been bought. It also includes using the Internet for issues such as reverse auctions, marketplaces, etc. to lower the cost of goods and services acquired by government. Chapter seven challenges this approach arguing that competing policy motives and reforms may erode e-procurement. This is in particular a danger since procurement in most governmental settings constitutes a marginal proportion of the total budget. Also, we argue that government labels suppliers, wholesalers, and procurement officers from an instrumentalist approach, and thus overlook the importance of interpersonal barriers to implementation of e-procurement.

Chapter eight (*Instrumental Digital User Democracy*) evaluates the formal digital access channels for exercising involvement of the users in the governance of local governmental institutions. The chapter is based on an analysis of web-based channels for user and citizen involvement in decision-making processes within the areas of eldercare, childcare, schools, and municipality councils. Rather than painting an idyllic picture of citizen digital access to information and interaction, the chapter suggests that the public sector has made no or very limited digital progress along the governance avenue.

In chapter nine (*Evaluation of IT Applications*) we present an impact analysis from the micro and the meta perspectives, respectively. The chapter identifies the different approaches to cost-benefit methods of Internet investments and provides an overview on what aspects the various approaches shed light. Moreover, we provide two examples of cost-benefit analyses of IS in the public sector. The chapter suggests that evaluations of IT applications should include content variables (capabilities, interaction, orientation, and values) and flow variables of the communication process, i.e. the variables of volume, data integration, diversity and span.

Chapter 10 (*Development Of E-Government Applications*) addresses the development of IT- application for government arguing that the ability to cope with IT-project challenges is equally poorly distributed among the consultants, governmental institutions, and suppliers involved in the projects. In government, particularly risk aversive and formal check-and-balance techniques are standard reactions facing potential failures. We need to start seeing the possibilities, rather than the dangers solely.

Chapter eleven (*Conclusions*) concludes the book and formulates six action points to propel the implementation of PPR. The action points list diagnostic principles rather than a real tool-kit for the actual process rebuilding. Also, the chapter calls for further input from organizational science, public administration, economics, and information systems. In particular, input from public administration is encouraged so an active role is played rather than just an analytical/ impact assessment role.

Chapter 2

THE ACTIVITY AND CUSTOMER CENTRIC APPROACH

1. INTRODUCTION

The customer and activity centric approach is a cornerstone of the PPR-approach – and is provocative in its assumptions and analysis. The argument that individual activities and networks of equal importance to, (and in some instances replacing formal and contractual regulation of public sector activities), is positioning itself in an academic minefield. As such, the PPR-approach will be a target for critique by practitioners, consultants, and IT-suppliers.

This chapter argues that a better proposition is to use IT in government by centering IT in the activities and direct the applications to the customers, rather than towards the formal organization and in-house needs for optimizing the *internal value chain*. The mapping of individual public employees and their individual customers can help build a stronger and more valuable linkage between financing, organizing, and implementers of the public services. This could help reduce staff hours, consultancy payments, and efforts spent on self-invented, not documented, and seldom used IT-projects.

Mapping the activities focus on the *activity molecules* and carefully examine the components. Attempts to transfer actors from the five other components of the activity molecule (content; the division of labor; rules for communication; users tool-capability; and the technology components) is likely to be met by power plays and political games. This appears to be even more prevalent in the public sector, than in the private sector.

2.   FORMAL INTERNAL AND EXTERNAL ORGANIZATIONAL BOUNDARIES

Many attempts to use IT to assist downsizing, rightsizing, cutting red tape, reinventing government, and new public management (Osborne and Gaebler 1992; Farnham and Horton 1996; Ferlie et al. 1996; Box 1999; Lane 2000; Stamoulis et al. 2001) have been inspired by the value chain and SWOT models and the work that the models were constructed on such as the transaction cost model (Coase 1937). In the public sector most of these attempts were perceived as badly masked budget cuts.

This is a fair critique, as many of these approaches were often more part of a political crusade against the public sector, than constructive attempts to build services that optimized the customers' need. Two of the most protein examples of formal organizational views where this crusade was encapsulated, are from some of the most widespread models used in training and education at the manifold business school programs: the value chain analysis and SWOT analysis.

Although there have been alternatives (as the *value shops* and *value network* models suggested) (Stabell and Fjeldstad 1998), the Porter view is still prevalent among many of the consultants, suppliers, and advisors on IT-implementation for private and government use. Also, the IS-research community has by large been part of establishing the Porter hegemony (Pedersen et al. 2002).

Also, the terminology on how to orchestra business operations, eliminate transaction costs, etc. has been fueled by the business process reengineering (BPR) agenda that swept through the management floors during the 1990s (Hammer 1990; Hammer and Champy 1993; Champy 1995; Hammer and Stanton 1995; Hammer 1996; Champy 2002; Champy 2002).

In the private sector, there has been a keen regard for competition as a key driver for uptake of IT, with a focus on improvement of internal and external value chains in order to stay competitive (Porter 1985, 2001) (Moreton and Chester 1996). The internal value chain model pictured in Figure 2.1 have been the focus for many studies on implementation of IT. Figure 2.2 illustrates an example from the mid 1990s on possible IT contribution in the private sector.

Regarding the internal value chain, one of the important observations and common misunderstandings we often have encountered from students and managers trying to use the internal value chain for the government setting is the perception that each step corresponds an increase in value. Rather, the model pictures represent increases in costs, and it is the cumulative costs that should be matched with the benefits it brings to the customer. The difference between the costs and the value to the customer is what creates the profit.

The model for the internal value chain outlined in Figure 2.2 ilustrates the important distinction between primary and secondary activities. The overall impression is that the spread of IT to the primary activities is very limited. In the past 30 years the major emphasis has been on support activities. By most accounts, applying the value chain in the public sector would be hazardous. The "input" and "output" picture of the public sector is primarily related to knowledge work, and the input and support activities are by nature different to activities in an automobile production hall.

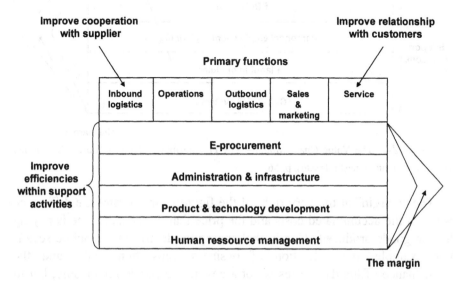

Figure 2-1. The Value Chain Model - *Source.* Porter (1985)

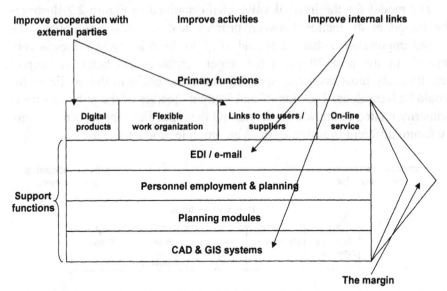

Figure 2-2. The Value Chain Model – The IT-contribution Note. - *Source.* Developed after Moreton and Chester (1996), p. 56.

The "margin" at the very right of the figure, demonstrates the difference between the accumulated costs and the price that the demand side is paying for the goods produced. This is challenging to identify in the public sector. For example, the collection of business transactions data, and the maintenance of the data bases is not a cost to the public sector only, but to the companies and citizens as well.

The current trend with online forms etc. available at the net does not transfer resources from the public sector to the private sector. A key concern is whether the ease with which the public sector can (by asking citizens and companies to enter data at a webform) retrieve data, will lead the public sector to ask for yet more data. Whereas the information technology could lead to one entry point for the public sector, the reality is that most IT-systems are segmented with no data transfer between the public agencies and no strategies as to how the IT-systems can benefit the endusers.

Furthermore, the value chain model operates at a formal organizational level, for example a municipality or a department within a ministry. Although this is in line with budget allocation procedures in most countries, the key to boost IT in government will from a PPR-approach, be to replace the formal organizational view with an activity centric view as argued in this and the subsequent chapters (particularly chapter 6). This would be more in line with our PPR model. Most of the limitations and shortcomings of the internal value chain model appears to be applicable to the external value chain as well.

Most critical is perhaps that what has been labeled as the Porter hegemony (Pedersen et al. 2002). This is being adopted in training of future managers for IT suppliers as consultants within the public sector. We even encounter public sector training programs where value chain analysis and even more problematic SWOT-analysis appears to be the most frequently used and remembered models presented for the students.

The irony of the public sector, as emphasized in chapter 5 of this book, is that the market/ demand side is not yet a true strategic parameter for public sector IT-applications. This will have to be changed before the SWOT-model recapped in Figure 2.3 below, makes sense to follow for strategic actions on new generations of e-government applications. The entries in the cells are inspired by an example from the private sector (Chaffey 2002) illustrating the problems using the SWOT-analysis for the public sector.

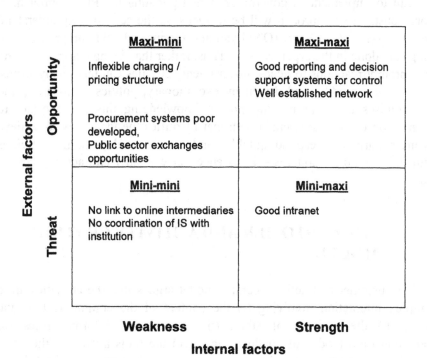

Figure 2-3. The SWOT-model

Thus, SWOT analysis could lead to minimizing external factors, maximizing internal factors (Mini-maxi strategy) and an improvement of the link to online intermediaries and the coordination of the IS-activities within the organization (mini-mini strategy). Yet, the underlying problem for the public sector is three-fold. First, the public sector is not *one* organization, but a fragmented set of institutions and activities (please consult chapter 9) that often fights with other departments that share the same budget. The external threats are often from other public departments or politicians that try to cut the budget.

Second, most of the public sector does not have any up-stream value chain to semi-producers or manufacturing companies. Instead their primarily up-stream and down-stream flow is a flow of data, information and knowledge linked to people and processed by people.

Third, there indeed already is plenty of exchange of data between government and their customers (see chapter 3 and 4). The problem is - who initiates and owns this digital communication and chooses the digital format, providers, and storage?

These three issues make the competition, value chain and SWOT analysis difficult to implement in government when pursuing the PPR-approach. A more constructive approach will be to focus on the activities to understand the *contrived value chains* (O'Sullivan and Geringer 1993) comprising how things are done in the organizations. Thus, rather than being competitive and have prompt reactions to needs, government activities can take many forms, react slowly, muddy, and driven by evolutionary, politics, rationality, and compromises in a big melting pot. Acknowledging this is important to progression on the value chain path that identifies the ideal way to achieve business purposes, respond quickly, and matches value-adding activities with the available resources – in essence our customer and activity centric model.

3.   THE CUSTOMER AND ACTIVITY CENTRIC MODEL

Our customer and activity centric model argues that the activities are a complex interaction involving (i) the content of the communication and work, (ii) the division of labor, (iii) formal and informal rules for communication (codes of conduct, etc.), (iv) the tools available, the users capable of using them, (v) the actors working in the units, and the (vi) IT-network linking the five other elements through wires, infrared, bluetooth, 3G etc. The six atoms or components in the activity molecule are dynamic in the sense that each of these changes and can impede changes to other molecules. The link between each of the six components provides an equally important way to look for triggers for change and for the limitations of top-down management. Personal and professional network hubs become essential to master in order to look for change in government.

In our profileration of the PPR-model we have been inspired by the knotworking model (Engeström et al. 1999) although we underscore that there are manifold dimensions where our view is not in line with their model and thinking. Therefore parts of the customer and activity centric model derive from the Engeström and Engeström model but the whole and the context of the parts that are used in the PPR-model are far removed from the context and roads Engeström and Engeström are following in their research.

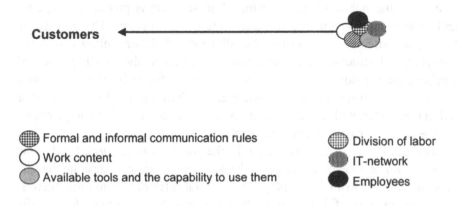

Figure 2-4. The Customer and Activity Centric View of Government

The alignment of the work and communication content in the public services and the resulting product with their customers can follow two roads: reduce the *negative and unwanted* communication and work content versus using IT to improve the *positive and the desired* part of the public sector. An example of the unwanted communication is transaction costs and the use of IT to for example streamline procurement. This problem is, however, that the push towards transaction cost reduction is by large a *departmental and bureaucratic issue,* whereas the overall qualitative aspects are more a *policy level* issue.

The individual worker, the street-level bureaucrat, the office clerk, the policy officer, and the immigration officer need to experience a synergy between the general policy instructions regarding what they should focus on and what type of activities should constitute their work content and the relation of this to the customer. Overall, job specifications should be descriptive of what and how the activities performed/ expected by the worker link to the customer rather than how they link to in-house standards/ expectations.

The second dimension of the activity molecule is the *division of labor.* In the discussion of the public sector, the legacy approach and the detailed description of each workers tasks is still useful guidance in pursuing the optimal organization structure (Mintzberg 1979; Hedberg et al. 1997; Mintzberg 1998). Yet, the governance approach might be more fruitful to follow, to understand how the employees undertake work and perform their activities (Haque 2002; Marche and McNiven 2003). Clearly there is a need for a division of labor within government but it is a concern when more time is spend on defining what is not within an area or giving reasons why this person should not complete the activity, rather than simply getting the job done.

Equally worrisome is the attempts to create lock-in impacts between the customers and public sector by using IT to see who is processing the case and making one person in government the contact person. The problem is that most attempts to define the division of labor follows existing governmental structures and pays more attention to the existing stock of workers, than it does to the division of labor in the light of the activities government delivers. Thus, the principles for defining the division of labor will have to start with the customers' needs by outlining what competences, data, etc. are necessary to solve the problem/ issue at stake.

The third part of the molecule is the *formal and informal rules for communication*. One of the largest mistakes one can do is to assume that the only information available is the current digital information and that there is a certain amount of information that can not be accounted for. While acknowledging the importance of being aware of tacit knowing and knowledge (Polanyi 1958) and challenges to codification (Boh 2003), it is a even bigger mistake to stop searching for information that can be digitalizing. Our point here is that too often analysis is stopped for rhetoric reasons. Rather than asking the question of what can digitalized, the question should be what can not be digitalized? This will bring the discussion in favor of IT, and have the opposition lift the burden to prove why red-tape areas, cross-institutional arrangements etc. cannot be digitalized.

The forth part of the activity molecule consists of the *tools and resources available and the users capable using them*. The notion of resources are important since IT expenditures could be spend on other activities, perhaps more closely listen to customers. Overall, and in the long run, this line of thinking is the most constructive way to estimate which resources are available for digitalizing the activities and bringing them closer to the customers. At the more hands on level, the resources also include the IT-tools available and the employees' capacity to use these. The irony of the software development in particular in the past 10 years is that programs have been easier to run and that only specialists or people with a very specialized need (for example those with the need to use a statistical package as SPSS), go to IT-courses. The lion's share of courses on IT are taken by project management and overall operational and strategic management challenges.

The fifth element is the *people working in the public sector*. As will be discussed in more length in chapter 6, mobility of the staff in the public sector is a key issue involving not only technical issues but of equal importance human resource dimensions. Social issues can easily pose limits to transparency and the actors capacity for ongoing learning. Also the actors and their communications partners do not have the ability and incentive to find and practice new forms of interaction and trust. Governments rarely experiment with technology in so far as they rely on trust-worthiness and being accessible and accountable. Introducing new technologies such as chat and virtual workspaces are often met with questions such as how much trust can there be in the systems? Is there any guarantee that the communication and files are confidential? Etc. The irony is, however, that the employees seem often more concerned about these issues than their clients/ customers do.

The sixth and final element is the *IT-network*. This is a constant challenge with regards to interoperationability, network integration, security, transmission and storage capacity, add-ons, support, driver maintenance and upgrade, and upgrades to newer versions/ applications. Although there are severe technical challenges, the drivers to design and choose new applications might be equal grounded on economic reasons has been demonstrated in the Open Source implementation from Beaumont Hospital, a large Irish public-sector organization:

"For Beaumont, the drive to OSS was primarily due to the necessity of reducing cost. The IT manager was very frank that it was not driven by any doctrine or anti-Microsoft ideology...Free access to source code was not really a factor in Beaumont's decision to deploy OSS solutions. The IT manager admits that open source software in the Beaumont case amounts to "zero cost or as cheap as possible."

Thus, even though they have been seeking OSS solutions, they are more guided by the zero or low cost availability rather than open source code. Indeed, this is evident in their choice of Star Office rather than the pure-play open source equivalent Open Office. This decision was taken due to the availability of support directly from Sun. Access to some form of external support provides a degree of reassurance at all levels in the organization, especially when contemplating a major shift in operating paradigm." (Fitzgerald and Kenny 2003).

3.1   Linking the clusters of activity

The customer and activity centric approach outlined above is challenging at individual worker level but even more challenging when linking clusters of activities. The customers of the public sector will often have the experience being in contact with different offices, unaware who can take over when another person is out, and have to deliver information in a different format. From a worker's point of view this will be easier to change as compared to power and policy issues that can emerge when trying to align the different clusters of activity.

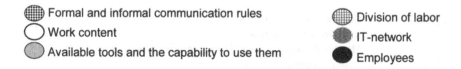

Figure 2-5. Linking the Clusters of Activity

For the intradepartmental challenges on "getting things done", it might be useful to apply the power and politics approach in trying to implement PPR (Marcus 1983; Pfeffer 1997). Strategies from this point of view suggest to map the competing actors and groups and negotiate on the means and ends. From our point of view, awareness of the power base and its key areas is essential. Areas such as position, resources, personal issues, knowledge, expertise, and symbolic issues are key features of e-government. In Table 2.2 we have summarized the power bases and the elements that help determine the strength of the individual power bases.

Table 2.2 Power bases workers will use to fight the customer and activity centric approach

Power base	Elements
Position	Status in hierarchy
	Power to change structures, rules, regulations
	Control of strategic decision-making
	Control of operational decision-making processes
	Political access and access to decision arena
	Staff support
	Contacts for information
Resources	Control of scarce resources, budget and technology
	Ability to reward or punish staff
	Be persistent and spend time
	Pool energy
	Work around roadblocks
	(Don't) use organizational rules
Personal issues	Involvement in interpersonal alliances, coalitions, and networks with links to the informal org.
	Capability to deal with decision-maker

	Able to exert charismatic leadership to get others to follow
	Able to cope with uncertainty
	Reputation
Knowledge &	Information specific to the change situation, Use data to convince
expertise	Skills specific to the change situation
	Knowledge and expertise unique to situation concerned
	Overall professional credibility
	Tradition
Symbols	Quality of accommodation
	Use of expenses budget
	Membership of high-level decision-making processes
	Receipt of company perks
	Unchallenged right to deal with those outside the organization
	Access to the ear of top management

Source. Inspired and developed after Greiner and Schein (1989), Senior (2002).

The tragedy is that most IS application has little awareness of the power issues that in many studies have been found to be critical for adoption of IT. The transition to the customer and activity centric approach is likely to foster even more power fights between individual workers using the power bases captured in Table 2.2.

3.2   Free radicals

In chemistry, free radicals are uncharged molecular species with an open shell configuration. These unpaired electrons are highly reactive and play an important role in many chemical processes. Within chemistry there are three main processes: initiation, propagation, and termination:

"(I) *Initiation reactions* are those which result in a net increase in the number of free radicals. They may involve the formation of free radicals from stable species...or they may involve reactions of free radicals with stable species to form more free radicals;

(II) *Propagation reactions* are those reactions involving free radicals in which the total number of free radicals remains the same;

(III) *Termination reactions* are those reactions resulting in a net decrease in the number of free radicals. Typically two free radicals combine to form a more stable species, for example: $2H\cdot \rightarrow H_2$" (Wikipedia 2003).

We use the term free radicals in a similar sense since the ambition is to free people and make them move to the activity clusters where there competences, time, and resources are in need. Thus, rather than thinking about actors being linked to one molecule, some of the actors will be able to move to numerous molecules within the organization at a given time. IT has an important role to play in this by making the user interface, data structure, etc. aligned. Equally, the four other parts of the molecule need to be adoptive for the free radicals.

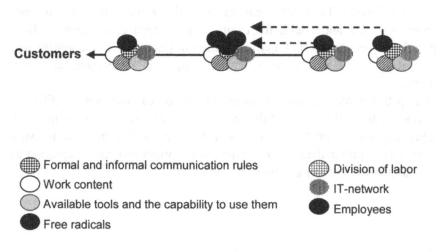

Figure 2-6. The free radicals and the activity molecules

Although we often see the public sector described as one unit, the reality is that often the public sector is fragmented or segmented (please consult chapter 9). Segmentation and fragmentation can materialize within the department by units or people that seek to protect themselves by fighting corporation on all six dimensions of our activity-model by for example having informal rules that are socialized within the group and hard for the rest of the organizations to communicate with. It can be by having rigid rather than flexible division of labor resulting in for example one person's desk being overloaded and another's is clean without the assistance to help the first person, or it could be by insisting that proprietory standards for the data documentation and communication, although the proprietory standards might not serve any other goals than simply keeping people working in their own unit rather than seeing the competing department getting one more employee.

3.3 Horizontal and vertical integration

The ability for workers to swiftly move from one cluster of activity to another is bounded by the ability of the five other components in our molecule. Thus, the very existence of free radicals can be cumbersome and in part due to power play strategies are easier to seek horizontal and vertical integration between the clusters of activity within the government.

Vertical integration is often niche oriented and combines upstream and downstream activities. In the domain of the public sector, upstream integration can mean integration of activities related to building permits from the different offices in the municipality. Horizontal integration focuses on more subjects and could, for example, be citizen cases across offices within the governmental unit, between different municipalities, counties, and even states. Language can be a barrier along with differences in legacy systems.

The path for vertical and horizontal integration can take a quite different turn now than during the 1990s. What we might see is an ad hoc and incremental integration that grows from the individual employees network and activities, rather than see the grand-scale organizational integration as the most important driver or observable integration locus.

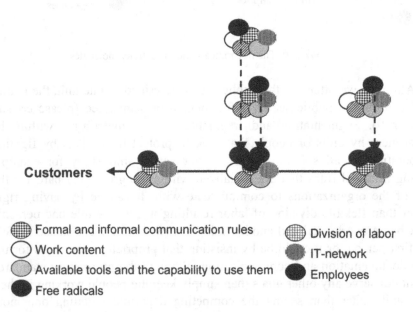

Figure 2-7. Horizontal and vertical integration of the molecules

3.4   The initiators and target stakeholders for reorganization of the public sector

In the previous sections we have outlined the dimensions of the customer and activity centric PPR-approach. Recalling, that we have two legitimate initiating and final points for the activities (the customers and the formal decision-makers), we will in this section elaborate on how this corresponds to the activity approach.

The customers are in Figure 2.8 split in three groups: companies, citizens, and decision-makers. The formal decision-makers include politicians but can also include decision-making bodies within semi-governmental units and quangos. By mapping each cluster of activity with the citizens, companies, and the formal elected decision-making, the residual can be eliminated. The residual is by other terms labeled in-house projects and overhead costs.

They key mission with PPR is not to reduce overhead costs, but rather to impede a change that has much impact. Also, we underline that the ambition with this mapping is not to eliminate the public sector but to eliminate the activities that can not be mapped to the customers. The intended consequence is that government will spend less time on self-invented IT-projects that have no links, justification, or benefits other than an activity opportunity.

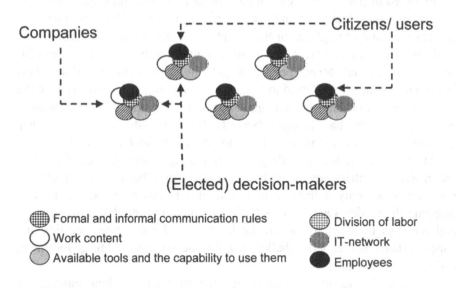

Figure 2-8. The link between companies, citizens, decision-makers – and the elimination of overhead/ dead waste

4. CHALLENGES FOR THE MODEL

Three severe challenges need to be considered: I) the timelag issue in mapping the activities towards the enduser, ii) the challenge on whom and how to address the linkage, and iii) the elements of the public sector that primarily comprise negative regulation, i.e. parts of policing, environment regulation, and taxation.

One of the major challenges is the time lag issue in mapping the activities towards the enduser. We can map the existing number of people working in the public sector and possibly the time some of the personnel spend in direct consumer contact, including their time spend on documentation and preparation for the contact. For some of the activities there is a time lag in measuring this. The more we extend the definition of consumer contact, the more the time lag problem escalates. Thus, from one perspective all public employees are in contact with the customers, it is only a matter of waiting and identifying the linkages. Despite acknowledging this issue, this potential cost-driven approach is not shared by the PPR concept.

The second major challenge is related to *who and how to address the linkage between the consumer and the individual workers*. On the who-dimension, a critical challenge is to consider the range of stakeholders that are involved in public services and aim for an inclusive and broad approach, rather than an exclusive and narrow definition of users. The users might be the travelers and immigrants of the society, as in the Australian on-line visa application procedure where the visitor can go directly to a website and fill out an application form, pay, and get the visa granted online. This information is then transferred to the immigration authorities that retrieve the information when the person goes through customs. This application procedure clearly has brought benefits for the end-consumer and has illustrated that the end-consumer need not even to be within the country.

At the domestic level, kindergarten, schooling, hospitals, and elder care are in some countries are all run by government, in other countries partly, in other countries only a fraction of the service is run by government. Yet, mapping the students and parents to the activities in school and the partners and relatives to the activities in the hospital and elder care facilities that concern them, are equally challenging for the socialist, semi-government, and market economies.

The *how dimension* of customer identification can be done through for example log-files. As pointed to in chapter 4, many of the public information infrastructure systems are transactional oriented which could make the mapping easier. This could, with few efforts help answering who and at what frequency different actors are in contact with customers. More advanced analysis on the content of the digital communication can also be conducted, although this would require more effort. Analyzing the log-files clearly assume that these are available to for example, the IT department. In times of outsourcing of applications, ASPs, and in some countries, confidentiality and concerns about the employees right to privacy, clearly raise more challenges to following this approach. Also, there might be data that due to national security is in the ownership of government and classified as confidential. Files within the national intelligence like the British MI6, FBI and CIA belong to this category.

Regarding the *regulation dimension*, the main point is that we need to focus on key processes and sub processes rather than on government per se. For example, the police departments in countries such as Denmark and France issue driver licenses and passports without any use of IT in their interaction with customers. We use the term customers because today most of these services in government are paid by the enduser rather than financed through the general taxes. In other countries such as Finland and Singapore, the application for, renewal, and payment of passports and driver licenses can be completed online. In the Finnish and Singapore case, the process is automated although it is still possible to ask some clarifying questions through e-mail. If we get a copy of each employee's logfile for external communication through the Internet (i.e. filtering all IP-numbers that belong to their own department), we could use this information to access whether some employees do not fit in to the PPR-thinking. Clearly, there are examples of regulation where it is hard to map a direct link such as directives and legislation on syntax rules, data dictionaries, document standards utilized in business transactions with the public sector, regulation on encryption and provision of certification measures, and (de-) regulation of the telecommunication market.

5.   CONCLUSION

This chapter has argued that a vital part of the PPR method is to map individual public employees to their individual users. This can help (re)build linkages between the financing, organizing, and implementing of public services. The six components of the activity clusters (content of the communication and work; the division of labor; formal and informal rules for communication; the tools available and the users capability of using them; the employee, and the technology component) are clearly challenges to seperate and realign. Even more challenging will be to bring the free radicals in to play and this is likely to be met by power and political games. The chapters in this book demonstrate that the in-house and transaction focused IT-applications dominate the picture, rather than the radical and revolutionary thinking as prompted by the PPR-approach.

This chapter has identified three key challenges for the customer and activity centric approach: time lag, inclusion/ exclusion, and negative regulation. Indeed these three areas will raise concerns when realigning the IT applications. It is equally important to be aware of these shortcomings is to keep the overall picture straight and carefully consider whether the three areas of concern are the exception or the rule. We believe that the former is true.

Chapter 3

THE DOMAINS AND DIRECTIONS OF IT IMPACTS

1.   INTRODUCTION

Departing from the previous two chapters that have set the scene for the PPR-approach and argued what and how IT in government can be approached, we have taken in this and the following chapter one step back in time to identify the impacts of IT so far.

The primary goal in this chapter is to advance our knowledge about the impact of IT on what we label the political system which incorporates the public administration that is the key focus of the PPR-approach. In many discussions of these impacts, there is still a tendency to emphasize either an utopian pattern based on an idealization of the positive benefits that IT will bring to citizens, public administrators, and politicians or an Orwellian vision in which the effects of ITs are generally undemocratic, inequitable and dehumanizing (Donk et al. 1995).

This chapter provides a systematic, empirical examination of the impacts of IT in the domains of politics and public administration. We explore the extent to which the major transformations attributed to IT have occurred during what we call the "golden age" of IT (from the late 1980s until the turn of the century) – a period of rapid expansion of IT investment and the routinization of the technology into behavior and practice of all types of actors and organizations.

Conceptually, this chapter suggests that there does seem some utility in applying our proposed taxonomy of IT impacts within four broad domains:

capabilities, interactions, orientations, and values. *Substantively*, the chapter specifies definable, if complex, patterns of IT related impacts. About half of all reported impacts, and the greatest number of positive impacts, are identified regarding the effects of IT on the capabilities of government. The highest incidence of positive impacts related to IT in a single category is the aspect of capabilities that focuses on increases in efficiency. The highest proportions of negative impacts from IT are in the areas of health, safety and well-being, individuals' privacy; the effects of IT on job quality; and the protection of legal rights.

This chapter is a slightly revised and shorter version of a paper co-authored with James N. Danziger. The methodology of our studies of impacts have been documented in Danziger and Andersen (2002) and Andersen and Danziger (1995) and is not included in this chapter.

2. CONCEPTUAL FRAMEWORK AND OVERALL RESULTS

The particular domain of our inquiry is the uses of IT in *public administration and politics*, which includes those structures, processes, actors and policies that determine or implement the allocation of public values in the collectivity (after Easton's (1965) classic definition of the political system).

We focus on IT related impacts in the political system, and especially in the domain of public administration. The boundary between public administration and politics can be somewhat blurred. We include in our analyses those impacts of IT which do have a substantial effect on those who make decisions and take actions on behalf of the state, at its various levels. It seems indisputable that applications of IT are increasingly pervasive in the world of public administration.

One constructive contribution to our understanding of the actual impacts of IT on public administration is to assess the body of recent social scientific research that provides sound, empirically grounded, and relevant evidence about the extent, nature, and directions of those impacts.

In this chapter, we provide one such systematic survey of research articles in key international journals that could be reasonably expected to include studies of IT in the public sectors of developed, industrialized democracies. The survey enables us to establish whether the recent research specifies any particular patterns of impacts. We review those effects of IT in the public sector that are documented in empirical studies conducted by the article's author(s). We include studies where it is possible to clearly identify the empirical analysis and results. We do not include author's reports on research conducted by others, "arm-chair" theorizing, or studies that focus on IT infrastructure development, implementation issues or expectations to possible outcome of IT use.

Despite the apparent physics analogue, we recognize that the concept of *"impacts" of IT* encompasses a broad range of processes. Individuals, role relations and organizations can be viewed as interacting, organizing and reorganizing constantly (Giddens 1990). These processes of structuration might be altered or shaped by the uses of IT in a variety of ways that are often subtle, complex, gradual or delayed, and that are difficult to measure with precision (Markus and Robey 1988; Orlikowsky 1996; Kling and Lamb 1999; Castells 2000).

It is also the case that human agency often shapes the technology-in-use (Danziger and Kraemer 1986; Smith and Marx 1994; Williams and Edge 1996). Thus in this chapter, we accept research findings where a certain effect can be attributed to IT even when there are interactive processes between the technology and the actors and when the causal relationship cannot be demonstrated with precision. We consider IT impacts at both the individual and the collective level. Individual impacts can occur for those in a variety of roles, such as public employee, manager, client or citizen. The collective level covers a particularly broad array of actors, such as virtual teams, workgroups, organizations, companies, local governments, political interest groups, state agencies, international nongovernmental organizations, and supranational institutions.

As a conceptual framework to guide our review, we utilize a taxonomy composed of four main domains of impacts, which reflect classic themes in political science: capabilities, interactions, orientations and value distributions. The taxonomy was initially developed by Danziger (1986). Within the four domains, we specify 22 categories of impacts which were formulated by means of an inductive process grounded in the actual findings in the research literature (Andersen and Danziger 1995; Danziger and Andersen 2002). Table 3.1 lists the 22 categories in our taxonomy.

- The impacts on the *capabilities* of a political unit are measured by examining whether IT has had any effects on the manner in which the unit (individual or collective) deals with its environment, in an attempt to control the environmental effects on its behavior and to extract values from the environment. We particularly consider alterations in capabilities associated with the impacts of IT both on the quality of information available to political actors and also on changes in the efficiency or effectiveness of performance.
- The impacts on the *interactions between the political units* assesses how IT affects patterns of power and control, communication among units, the coordination of tasks or policies, and the cooperation among actors in performing a function within the public sector. It also considers the

relations between the public sector (e.g., governmental agencies, public administrators) and citizens or private sector actors, as well as the relations among citizen groups.

– The effects of IT on *orientations* are measured by the impact of IT on the political unit's cognitive, affective and evaluative considerations. For example, we consider whether quantitative considerations have gained weight relative to qualitative arguments in political decisions and actions. Also, we survey whether IT causes actors to structure problems differently. And we explore whether actors, such as street-level bureaucrats, perceive that their discretion has been altered by IT.

– Finally, the impact of IT on *value distributions* is measured by examining whether a political actor experiences a shift in values that is attributable to IT. We look specifically at values associated with the enhancement of the citizen's private sphere, legal rights, and levels of health, safety and well-being, as well as examining the job satisfaction and job (domain) enlargement of public employees.

Table 3-1. Conceptual Domains and Specific Categories of IT Impacts

I. CAPABILITIES	Information Quality
	1. Data access
	2. Data quality
	Efficiency
	3. Productivity gain
	4. Staff reduction/substitution
	5. Improved (managerial) control
	6. Time-saving measures
	Effectiveness
	7. Improved decision processes
	8. Improved products and services
	9. Improved planning
II. INTERACTIONS	10. Improved coordination/ cooperation
	11. Citizen-public sector interaction
	12. Private sector-public sector interaction
	13. Citizen-citizen interaction
	14. Organizational control and power
III. ORIENTATIONS	15. Emphasis on quantitative criteria
	16. Structuring of problems
	17. Increased discretion
IV. VALUE	18. Protection and improvement of the private sphere
DISTRIBUTIONS	19. Job satisfaction and enrichment
	20. Job enlargement
	21. Protection of legal rights
	22. Improved standard of health, safety and well-being

Overall, there are clear differences in the distribution of IT related impacts on public administration across the four analytic domains. Nearly half (47%) of the specific findings deal with impacts of IT on capabilities, 29% deal with the impact of IT on interactions, 19 % identify impacts on value distributions, and only 6% of the findings focus on the impact of IT on political orientations. With respect to the direction of the impacts of IT, the research concludes that the impacts have generally been positive. Across all domains, fully 74% of the specific impacts are positive, while only 19% are negative. The research concluded in 8% of the cases that the impact of IT did not result in a significant direction of change in a category of interest. Finally, mixed effects (that is, both positive and negative IT based impacts in a single category) were reported in 13% of the cases.

IT has typically been touted as a tool that increases the efficiency and effectiveness of governmental operations (Council-for-Excellence-in-Government 2001). Both the substantial proportion of IT impacts on capabilities and also the high proportion of positive impacts in this category seem consistent with this expectation. In detailed analyses below, we examine whether specific aspects of capabilities are most extensively affected by IT. Then we will explore the impacts of IT on interactions, including a consideration of why nearly two-fifths of the effects on interactions are negative or neutral. We will address the apparently limited impacts of IT on political orientations. Finally, we consider IT related effects on value distributions, and especially the high percentage of negative impacts.

Table 3-2. Impact of IT on Capabilities, Interactions, Orientations and Value Distributions

Variable	Impacts				
	Positive (%)	Negative (%)	Neither positive nor negative (%)	Total (N)	Studies reporting mixed impacts (N)
Capabilities	84	8	7	108	10
Interactions	65	20	15	66	12
Orientations	85	15	0	13	1
Value Distributions	56	44	0	43	7
Total	73	19	8	230	30

3. IT IMPACTS ON CAPABILITIES IN THE PUBLIC SECTOR

The empirical research reports that the highest proportions of both impacts and also positive impacts attributed to IT are identified in the area of capabilities (Table 3-2). Table 3.3 details these impacts, examining the three different categories: (1) information quality impacts (data access and data quality); (2) efficiencies (productivity gains, labor reductions and substitutions, improved managerial control, and time-savings measures); and (3) effectiveness impacts (improvements in decision processes, products and services, or planning). The percentage of positive impacts from IT is consistently high across all nine categories, and it is particularly striking in the area of efficiency, where fully 84% of the findings are positive. In the specific research studies, benefits associated with capabilities are most common within activities characterized by routine behavior and actions by public administrators.

Table 3-3. Impacts of IT on the Categories of Capabilities

Variable	Impacts				
	Positive (%)	Negative (%)	Neither positive nor negative (%)	Total (N)	Mixed (N)
Information quality					
1. Data access	82	14	4	28	3
2. Data quality	85	15	0	13	1
Efficiency					
3. Productivity gain	79	7	14	14	1
4. Staff reduction/substitution	50	0	50	2	0
5. Improved control (management)	94	6	0	18	1
6. Time-saving measures	100	0	0	4	1
Effectiveness					
7. Improved decision processes	86	0	14	7	1
8. Improved products and services	81	6	13	16	1
9. Improved planning	83	0	17	6	1
Total	84	8	7	108	10

Note: Tables 3-3, 3-4, 3-5, and 3-6 indicate the number of studies that report positive, negative, neutral and mixed effects of IT on the particular category. Thus, an article might be listed under several impact categories and might report effects in more than one direction. The "Total Impacts" column indicates the total number of times that an impact is reported. The far right "mixed" column reports the number of articles in which the impacts of IT in a category are reported in more than a single direction.

3.1   Information Quality

Almost 40% of the total impacts of IT on the capabilities of the political system are reported in the area of information quality. A high incidence of IT improvements to information quality might not seem too surprising. Yet it does seem notable that, fully three decades after IT generated its early impacts on government in the areas of data quality and data access (Kraemer et al. 1974), information quality improvements continue to be reported at such a high level.

The studies report a higher absolute number of positive impacts (Easton 1965) generated by IT in the area of *data access* than in any other single category of IT impacts in the entire analysis. Overall, 82% of the findings regarding data access are clearly positive, and no article reports only negative impacts in this category. The empirical research documents that the citizen's access to data, and especially to data of higher quality, has improved significantly. Examples such as Santa Monica's Public Electronic Network (PEN), the Cleveland Free-Nets, and the Community Memory Network in Berkeley in the United States and Hamamatsu prefecture in Japan are indicative of citizens' increased information access opportunities through the use of IT (Schuler 1994; Sekiguchi and Andersen 1999). However, there does seem to be a tendency for some of these citizen information systems to be modified over time in ways that reduce citizen involvement and mobilization, suggesting that political actors can introduce obstacles which counter the democratizing effects of the technology (Steyaert 2000).

Eleven findings indicate that IT has improved *data quality* for those in the political world. It is within certain areas of the finance function that the studies most frequently report beneficial impacts of IT on data quality. There are fewer reports in the research, although still positive effects, from improved data quality in areas other than finance, such as police and planning (Northrop et al. 1990; Andersen and Madsen 1992; Kraemer et al. 1993; Hertzum 1995). In the police function, for example, current applications of IT provide patrol officers with data about suspects and crime patterns that are of higher quality, are more easily accessible, and are shared across more jurisdictions (Northrop et al. 1994). Also, increasingly powerful GIS (geographic information systems) provide data of greater relevance and specificity which meet the needs of public administrators on a range of actions, from needs assessment to facility location to targeting citizen groups with "geodemographic" data (Brown 1996; Dulio et al. 1999).

Broadly, Zuurmond (Zuurmond 1994) argues that public organizations are moving from the functional, generally hierarchical structures described by Max Weber (Weber 1958), to more flexible, organic and horizontal structures. Zuurmond demonstrates that this shift in organizational structure is substantially facilitated by IT, as it provides greater data access and higher quality data to employees within and across organizational levels. In a related way, Snellen (1994) notes that many IT systems have evolved from back-office systems to front-office systems and that increases in information quality have supported the expansion into domains of use that support not only routine, administrative decisions but also those which serve as an integrated part of general administration. In general, these studies indicate that this greater data access and high data quality have associated benefits, as IT increases the information power of public administrators, resulting in improvements for managerial control, decision-making, and planning (as noted below).

3.2   Efficiency

Efficiency in government operations is reported in terms of four phenomena: productivity gains, staff reductions, managerial control of subordinates and processes, and time-savings. Overall, the research is unambiguous in concluding that IT has enhanced efficiency. Next to information quality impacts, this is the area where the largest number of impacts is identified in the research, with a very high proportion of positive impacts. However, the number of reported impacts is quite varied across the four specific domains.

We found only two empirically grounded studies identifying *staff reductions*. It can be very difficult, as shown by Kaneda's (1994) study of Japanese local governments, to transform IT related cost savings into the actual net reduction in personnel or into changes in statutory requirements or organizational culture regarding the hiring and firing of public employees. These points are also supported by the research findings of Sekiguchi and Andersen (Hertzum 1995).

Four studies do conclude that there have been direct *time-savings* as a result of IT. Agencies providing cash and service benefits to clients, for example, use computer matching systems to identify overlaps in provision far more quickly (Clarke 1995). When we consider the prominence of time-savings as a theme in the early rhetoric about the benefits of IT, we might expect this finding to appear more frequently in the research. It is possible that current studies assume such time-savings are obvious and hence do not attempt to document them. Alternatively, it might be that the substantial time savings in many domains of work were associated with the initial applications of IT and further improvements are now more difficult to achieve. It is even possible that some of the continuing impacts of IT on many jobs also generate new demands on workers' time.

There is much more extensive evidence in the research that there are significant *productivity gains* attributable to applications of information technology in public organizations. Several studies, especially those examining local governments, conclude that employees have experienced substantial increases in productivity as IT has enabled them to handle more cases and/or more extensive amounts of information (Kraut et al. 1989;

Brudney and Brown 1992; Norris 1992). In the Swedish social and health services, for example, computerized case management systems have increased the number of cases that an employee can analyze, and IT has been especially helpful in the face of frequent regulatory changes that alter the composition of the client group (Ingelstam and Palmlund 1991). Public safety is another government function where the research finds positive IT impacts on productivity, as automated systems enable staff to work actively on a larger number of cases and to clear more cases (Sinclair 2001).

Interestingly, improvements in *managerial control* are the most frequently reported category of IT based efficiencies in public administration. For example, the empirical research identifies improved management performance resulting from the uses of IT within the Dutch social services (Zuurmond 1994), human resources management in the United States (Garson 1992), document administration in Danish ministries (Hertzum 1995), and case administration in the Dutch ministries (Snellen 1994). Some studies suggest that IT is particularly valuable to "knowledge managers" who directly use operational and performance data in order to monitor the work of subordinates and to allocate financial and material resources. However, there are also many public managers who use IT more indirectly, relying on support personnel (i.e. administrative staff, policy analysts, information officers, etc.) to interpret the unit's IT based information. The manager then uses these summarized data and interpretations to control staff and operations (Kraemer et al. 1993; Overman and Loraine 1994).

3.3   Effectiveness

The impacts of IT on the effectiveness of public administration are measured through three indicators: improved decision processes; improved planning; and improved products and/or services. In the research, 29 findings regarding effectiveness were identified, fewer than for either information quality or efficiency. Effectiveness impacts were positive in fully 83% of the findings. In fact, while there were some null findings, there was only one negative finding regarding IT and effectiveness.

Several studies focus particularly on GIS, which have produced benefits for both decision-making and planning. For example, digitized maps of the government's jurisdiction and service areas have facilitated the planning regarding location of and implementation related to such programs as public utilities, roads, redevelopment, etc. The GIS systems have also supported modeling in such areas as economic and demographic analyses (Brown 1996). IT applications such as database systems and productivity software (e.g., Microsoft Office, Lotus Domino & Notes, WordPerfect Office) enhance the capabilities of public officials to draw upon a richer array of information and to undertake more sophisticated analyses in the policy process. Improvements in information-analytic capabilities, such as forecasting and scenario-building, have been shown to result in improved decision making, in such areas as financial management, economic policy planning, human resource management, and public safety (Andersen and Madsen 1992; Garson 1992; Kraemer et al. 1993; Northrop et al. 1994).

Most of the studies which identified improvements in effectiveness attributable to IT relate to the public sector's *provision of services and products*. Many IT systems facilitate the citizen's ability to gain access to government service providers and the government's ability to target public goods to appropriate citizen-clients. These effects of IT improve the responsiveness of government units to citizens' specific service needs (Norris 1992). Key examples of such enhancements are the "one-stop shops" of local governments (Ducatel 1994; Bellamy et al. 1995; Steyaert 2000), Internet-based communications between citizens and public administrators (Hepworth 1992), and systems for general document administration (Northrop et al. 1994; Hertzum 1995).

4.   IT IMPACTS ON INTERACTIONS

One of the most powerful attributes of IT is its capacity to facilitate patterns of communication and engagement among political actors. Overall, more than one-fourth of the findings deal with these impacts of IT on interactions involving the public sector and politics. During the period analyzed, the substantial majority of the documented impacts on interactions are related to changes in the internal operations of a governmental unit. These are reflected in Table 3.4 in the fact that nearly three-fifths of the findings that address the effects of IT focus either on the shifts in intra-organizational control and power (36%) or on coordination and cooperation between governmental units (26%). The remaining two-fifths of the impacts register a change in the relations between citizens and government, between the private sector and the public sector, or between citizen groups.

The majority (65%) of the findings report positive impacts of IT on interactions in the political world. This proportion of positive impacts is generally similar for two of the three interaction categories with the most frequent reported impacts: organizational power and control and coordination/cooperation. It is noteworthy that several categories of interaction effects are characterized by a relatively high proportion of negative or mixed impacts, including citizen-public sector interactions. We consider below why the impacts of IT on these important domains of interactions are almost as likely to be negative or unclear as they are to be positive.

Table 3-4. IT Impacts on Interactions

Variable	Impacts				
	Positive (%)	Negative (%)	Neither positive nor negative (%)	Total (N)	Mixed (N)
10. Improved coordination/ cooperation	71	12	18	17	2
11. Citizen-public sector interactions	53	32	16	19	4
12. Private sector-public sector interactions	75	25	0	4	1
13. Citizen-citizen interactions	100	0	0	2	0
14. Organizational control and power	67	17	17	24	5
Total	65	20	15	66	12

Note: See note in Table 3-3.

4.1 Coordination and Cooperation

IT has resulted in increased coordination and cooperation in 71% (seventeen) of the documented cases. Computer-based modeling, electronic registration of users/citizens, and computer-supported collaborative work are examples of the IT uses that have increased coordination and cooperation between the different units in public administration (Norris 1989; Brudney and Brown 1992; Garson 1992; Snellen 1994). In one example, IT has enabled different units of the police force (including remote units) to cooperate in the search for possible suspects, to compare the "modus operandi" (M.O.s) in unsolved cases, and to coordinate the actions of multiple units, even across jurisdictions (Northrop et al. 1994). IT has also enabled various social service agencies to coordinate with each other in determining the eligibility for public services of a particular individual or household, as well as cooperating in the actual provision of a bundle of services and financial aid (Zuurmond 1994).

4.2 Interaction Patterns: Citizen-Public Sector, Business Sector-Public Sector, and Citizens-Citizens

As IT has improved the access to public information for citizens (Scheepers 1994; Hertzum 1995) and companies (Hepworth 1992; Grupe 1995) and has facilitated communications between these groups and public sector employees, the interactions between these groups have generally increased. We identified 25 reports of IT related impacts on such intergroup interactions. The great majority of these findings describe the interactions between citizens and the public sector. Several studies explore the introduction in some local governments of an electronic "front-desk" where public employees can access a range of databases which provide citizens with information and initiate actions in response to citizens' specific needs. Some local governments have introduced videotext systems or web-based systems to streamline this function or to allow citizens to make direct inquiries electronically (Steyaert 2000). Also, GIS systems over the web have improved public participation in such areas as environmental decision-making (Brudney and Brown 1992; O'Looney 1997). These systems enable citizens to search for and visualize useful information and then to communicate to relevant units of the government by a means that can be considerably easier than face-to-face connection. Such linkages can also make it more difficult for public personnel to suppress or retain information which citizens have a legitimate right to access.

Among the 19 findings focusing on the interaction between citizens and the public administration, only half conclude that there have been positive impacts, while about one-third identify negative impacts. The positive interactions primarily relate to the provision of services (Arterton 1988; Hoff and Stormgaard 1991; Northrop et al. 1994). Hoff and Stormgaard (1991), for example, analyze an information system that enables public employees to check electronically whether a citizen is entitled to a given benefit. Normally, a generalist employee will deal with citizens at a "front-desk," using an expert system linked to a range of specialized databases to answer citizen requests. In the 1990s, a number of Danish local governments introduced videotext systems that gave citizens the opportunity to retrieve information themselves about a number of services and other government programs. Such systems seem to empower citizens by reducing or breaking the information monopoly of the public administration.

Such changes associated with IT can increase the transparency and predictability of the citizen's engagement with the public administration; but these processes can also result in negative effects on these interactions. One-third of the impacts in the analyses we studied were negative. In the Dutch social services, for example, IT has limited the flexibility available to public administrators in handling particular cases, thus reducing the possibility of individualizing services to citizens (Scheepers 1994). Similarly, Ingelstam and Palmlund (1991) conclude that one consequence of computer-based case management systems is that the administration has reinforced its domination in relations with citizens/clients in Sweden.

Active political participation via IT – the stuff of "digital democracy" and virtual government visions – has been extensively discussed and subjected to numerous experiments (Becker and Slaton 2000). Yet the studies in our analysis provide few empirical conclusions regarding clear positive effects in this area. Steyeart (2000) concludes that the information systems in Flanders are not constructed to encourage communication from citizens to their local governments. And Dutton and Guthrie's (1991) study of Santa Monica's public electronic network (PEN) illuminates government managers' struggles to gain control of network developments affected by citizen groups, as well as interagency competition. Although no single actor succeeded in gaining control, PEN did not ultimately serve as a strong medium for civil, civic engagement. Snellen (1994) points out that although the automation of a range of tasks in several Dutch ministries has resulted in operational improvements on the majority of routine decisions, the process has not established any formal mechanisms which incorporate citizens in more active decision-making roles. This implies that IT might support the making of decisions about citizens, but automated systems have generally not furthered the goal of enabling the citizens to shape their interactions with government more fully.

Several studies conclude that IT has increased political communication or interactions between citizens. Arterton's (1988) study finds that IT has facilitated a moderate increase in participation, although the costs related to that increase have been considerable. Similarly, Schuler (1994) describes the contributions of IT to citizen-citizen interactions in various pilot projects or experiments that have encouraged the growth of citizen networks. Leizerov (2000) details a case study of political mobilization, in which geographically diverse individuals used the Internet to share information and then to organize citizen advocacy groups into social movements that worked collaboratively against Intel Corporation's introduction of a new chip with a personal identifier.

Only a few findings focus on public sector-private sector interactions. It is now possible for companies to utilize IT to collect better and more extensive information from the public sector. This typically enables private sector actors to understand and relate more effectively to public policies and governmental agencies. At the same time, many private sector actors are now required to submit data to public agencies in increasing amounts and on a more frequent basis. As IT facilitates the expansion of information in the public sector, the commercial value of information collected and processed by such units as state agencies and local governments has increased. Given this rich data regarding government activities, citizens, and the environment, there is growing demand for publicly-held information to serve the commercial interests of marketing firms, financial investors, contractors, R and D firms, consulting firms, and so on (Hepworth 1992). Such demands for public information and interest in data mining by private actors generate policy challenges for public administrators, not only regarding privacy issues and from a legal point of view (that is, who has legitimate access to what "public information"?), but also in terms of pricing. If a public agency does provide information to a nongovernmental actor, should the price reflect merely the costs of reproduction, or should it also reflect the full cost of collecting and processing the information (Grupe 1995)? Several countries, including Denmark, have prepared circulars and directions advising public administrators how to respond to such issues. However, there is room for substantial interpretation in these regulations and thus continuing uncertainty regarding how much of a "public good" such information should be.

4.3   Organizational Control and Power

Twenty-four findings deal with organizational control and power relations. Among these, 67% are positive, 17% are negative, and 17% are characterized by impacts that are not clearly positive or negative. Some of these studies examine the power relations among those within the public sector, such as functional experts, knowledge workers and managers, while other studies focus on the power balance between citizens and government. Regarding intraorganizational control, there has been considerable attention in the literature on how IT can contribute to the pursuit of key functional objectives (e.g., total quality management, business process reengineering) that emphasize the capacity of management to establish greater control over middle-level personnel by setting up work teams rather than offices. Seen from this perspective, IT has had a positive impact for public managers, even if the findings of Overman and Loraine (1994) are correct that the impacts of IT have a more symbolic than substantive value in terms of cost control, planning, or quality control. Examples of interorganizational control attributable to IT include the management of social security and the oversight of agencies by their state legislatures (Miewald and Mueller 1987; Dyerson and Roper 1991; Ingelstam and Palmlund 1991).

In some of the empirical studies, the impacts on intraorganizational control are more ambiguous. Clement (1994) finds, in his study of telephone operators, library assistants and secretaries, that IT has been a factor in redistributing control toward those lower in the organizational hierarchy. However, in his study of gender and job functions, Norris (1992) concludes that IT has not changed important aspects of control and has not created friction among work peers or between employees and managers. Dunkle et al. (1994) report that the distribution of IT resources within U.S. local governments has been relatively stable among functional units across the period 1975, 1985 and 1998, inferring that there has been no redistribution of intraorganizational power associated with those resources.

While most studies deal only indirectly with the impacts of IT on power relations between government and citizens, this topic is a core concern in

Rodan's (1998) analysis of the relationship between the government of Singapore and the impacts of the Internet. While Singapore has been committed to creating one of the most wired societies in the world and to supporting IT development to drive its success in the new economy, its dominant People's Action Party has been unwilling to surrender its authoritarian political control. Given the presumed effects of the Internet in loosening such control over politically-relevant information, the government has responded aggressively. Its policies regarding IT have emphasized the extensive use of court prosecution, censorship and surveillance to insure that no serious opposition to PAP rule is facilitated by the Internet. Even Internet-based information sources from outside Singapore are effectively controlled by restrictive public policies, which punish carriers of material judged to be anti-government.

5.   IT IMPACTS ON ORIENTATIONS

As indicated in Table 3.5, only a few articles deal explicitly with the impacts of IT on the orientations of those taking action and making decisions in the political system. We assessed three potential impacts of IT on orientations: an emphasis on quantitative criteria; the manner in which policy problems are structured; and increased discretion for public administrators. There are only four empirically grounded findings in the articles that directly address the latter two categories of impacts. Three studies present findings regarding the impacts of IT on public administrators' **discretion**. In the Netherlands, Snellen (1994) finds that the application of IT to quantify programmatic elements and policy options within the social services has reduced the scope of discretionary action for case administrators. In contrast, several other studies conclude that public administrators experience greater discretion over decision and action as IT enables them to access richer data which inform their decision-making on individual cases (Weikart and Carlson 1998).

In the research examined, most of the conclusions about IT related effects on political orientations focus on the growing emphasis on **quantitative decision criteria**. Regarding such an emphasis, there are two general normative perspectives. One perspective argues that extensive quantitative data improve decision-making by providing relatively objective information which aids rational thinking and which actually makes it easier to introduce qualitative viewpoints in appropriate ways, within an analytic framework. The alternative perspective proposes that IT privileges what Joseph Weizenbaum (1976) calls "instrumental reason" – an orientation which devalues qualitative thinking and arguments in the decision process, relative to quantitative analyses, to the detriment of sound decision-making.

Table 3-5. Impacts of IT on the Orientations of Political Actors

Variable	Impacts				
	Positive (%)	Negative (%)	Neither positive nor negative (%)	Total (N)	Mixed (N)
15. Emphasis on quantitative criteria	89	11	0	9	1
16. Structuring of problems	100	0	0	1	0
17. Increased discretion	67	33	0	3	0
Total	85	15	0	13	1

Note: See note in Table 3.3.

The studies in our analysis conclude that the uses of quantitative data have become more extensive as IT has become a key instrument in policy processes. Fully 89% of the findings conclude that this emphasis on quantitative criteria yields overall benefits by facilitating useful comparisons and more accurate calculations (Kraemer et al. 1993; Scheepers 1994). Andersen and Madsen (1992) examine the use of IT based regional and macro-economic models in Danish local governments, the Employment Service, and economic policymaking. Their study finds that the quantification of economic effects from proposed legislation and policies is becoming an increasingly important element in the decision process. However, the study also concludes that very few of the actors who directly or indirectly use the information from the models understand the basis of data and calculation methods of the models.

6.   IT IMPACTS ON VALUE DISTRIBUTIONS

Table 3.6 lists the five areas of potential impacts from IT on the distribution of values within the political system. Interestingly, the research findings associated with IT related impacts on value distributions reveal the highest proportion of <u>negative</u> impacts (44% of the total). This is more than twice as high a percentage of negative impacts as for interactions, three times higher than for orientations, and five times higher than for capabilities. The proportion of negative impacts from IT is particularly high on matters associated with standards of health, safety and well-being (where the only two findings of IT impacts are negative) and on the protection and improvement of the individual's private sphere. Negative impacts are also high regarding job satisfaction and protection of legal rights.

Table 3-6. IT Impacts on Value Distributions

Variable	Impacts				
	Positive (%)	Negative (%)	Neither positive nor negative (%)	Total (N)	Mixed (N)
18. Protection and improvement of the private sphere	22	78	0	9	1
19. Job satisfaction and enrichment	63	38	0	16	5
20. Job enlargement	80	20	0	10	0
21. Protection of legal rights	67	33	0	6	1
22. Improved standard of health, safety and well-being	0	100	0	2	0
Total	56	44	0	43	7

Note. See note in Table 3.3.

These studies identify several areas where IT impacts are associated with the erosion of **the private sphere**. The government's utilization of IT to collect and process personal data about individuals' jobs, purchasing patterns, marital status, and so on is a generally accepted public activity for public administrators in social welfare systems like Denmark and Sweden (Ingelstam and Palmlund 1991; Grupe 1995). However, the widespread utilization of personal data by certain political actors, such as those in social services, law enforcement, or political interest groups, is characterized in most studies as an undesirable diminution of the citizens' private sphere. This judgment seems especially evident in countries that emphasize individual freedom, such as the United States (Frenkel 1988). Rodan's (1998) study of Singapore described above, is a particularly clear example of the negative uses of IT for government surveillance of citizens and political groups.

Even in Sweden, the expanding collection of personal data in governmental information systems resulted in a public backlash, led to the founding of an organization to ensure that the citizens' information privacy rights are not ignored, and stimulated the passage of one of the first national policies to protect those rights (Ingelstam and Palmlund 1991). Many countries are re-assessing the desirability of integrating files on individuals across multiple agencies and government levels and are attempting to resolve the tradeoffs between the government's legitimate need for information and the citizen's rights to limit the collection and use of personal data.

In general, the impacts of IT on job enlargement and job satisfaction seem somewhat contingent on the type of work and the organizational culture of a specific context (Scheepers 1994; Snellen 1994). In our analysis, nearly all of the instances of *job enlargement* impacts of IT on the work environment of knowledge workers have been positive. These studies note that IT has enlarged the domain of work and increased the variation in tasks performed by public employees, across a variety of types of public agencies and levels of government (Henry and Stone 1994; Northrop et al. 1994; Zeffane 1994).

The effects are considerably more mixed with respect to IT related impacts on *job satisfaction*. For example, workers find that telecommuting can produce both positive and negative impacts on their job. Moreover, in some cases employees report that IT has increased their job satisfaction, as they are more in control of their own work situation, less dependent on information from others, or dominated by others with greater "information power" in the workplace. But there are also negative effects in more than one-third of the studies, due to such consequences of IT as social isolation and reduced synergism from the reduction of face-to-face peer interactions. Clement (1994) concludes that there are demonstrable negative impacts of IT on the work environment of particular classes of workers, such as women in clerical positions. And IT causes some public employees to report lowered job satisfaction as it increases the time pressure on completing tasks. Moreover, the absence of IT skills, especially given the frequent changes of information systems-in-use, generates job anxieties for some end users.

The research concludes that the uses of IT to protect the *citizens' legal rights* have been somewhat more positive than negative. In Scandinavia, the development and legitimization of the modern welfare state are closely connected with IT based systems which aim to ensure that citizens are treated in a fair and equal manner and that they receive the services to which they are entitled (Hoff and Stormgaard 1991; Ingelstam and Palmlund 1991). Elections constitute another area where IT has generally had a positive impact. Computer processing of ballot papers usually assures quick election results in which people can have greater confidence than hand counts (Saltman 1988); however there can be problems associated with the accuracy and reliability of computer use in the voting process (Frenkel 1988), a fact brought into dramatic relief in the U.S. presidential election of 2000.

7.   CONCLUSIONS

This chapter has assessed a set of empirical studies that examine the impacts of information technology in the public sector. Our substantive goal has been to ground discussions of such impacts in a strong social-scientific foundation. Of the 230 specific findings in recent empirical research, nearly half of those findings are associated with changes in the capabilities of political units that are attributable to the uses of IT. There are a substantial number of findings associated with all three categories of capabilities in our study: efficiencies, effectiveness and information quality. More than one-fourth of all the findings address the ways in which IT shapes the interactions among political actors, particularly regarding aspects of either coordination or control. The impacts of IT on the distribution of values among political actors are the subject of one in six of the findings, with the effects on the quality of the work environment being the most prominent categories. Few of the empirical findings reported on IT impacts on the orientations of political actors, except to conclude that quantitative criteria have become more a prevalent element in decision and action.

Our systematic review of research findings does not reveal a clear pattern of positive or negative effects from IT– the picture is more complex. Figure 3.1 provides a graphical mean to consider the proportion of positive and negative effects from IT on each of the 22 specific categories in our analysis. As a category is closer to the <u>bottom</u> of Figure 3.1, the proportion of findings reporting positive IT related impacts increases. A striking aspect of looking at the data in this manner is that positive impacts from IT (the black bars) are quite predominant for many of the categories. Conversely, on only six of the twenty-two categories are there 25% or more negative impacts (the light bars). With regard to the four broad domains, there does not seem to be a strong pattern among the specific impact categories at the two extremes. However, many of the categories that are associated with efficiency and rationality effects do tend to be the ones that report the highest proportion of positive impacts. Also, many of the categories which involve the more subjective impacts of IT on people as they relate to government, whether in their roles as private citizens or public employees, tend to have relatively lower proportions of positive impacts.

Based on the empirical research analyzed here, we might tentatively conclude that, in general, the clearest positive impacts generated by IT on public administration are in the areas of efficiency and productivity of government performance, in both internal operations and service functions. There are also substantial information benefits, such as improved data access and quality for both public administrators and citizens. The most prevalent negative impacts from IT are reported in areas such as IT related effects on citizens' private and legal spheres and their interactions with government, and on public employees' work environments and power relationships.

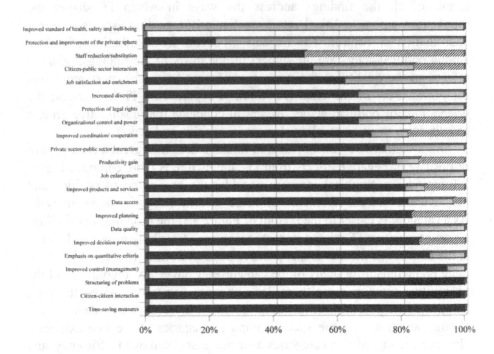

Figure 3-1. Distribution of Positive, Negative and Neutral IT Impacts, by Impact Category

At the broadest level, this chapter has raised the issue of whether IT has transformed public administration. Given the standard political science notion of transformation in terms of fundamental change, the articles in this study suggest that the answer is no. The articles offer little evidence that IT has caused a major redistribution of values and power in the public sector, or has resulted in a basic alteration in actors' orientations, or has dramatically restructured interaction patterns. Even in the domain of capabilities, the area where the most intensive IT based changes are reported in the research, it seems hyperbolic to characterize the changes as revolutionary.

In our analytic reading of the research published on impacts, we are persuaded that IT is penetrating ever deeper into virtually every aspect of public administration. The research provides considerable evidence that the impacts of IT on public administration are often substantial and result in many significant modifications of behaviors and structures. Moreover, if one considers the history of other major technologies, it is quite likely that the changes from IT will be pervasive, but will typically be gradual, lagged in time, and often subtle.

Chapter 4

DIGITAL WHEELBARROWS IN LOCAL GOVERNMENT

1. INTRODUCTION

Despite the rapid IT uptake in organizations, the research on the relationship between organizations and IT has not or has only marginally undergone changes during the past ten years (Myers et al. 2000). Throughout the 1970s, 1980s, and 1990s researchers suggested that digitalization should be approached from ones angles apart from only the technology domain. They argued that changes in technical opportunities are mediated by a rather complex interaction between technology, organizational structures, and actors (Leavitt 1970; Marcus 1983; Zuboff 1988).

Although we have witnessed a move towards the networked and imaginary organization (Hedberg et al. 1998), the two cases explored in this chapter witness a high focus on transactions and re-use of digital data (Coase 1937, 1960; Williamson 1975; North 1981). In government, this shift is perhaps less prevalent than in the private sector. Government appears to be more eager on using IT as a technology to substitute activities and people rather than as a technology to help analyzing the activities and possibly improve these. Also, rather than opening up the organization, IT has followed existing structures and evolved in areas less involved with customer interactions.

This chapter examines governments' i) ability to use data for transactional purposes within their own domain ii) the capability to use exchange data across organizational boundaries, iii) use of data to enhance their services. All three areas are within what technically could be expected to have evolved after the widespread adoption of computers and connectivity network capacity have been installed.

The chapter identifies a continuously and successful *reliance on transaction and process improvements* and no or only marginal use of data to improve the core of services. Governments' obsession to get yet bigger and more digital wheel barrows, digital storage containers as well as digital waste dump sites outweighs attention on how governmental services can be improved and transformed. Thus, whereas the figures on the overall uptake of IT in government are encouraging, the uptake of Intranet is discouraging. The widespread uptake of Intranet can cement and glue the government units by fostering integration with structural barriers (Giesbers 2001) and create barriers of accessibility and transparency from the customers point of view.

This chapter reveals that even when process and transactional improvements occur, institutional arrangements and governmental payment and reimbursement schemes can make actors and institutions *reluctant to report such impacts,* especially considering that budget costs etc. might be the consequence of such reporting.

2.   THE UPTAKE OF IT

The uptake of intra- and interorganizational information systems progress in many cases at grass-root level and lead to islands in government having intranet services, rather than a unified, organization wide implementation (Lamb and Davidson 2002). Onwards, the dream that uptake of IT-application as SAP would be associated with organizational information order and agreement on standards for data storage and exchange rarely has been fulfilled (Hanseth and Braa 1999). This appears to be the status for both the transactional oriented activity areas as e-procurement (please consult chapter 7) and non-transactional activities.

This is surprising since studies have pointed to an early emerge of a digital infrastructure in local government during the 1980s and early 1990s with document management systems as the key application area (Northrop et al. 1990; Kaneda 1994; Hertzum 1995). On examining the studies from the 1980s and early to mid 1990s, one could expect that the use of data has shifted from a transactional focus to a more analytical focus, and thereby has enabled analysis on, such areas as the quality of the services, and the use of IT to help detect fraud.

During 1999/2000 and 2001/2002 we have conducted surveys on municipalities' uptake of IT (Andersen and Nicolajsen 2001; Andersen and Juul 2002). Our surveys confirm the general positive image of the municipalities' use of IT identified in other studies of government adoption of IT (PLS-Rambøll-Management 2000, 2001, 2002; Statistics-Denmark 2002; 2003). Having equipped all governmental offices and personnel with local area network (LAN) and personal computers (PCs) and a high diffusion of home offices for the employees, the Danish public sector is driving towards the next stage in informatization with widespread intra- and internet use, wireless network, and mobile services.

A turning point for the adoption of IT surfaced in the mid 1990s. Within three years from 1993, close to all merged to having electronic archives, management, or mail systems with 1995 being the peak for introducing these technologies. By 1996, about one-third (35%) of the national government, 51% of the municipalities and 64% of the counties reported electronic handling of incoming mail and electronic case handling.

Table 4-1. Introduction and use of electronic case handling and electronic mail in Danish national and local government during the mid 1990s (percentage)

Level of government/ year		No use of electronic archives, management or mail systems	Electronic archiving or electronic case handling systems introduced	Electronic handling of incoming mail and electronic case handling
National	1993	31	20	0
	1995[a]	15	49	2
	1996[a]	4	46	35
Municipalities	1995[b]	11	38	6
	1996[c]	2	28	51
Counties	1995[b]	7	57	0
	1996[c]	0	14	64

Note. a= spring, b=primo, c=ultimo - *Source. DMITAR* (1997)

Although the uptake of IT by government has progressed since the mid 1990s, government still transmits documents between departments rather than between the citizens and companies. Thus, in 2003 about 30% of the public sector institutions received more than 25% of the documents in digital format from other public organizations, whereas only 14% of the public

Table 4-2. Percentage of public sector organizations receiving more than 25% of document in digital format from citizens, companies and other public organizations, 2002 (percentage)

	Percentage of public sector organizations receiving more than 25% of document in digital format
Citizens	14
Companies	18
Other public organizations	30

Source. Statistics Denmark (2003)

sector received more than 25% of documents in digital format exchanged with citizens and 18% with companies.

3.   TRANSACTIONAL USE OF DATA

In 2002, 79% of the Danish municipalities had an Intranet (defined as more than one department having access to the content), whereas 63% of the municipalities had an Intranet in 2001. Also, eight of ten municipalities had an Intranet that encompasses both central administrative offices/ city halls and individual governmental institutions. The primary institutions using the Intranets are in this case eldercare institutions (74%), schools (73%), public libraries (69%) and childcare institutions (68%) (Statistics-Denmark 2002, 2003). The high penetration of Intranet is explored below with respect to availability of data and whether larger municipalities less frequently have to re-key data.

3.1   Availability of data

In our survey data from 2002, 88% of the respondents stated that they had access to shared data bases. Only 26% of our respondents reported that they to a larger degree/ often re-key the same data. Shared data bases/ programs encompassed accounting/ financial data and document management. Also, 70% reported that data was available at the desired time and place. Thus, the respondents did not find that they had to spend a long time searching for the data when they needed it.

Our survey also found that the central offices have access to data stored outside their own organization, more frequently than institutions. Thus, the alignment of the data structure is towards the city hall administration, rather than the activities performed at institutional level. This is in contrast to the principles in the PPR-concept that would argue that if any imbalance should occur it would have to be in favor of the decentralized institutions since these are more directly involved with citizen contact.

Even more troubling is that we found that the physical planning departments are in the top range of data exchange and data availability whereas schools, childcare, and eldercare institutions are the least frequent to report that data are available across institutions.

This is confronting to the PPR-concept since we find that the least customer oriented processes are the ones where most data is available. The PPR-concept would argue that this is an indicator of a practice for digital storage and exchange that is more administration oriented than customer-centric. On the positive side though is that all areas have an availability higher than 50%, implying that the respondent is likely to find the needed data from institutions at the right time and place.

3.2   The issue of scale and scope

Due to more IT resources and more staff trained in process improvement, statistics, etc., we expected that the larger organizations would less frequently re-key data that they receive in digital format. This argument of return to scale is firmly founded in the economic literature on (dynamic) economics of scale and scope.

The scale arguments have been rooted in (more) effective use of indivisible production factors, switching costs, geometric properties and reserve machinery/ maintenance in a static or dynamic learning (decrease in marginal costs). The *scope argument* argues for the economic rationality in having different activities under the same roof (decrease in total cost). Along the same line, one could expect that the larger organizations have greater returns to scale in areas such as social security (Ingelstam and Palmlund 1991; Scheepers 1994) and police (Northrop et al. 1994).

Yet, with a γ-value at 0.23 and a p-value at .0321 we found a weak but *positive correlation between size of the municipality and the re-keying of data.* Although the majority of the municipalities report that they do not or only rarely re-key the same data twice, the statistical test suggests that the larger municipalities are more likely to re-key the same data. Close to one-third (29%) of the larger municipalities report that they re-key the same data. More than two-thirds of the respondents in the municipalities with less than 10,000 citizens responded that they never or only to a limited degree have to re-key data.

Table 4-3. Re-keying of data correlation with number of citizens.

Number of citizens	Are the same data entered more than once?				
	At no or only limited degree	Some times	Often or to a large degree	Total (N)	γ P
<10,000	69 %	10 %	21%	100% (48)	0.23
10,000-20,000	59 %	14 %	27%	100% (44)	0.0321
>20,000	46 %	26 %	29%	99% (35)	

Note. The answers are transformed from a seven point Lickert Scale

Various explanations could aid our understanding of the picture formed by the data displayed in Table 4.2. Large municipalities are likely to have *more divisions* and institutions and therefore are likely to need to transmit data more frequently. As a result of the large frequency, they will be more likely to experience the need to re-key data.

Subsequently, larger municipalities might have *more IT applications* that fail to exchange data automatically. For example, the case worker that extracts data from one application may have to enter the very same data in possibly two other application such as client e-mail and case handling application.

4.   ANALYSIS OF DATA

The previous section demonstrated the use of digital wheel barrows to transport the data from one institution to another. The IT-transportation path primarily is from individual institutions to central functions within the city hall/ municipality central administrative functions. Also, we found the areas that are least likely to have direct customer involvement/ relevance are the ones with the most reported data availability. Clearly, the PPR here are at odds with the practice.

The second overall area we address in this chapter is whether the use digital wheel barrows is accompanied by analytical processes where the data is used as input to gain insight in the quality improvement of the services. Only about half the respondents reported that data was used for other purposes than transactions. There was no difference on this dimension whether it was large or small municipalities. Thus, the data are encapsulated in digital containers or forwarded through intranets and network drives as if they were waste dump sites. There is limited practice on how to move from the transactional mode to the analytical phase.

Resounding the concerns expressed above that data availabilities were highest in the non-customer oriented processes, the field of data analysis show similar results. Physical planning is the most frequent to use data to gain new insight and to redesign the quality of their services. 52 % report this, whereas only 41% and 42% respectively of the cultural and daycare institutions, report analytical use of data.

Despite the low frequency of the analytical mode of data usage, 61% of the respondents do not identify major inhibitors for this to start. 21 percent find substantial barriers for analysis of data. The barriers we have found most critical are
– The cost of the technical applications and implementation
– The overall readiness to start analysis
– The lack of technical appropriate software
The importance of technical barriers for progressing with collection and analysis of data varies with the size of the municipality. The larger the municipality, the less important are technical barriers. Analyzing the correlation between size (number of citizens or total expenditures), we found

a negative correlation (-0.26, -0.25) for number of citizens respective total budget as explanatory variables for the variance in the respondents' perception of the importance of technical barriers. The overall correlation is about the same whether measuring size by number of citizens or budget. Yet, there is significant different distribution for the mid-size municipalities' perception. If taking the number of citizens as an indicator, 62% found technical barriers not to play an important role.

Table 4-4. Number of citizens correlated with perception of technical barriers for data collection and analysis

Number of citizens	How important are inadequate technical solutions as a barrier for the municipality's collection and analysis of data?				
	No or only limited importance	Some	To a large extent	Total (N)	γ P
<10,000	48 %	19 %	32%	(31)	-0.26
10,000-20,000	62 %	7 %	31%	(29)	0.0443
>20,000	68 %	21 %	11%	(19)	

Note. The answers are transformed from a seven point Lickert Scale

Using the budget as an explanatory variable, confirm the negative correlation (γ=-.25) between size of the municipality and their view of inadequate technical solutions as a barrier for the municipality's collection and analysis of data. For the mid-range municipalities, however, 42 percent view these as important when correlating the expenditures and technical solutions, whereas 31 percent of the mid-range municipalities measured by population size agreed to this.

Table 4-5. Total expenditures correlated with perception of technical barriers for data collection and analysis

Total expenditures (Million USD)	How important are inadequate technical solutions as a barrier for the municipality's collection and analysis of data?				
	At no or only limited extend	Sometimes	To a large extent or often	Total (N)	γ P
<50	50 %	25 %	25%	100% (24)	-0.25
50-113	52 %	6 %	42%	100% (31)	0.0380
> 113	74 %	17 %	9%	100% (23)	

Note. The answers are transformed from a seven point Lickert Scale

5.   **EXCHANGE BETWEEN GOVERNMENTAL**
        UNITS AND BETWEEN GOVERNMENT AND
        PRIVATE SECTOR

With between two-thirds and three-quarters of all letters of discharge
(68%), laboratory test results (74%), and prescription letters (77%) in
December 2003 (MedCom 2004), the Danish national health network has
been successful in linking the private general practitioners (GP) and
pharmacies with the governmental run hospitals, laboratories, and state-run
health insurances. Yet, the governmental actors are the least successful
actors with only 21% of the messages to and from the municipalities and
59% of the reimbursement notifications from the health insurance being
included.

There has been intensive policy attention given to this field because of
the cost of the health sector, rather than the health data network per se.
Achieving and monitoring managerial benefits have been the goals for the
network. Therefore, the network has progressed and materialized with only
limited attention to the end-customers being left out in designing and
implementing the network.

With an annual flow of more than two million messages, the network has
gained transactional success using the EDI-technology. During the late
1980s and early 1990s extensive literature on EDI in the health sector
surfaced. The literature did not so much address the technical problems per
se or the problems with computers. Rather the focus was shifted to how to
use EDI inter- and intraorganizationally. Since then, a massive development
in the application and communication channels and improved user ability
has emerged. EDI is now regarded as the simple form of communication
between organizations and individuals. There have also been several studies
published suggesting that negative lock-in impacts could occur with regards
to costs of service and reduced ability to innovate the communication.

In 1992, Fuen County initiated the development of the Fuen health data
network. Communication was established via an electronic mailbox wiring
hospitals, general practitioners (GPs), pharmacies, and the regional health
insurance. The health data network involves communication with letters of
discharge from hospitals to GPs, laboratory and radiology reports to the GPs,
prescriptions from GPs to pharmacies, current information on the
occupancies of the hospital departments, waiting lists, treatment procedures
etc. from the hospitals to the GPs, reimbursement forms from the GPs and
pharmacies to the regional health insurance, and medical information from
the wholesale suppliers to the pharmacies/ doctors. The communication
follows the Electronic Data Interchange for Administration, Commerce and
Transport (EDIFACT) developed by the UN and approved by the

International Standards Organization (IOS) and Comite European de Normalisation (CEN).

Figures 4.1 and 4.2 display the number of messages per month from the very start of the health data network till the end of 2003 and the relative diffusion of the messages as compared to the total number of messages.

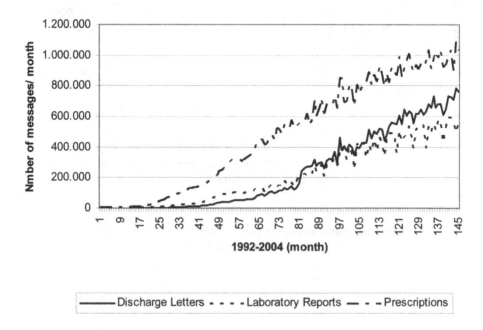

Figure 4-1. Number of messages, 1992-2003 - *Source*: http://www.medcom.dk

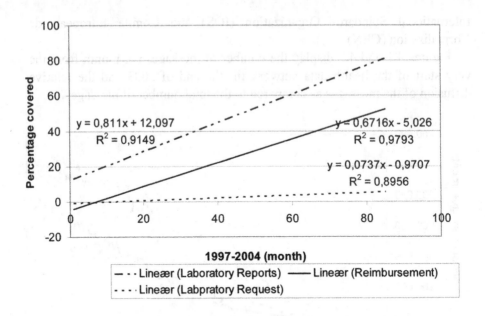

Figure 4-2. Actual messages relative to potential, 1992-2003 - *Source*:
http://www.medcom.dk

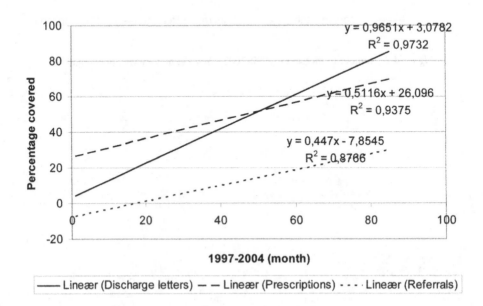

Figure 4-3. Discharge letters, Prescriptions and Referrals

Quick laboratory response is critical for increasing or expanding the number of patients treated, such as the case for adjusting the medication for diabetics. Although our data show mixed impacts on the networks' impact on timely laboratory response, it must also be kept in mind, that the incentive to report major impact on faster treatment etc. can be underestimated due to financial motives. Doctors' practices receive payment from the general health insurance. If they were to report major time reductions, the standard fees for the treatment of each patient might be reduced accordingly. A clearer impact can be identified when the question is rephrased and asks about time reduction in handling laboratory responses and letters of discharge. Here we witness time reductions up to an average of five minutes for receiving letters of discharge.

The net-benefit for the hospital and others has been low or even counter-productive due to the double-administration. In addition, the reason for not using computers in the doctors' practice was during the later part of the 1990s often explained by economic and professional arguments, rather than technical or unfamiliarity issues. Though the economic resources for developing the network is claimed to be sufficient, funding for transferring from one system to another might have slowed down the implementation process.

Before the network was established, the status of the computer facilities at the doctors' practices, the clinical departments at the hospitals and the laboratories were surveyed. Within the doctors' practices, about half of the respondents reported that they have used computers in their correspondence with national health insurance less than six months prior to the time that the connection to the network was established. The other half used it for more than six months. Yet, about two-thirds of the doctors have had electronic patient records more than six months prior to using the health data network.

Although this indicates a difference in technical abilities, a perhaps greater variance exists in classification and standardization of coding of the work. Within public administration literature, emphasis has been made about the autonomy of the actors and the street-level workers. Health care involves quite a number of street level workers, such as home nurses and cleaning staff that clean sick persons' homes (if they are being taken care of at home, instead of at the hospitals).

There is an enormous flow of data in connection with this service. Most of it is still not computerized since the classification in the municipalities varies greatly. So far, though, it has not been possible to get this part of the health sector, the municipalities, involved in the health data network. Also, there is a decentralized welfare service at work here providing the municipalities with autonomy to decide how much service they want to provide and the quality of that service. If all the data indicating the efficiency and effectiveness were exposed, privatization and standardization could be the answer. Also, centralization in steering might increase. The resistance towards this tendency is high in Denmark. In other countries, such as Norway and Germany, signs of centralization have already been observed.

While there has been substantial pressure from the county administration and at the national level, the intended users' need for the network varies. In general however, the need is sufficient to establish an interest and a commitment. About half of the respondents reported to have no discussions or plans for which educational requirements or challenges to the organization of the workplace could be posed by the network. With a general commitment to improve the treatment of patients, most of the initiatives are made, however, behind the curtain, i.e. administrative procedures. At the pharmacies, for example, more than three-quarters of the prescriptions are received through the network. The rest are either called in by phone or sent by fax. Furthermore, all prescriptions are computed in their internal computer-system allowing them to expedite billing to the national health insurance and print labels for the drugs.

By contrast, in the pharmacies' communication with the administration in the municipality, the records at the pharmacies are printed and then sent by s-mail to the municipalities. In the municipality, the records are entered again. Here, we point to an obvious need for the network. Yet, this seems to indicate that most of the participants, (public or private institutions) still approach networking as an internal matter, rather than as an interorganizational data network. One of the reasons for thinking this way is the relative limited resources for the network, especially in municipalities and hospitals. Another reason is --as suggested earlier-- economic motives. The limited personnel resources and economic resources are in most cases linked very closely.

As revealed in the previous section, the health data network had considerable success if measured by the *number of users*, their *satisfaction with the interface, time-reduction* in receive/ recording responses from pharmacy or letter of discharge, transmission of prescription, and retrieval of information. However, the network had *little or no impact on treatment, communication pattern, and organizational issues*. These results have implications both for the future of the Fuen network, its expansion to other areas within the health sector, and the development of nation-wide networks.

In developing and implementing the network, multiple actors have been involved. The increased policy attention received from international, national and local levels of government as well as from the private sector, also contributed to its recognized success. Besides, at the national and international level, multiple political and corporate actors have been advocating for the establishment of a network allowing the participating sectors to communicate faster and with increased accuracy.

The push for the computerized data network, and in turn for the electronic patient journal (EPJ) came from more than one place. The National Health Insurance and in turn the Ministry of Health as well as other insurance companies are among the stronger players. With the outbreak of the HIV-AIDS virus, a great demand for patient information arose from the insurance companies. Through lobbying they were able to change the law, and obtain access to the patient files kept at the GPs and hospitals. This paved the road for the electronic data network to include information beyond transaction forms, letters of discharge, etc. Prior to that Fuen County has been particularly active in the development of the network, through the funding of the Center for Health Informatics.

While the county runs hospitals (only a small fraction is privately run), the GPs tend to have private practices. The same goes for the pharmacies. As pointed out above, there is a multitude of institutions and actors involved in the network, each with a different need for being informed. For example, while the GPs' need to be informed might be high, they might not want to expose possible cost reductions as a consequence of their investment in IT, since the reimbursement per patient from health insurance will likely be reduced. Similarly, through computerization the hospitals can possibly save a part of their administration costs, although it is very difficult to estimate who and how much is saved by investing and participating in IOS, such as EDI.

For example, in a publication the Danish Ministry of Technology and Research estimated that about 30 % of the manpower resources at the hospitals are used for documentation and administration. They expected similar resources to be used by the GPs (DMITAR 1994). It is no surprise that this conclusion elicited a feverish response from the professional organizations and the hospitals. The 30 % were taken from an American survey, which, they argued, was not applicable to the Danish health policy area. The quarrel ended with the Ministry withdrawing the estimate.

Secondly, there is a complex organizational structure of the departments at the hospitals. Each of them is very eager to keep a firm grip on funds and make sure that funding is not lost to other departments. This is not to indicate that they do not want to be efficient, but that their willingness to expose results, documents, and departmental affairs in a computerized network can be limited. The network in Fuen focused on communication, but in order to gain the full benefit from a network, a computerized "base" must be present, which the health sector lacks. Also, within the hospitals one finds a very different organizational push for the network. There is a push from the administration, as well as the labs. But the clinical departments' eagerness in this matter falls short.

To summarize, the health data network is successful but primarily and early on in the private sector and scattered in regions. From a PPR-perspective it is noticeable that this success has not led to initiatives from health insurance to cut overall costs. This is partly due to the fact that administrative costs for GPs is a fraction of the total costs and in the hospitals where the administrative costs amount to about 30%, the adoption of MedCom has been scattered and it is yet to be demonstrated that the overall impacts had led to actual saving.

6.   CONCLUSIONS

This chapter has demonstrated that the government has excelled in acquiring and using the digital wheel barrows in the areas of municipalities internal communication, and in national laboratories and health insurance involvement within the health data network.

The transaction oriented health data network could imply that *local and corporate autonomy* is essential to make ongoing innovations and secure some degree of competition in a mostly publicly financed health sector. In Fuen, the number of GPs and pharmacies being wired is the engine behind the development. The relatively small scale of the network makes changes and quick feedback possible. National systems might come too late, address misleading or wrong issues, and be hard to change. We found a bottom-up organizational process for such systems much more attractive. Thus, networks should emerge at the lowest level possible (in this case at the county levels) initiated by local actors and interests, although this could challenge the control and autonomy of the Ministry of Health. Bureaucratic and professional resistance, and issues of privacy are likely to be substantial barriers for not only the completion of such a network but also development of similar networks.

This chapter has highlighted the centralization of success with the city hall office being more likely to receive and access data from the branches of government, than vice versa. Also, we pointed out that those areas removed from the customers are the more successful areas for data exchange. The health data network is an example of this and in the municipality we identified the area of physical planning as the most frequent area of data exchange.

Although the health data network has potentials and already has departed from solely using digital containers and digital waste dump sites, we found limited analytical use of the data in municipalities. This highly alarming finding is propelled even further by the fact that the physical planning is leading analysis whereas the areas with most frequent customer interaction submit.

Chapter 5

E-GOVERNMENT OBJECTIVES, MEANS, AND REACH

1. INTRODUCTION

The start of the 21st century has been turbulent when it comes to beliefs in what and to what degree IT can facilitate organizational and business changes. Simultaneously with the fading of enthusiasm regarding e-commerce in the private sector after the burst of the "dot-com" bubble, government has to an increasingly degree been expressing a firm belief that e-government could channel tasks from manual processes to electronic procedures. This is most predominant in the areas of internal administrative and services, legal control, and law enforcement. The IT enthusiasm has also been apparent in the active role of government seeking to transform society by pushing and pulling the private sector and citizens to adopt on-line government services.

In a review of literature on e-government themes and issues, we used the title "e-government: stray gods or wild cats" to capture the fragmented and segmented e-government initiatives and mostly ad hoc, discipline oriented, and small scale studies (Andersen et al. 2004). There appears to be few, if any, new substantial and fundamental research questions addressed in the e-government literature that has emerged so far. The use of solid research methods is seldom and experiments with the technology almost absent (Grönlund 2004).

Thus, there are many remedies from the e-commerce wave and it could be feared that e-government is more a signal of crisis rather than it is reflecting and facilitating a change in implementation of IT in government.

On the positive side, however, there is now so much *current* in the way IT is approached in government that new opportunities have emerged for both research and practice to alter organizational practice towards the PPR-concept.

This chapter identifies numerous variations in the domains of e-government and how and what part of e-government is studies which seems to suggest that there are *more issues that divide rather than unite scholars and practitioners* using the e-government term.

We will start the chapter addressing whether IT in government is a special case or equal to IT implementations in other sectors. The main argument pursued is that there indeed are special characteristics that at least the IS-community has not been able to address so far. At present, e-government research is primarily from the legacy of IS research and has failed to *incorporate disciplines such as public administration and political science.*

Changing this path could offer rewarding research and practice opportunities for materializing the PPR-approach. Thus, a key point in this chapter is that the IS-community has been unable to incorporate the more forward pointing concept of e-governance. For the PPR-concept it is equally important to be aware of the *how and when* questions captured by the governance approach and the formal questions of *who and why* captured by the government approach.

We then provide an overview of the policy and research e-government agenda with variations in objectives, means, and reach. Departing from the strategic and key e-government research issues, we propose an e-government stage model with four phases: cultivation, extension, maturity, and revolution. With the basis in the literature review, this chapter argues that we are in the first phase only and that significant challenges are ahead before maturing to the subsequent phases.

2.   IT IN THE PUBLIC ADMINISTRATION: A SPECIAL OR TRIVIAL CASE?

IT in government is not a new phenomenon. IT applications were adopted by public sector institutions about the same time as by businesses and the literature is rich with examples describing the adoption and use of IT applications within the public sector institutions (Danziger et al. 1982; Kraemer et al. 1995; Heeks 1999; Bretschneider 2003). It is beyond the scope of this chapter to discuss if, and in particular how, IT applications for public sector institutions might differ from those designed for private businesses. We discuss in this section characteristics of the public sector institutions, thereby identifying possible special conditions which IT applications, and furthermore e-government, should meet if successful adoption and implementation is to take place in governmental units.

In the PPR concept we focus primarily on public administration (the executive part), but have included decision-makers as a group of users of information etc. from the administrative body. One of the issues that remain a puzzle for most IS-researchers is how to define government and IT-applications used for government.

One approach is to take a rather narrow view of e-government, by defining government from a pure legacy perspective. According to this view all governmental activities are based on law and e-government applications driven by law enforcement. Supportive of this argument is that taxation through the internet has been a front runner in many countries. We subscribe more to the view that government is not only about law, but is addressing who gets what, when, and how (Laswell 1936). Thus, there is a range of structures, processes, actors and policies that determine or implement the allocation of public values in the collectivity (Easton 1965). Easton's model (see Figure 5.1) brings an awareness of the political environment of which public administration is part, and gives an insight into the complex way in which public services have emerged, been sustained and changed.

For example, some IT-initiatives are motivated by knowledge diffusion as the objective and the means (e.g. educational initiatives). Other IT-initiatives are motivated by objectives to boost foreign investments (e.g. information sites on the attractiveness of the region), or directly part of regulation and legislation (law information). Yet other applications are aiming to improve procedures of government in areas such as e-procurement. Each of these motivations can be directly linked to decisions taken by politicians, based on a rather complex interplay between demand and support for various positions and initiatives, decision-making processes, formulated policies and feedback from the political environment. Complementing the model outlined by David Easton, with a modern more in-depth *governance analysis* (Ham and Hill 1993), could help improve our understanding of *how* IT-initiatives and IT-practices unfold. Thus, the PPR concept is more oriented towards understanding the *how dimension* rather then other vital parts of the politics: who, why, and what.

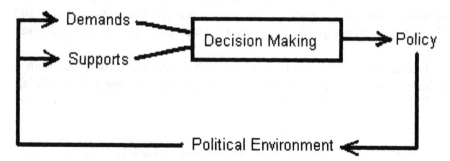

Figure 5-9. Easton's Classical Political System - *Source.* Easton (1965)

The *how dimension* of government's IT-initiatives and practices have many similarities to the lessons learnt from the private sector, yet we take the position that there are special needs necessary for studying IT in government. When we address the issue of whether government differs from the private sector, three positions crystallize: 1) there is no difference, 2) there is a difference, and 3) it depends upon which part of the public sector we focus.

Barry Bozemann (1989) take the position that "all organizations are public" in so far as they are subject to public authority with others arguing that the specific context among other things is constituted by the inherent political and regulated character of both goal-setting and performance (Allison 1984; Klausen 2000).

One of the key characteristics of government is that there are *many and shifting political actors setting the goals.* This picture is contrasting the formal picture of government as being governed by long term strategic plans drafted and decided by the politicians, leaders and managers of public institutions. The goals of government are subject to change whenever shifting political coalitions find it opportune, and they are typically diverse, broad and ambiguous (Hoff 1992). This produces "less direct market exposure (and therefore more reliance on appropriations), resulting in less incentive for productivity and effectiveness, lower allocational efficiency, and lower availability of market information; more legal and formal constraints; and higher political influences, including impacts of interest groups and the need for support of constituencies"(Thong et al. 2000).

At the managerial level, managers are left with "less decision-making autonomy, less authority over subordinates, greater reluctance to delegate, and a more political role for top managers; more frequent turnover of top managers due to elections and political appointments; difficulties in devising incentives for individual performance; and lower work satisfaction and organizational commitment"(Thong et al. 2000).

Furthermore, there are often *strict rules and regulations* as to how various tasks and jobs are to be accomplished, what is to be done and what is not to be done. The room for strategic maneuvering is therefore often very limited. A public institution can for instance neither change its line of production nor can it harvest and invest any profits it may gain from reducing the spending of resources or from performance pay (Klausen 2000).

Overall, the public sector is a very labor intensive workplace with a particular work culture. There are common expectations that public officials act fairly, responsively, are accountable, and honest. Although similar expectations do exist in the private sector, there are different and more legal means to seek these expectations being implemented within the public sector.

In the mid 1990s, Hutton (1996) pointed out that public sector organizations have a number of specific characteristics, including rigid hierarchies, a special work culture, multiple stakeholders for many processes, and boundaries that cannot be crossed. Within the public sector the changes in policy direction can be sudden and dramatic which in turn raise expectations of rapid changes of IT applications in due course for new policy implementation. Also, government has an overlap of initiatives between departments, resulting in often identical IT-applications across departments. Although there are those who are skeptic of governments, there are equally many who have unrealistic expectations of the impacts of government involvement. This often challenges IT-applications to incorporate and model issues that are not well described, but still carry high policy saliency and expectations. Finally, Hutton noted that staff is a crucial part of public sector organizations, which implies in our context, that very few of the IT-applications in the public sector are on physical products optimizations where robots, sensors, etc. are the key. Rather IT-applications are part of organizations which are essentially comprised by humans and not machines. An implication of these characteristics is that "soft" human issues are vital issues to consider when building and implementing IT applications for the public sector (McAdam 1999).

Table 5-1. Governmental characteristics

- labor intensive
- specific context constituted by the inherent political and regulated character of both goal-setting and performance
- political actors setting the goals (not the leaders and managers of public institutions)
- diverse, broad, ambiguous, overlapping, and over ambitious (with respect to impacts) goals are subject to change whenever shifting political coalitions find it opportune
- strict rules and regulations as to how various tasks and jobs are to be accomplished, what is to be done and what is not to be done, e.g. the room for strategic maneuvering is often very limited
- rigid hierarchies and boundaries that cannot be crossed
- less market exposure (indirect link to demand side), hence less incentive for productivity and effectiveness improvement
- special work culture
- expectations that public officials act fairly, responsively, and honestly

3.   E-GOVERNEMENT AT THE STRATEGIC AND RESEARCH AGENDA

Throughout the past five years the term "e-government" has secured a foothold in the vocabulary among politicians, practitioners, and researchers. The former UK eEnvoy, Mr. Alan Mather, stated that e-government "...is just like government, it is just smarter and faster" (Millard 2003). From the PPR-perspective it is appealing to fuel the demand side in making the e-services, e-democracy, and traditional services bigger and better using IT. Also, the ambitions on making the back office administration smaller and smarter is appealing with intra- and intergovernmental process re-engineering along with reengineering of the legacy systems and technologies. The underlying thinking that the service part gets decentralized and the control part gets centralized is far from being in line with the PPR-approach. Instead, we advocate the decentralization and ownership of the activities to the customers and decision-makers. The former UK e-envoy definition of e-government does not bring us closer to that situation. By contrast, this view will more likely reinforce existing structures and patterns.

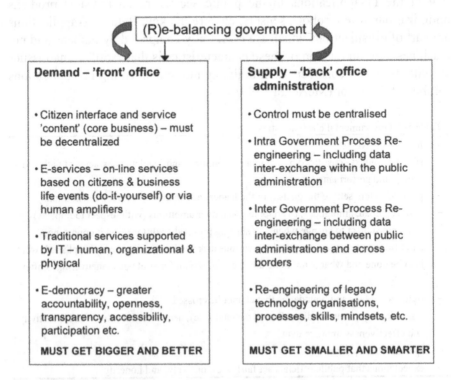

Figure 5-10. Bigger and Better Front Offices and Smaller and Better Back-Offices - *Source.* Millard (2003)

Other authors have suggested that changes will take place in public administration due to e-government, and as a result they advocate strategic visions as part of the transformation (Deb 1999; Luling 2001; Stamoulis et al. 2001; Watson and Mundy 2001; Armstrong 2002; Burn and Robins 2003) and propose guidelines for how to manage the transformation to the more dynamic interaction brought about by the technology (Lenk 2002; Tan and Pan 2003). A competing view is that "...this sounds all too familiar. Almost 20 years ago a similar debate arose...pitting proponents of new IT against those who suggested that existing organizational and political relationships would dramatically influence any use of new in technology" (Bretschneider 2003). Supportive of this view is that e-government applications appears to follow existing patterns of control and institutional view of participation rather than challenging these and there are rarely any experiment with new generations of applications. Instead, government adopt "old" technologies to improve formal communication channels to impede for example participation (see chapter eight).

The significance of e-government is easily traced in the political agendas throughout the world. At the supranational level, e-government has been on the agenda for quite a while (EU 2003; OECD 2003) with national governments catching up by formulating strategies for using technological applications and infrastructures in their work procedures (IAB 1999).

A number of Special Interest Groups (SIGs) have emerged within industry associations such as the Industry Advisory Councils (IAC) SIG on e-government, and within research communities such as the Association of Information Systems (AIS). Various conferences have recently included tracks on e-government as the American Conference on Information Systems (AMCIS). Also, the Database and Expert Systems Applications (DEXA) eGov-conferences and European Conference on e-government, which have specially focused on e-government have surfaced. These events have attracted an increasing number of researchers. Two particularly encouraging developments are the *uptake of e-government is the agenda of core public administration conferences* such as the European Group of Public Administration (EGPA) and International Political Science Association (IPSA) conferences and *journals* being devoted to e-government. This has been demonstrated by special issues (e.g., *Decision Support Systems* and *Information Systems Journal*) and entire new journals being launched on this topic (e.g., *International Journal of e-Government* and *Electronic Journal of eGovernment*).

Although there have been published specific conceptual papers devoted to define e-government (Deb 1999; Silcock 2001; Marche and McNiven 2003), e-government appears in a variety of labels and spellings such as e-government, egovernment, e-governance, egovernance, Egovernment,

Egovernance, one-stop government, digital government, electronic government, and online government.

It is important to be aware of the definition of e-government since there is a watery balance between broad definitions (digital information and on-line transaction services to citizens) and narrow definitions (e-procurement) with respect to creating opportunities and value as a rallying force (Laswell 1936).

The five broad terms e-government, e-governance, digital government, online government, and one-stop government and the spelling variations of these constitute our research entries to identify whether the research community has established a consensus of which of these to use. The information source for this search was the Social Science Citation Index (Web of Science) and ProQuest (ABI/Inform). We have included only *scholarly papers* for the period 1998-2003 whereas editorials, introductions to special issues, book-reviews, and contributions in conference proceedings were excluded.

Among the potential threats to the validity of our method is its failure to capture research on the impacts of IT on politics and public administration that were not published in these particular journals since we included scholarly journals only. We recognize that there are numerous other valid sources of empirical research, including other journals, online media, books, book chapters, conference papers, and so on.

A second threat to the validity to the compilation of the research is that we have relied exclusively on English-language journals, which introduce certain biases regarding scholars, countries studied, and epistemologies. As a result there are plentiful e-government initiatives and actions we have failed to incorporate in our conceptualization of e-government. The language bias affect developed as well as developing countries. For example, we have very few developed countries and economic power houses (as for example Germany and Japan) in our literature sample. Also, there is a clear under representation of developing countries. Yet, e-government application might be equal or more challenging in developing countries as compared to countries such as the US and UK which have been represented in our sample.

Third, the research methods in the studies vary, generating problems of comparability and generality when the findings are aggregated in the manner we utilize. About one-third of the studies we found are case studies and none of them used survey techniques. One quarter of the studies used data that were not collected by the authors themselves. Combining these in a e-government (melting) pot is clearly raising methodological concerns.

Forth, we do not weigh the findings in the individual studies on the basis of the strength of evidence supporting the inferences provided in the research. In turn, we do not argue that one finding is more correct than another. The lack of survey presence is one reason for not scaling the findings in the individual studies. Second, we assume that the journal's internal system of peer review provides a baseline of acceptability regarding the validity of the research and conclusions. Despite these possible shortcomings in validity, analyzing the articles in a sample of key academic journals is a reasonable method for assessing the body research within the "universe" of e-government.

Table 5-2. Number of research articles on e-government identified through Social Science Citation Index and ProQuest, 1998-2003

Keyword	Social Science Citation Index	Proquest
e-government	139	54
e-governance	17	5
Egovernment	14	2
Egovernance	1	0
e-government + e-governance	6	3
egovernment + egovernance	1	0
e-government + egovernance	0	0
e-governance + egovernment	0	0
Digital government	23	10
Digital governance	0	0
Online government	4	1
Online governance	1	1
one-stop government	6	1
one-stop governance	0	0
electronic government	48	14
electronic governance	5	0
Total number of citations	265	87

Source. Andersen, Henriksen, Ahmed, et al. (2004)

Our analysis reiterates that the terms e-government, electronic government and digital government by far outweigh the e-governance studies. This might be an indicator that research focuses on formal government rather than the activities of government.

Echoing section 5.2 of this chapter, we argue for supplementing the formal view of government, i.e. who gets what, when, and how (Easton 1965) from government by viewing government as a mixture and dynamic set of structures, processes, actors and policies that determine or implement the allocation of public values in the collectivity (Ham and Hill 1993).

Easton's model brings awareness to the political environment of which public administration is part of. The model provides insight into the complex way public services have emerged, sustained and changed. Yet, complementing Easton's model with modern more in-depth governance analysis can aid our understanding of how governmental IT-initiatives and IT-practices unfold (2000).

For example the use of IT to erode big government requires a necessity of understanding what big and what government is. Micheletti (Micheletti 2000) argues that "Bigness can be defined in terms of size or largeness (i.e., number of employees, relative costs, and spheres of involvement). It can also be defined in terms of its importance in society, which concerns the quality of government service (i.e., output and outcome of governmental effort), representation of the will of the people, and social representation ... Classical definitions [of government] focus on the need for government to be in control of its territory and in command of the tasks in its sphere of responsibility. Government ability to control and command are now being challenged by unclear horizontal and vertical separation of powers, regionalization and globalization, decentralization and devolution, and involvement of nongovernmental units in the policy steering process (i.e., governance) (World-Bank 2003).

Micheletti's observation emphasizes that the object of e-government application might be more difficult to identify than at first assumed and that the thinking in the articles we found (through the bibliographical study) appear to suggest a rather formal, and outdated, view of government. It appears to be a question of using IT in the context of formal control and command of resources and areas of responsibility.

Table 5-1. Definitions of E-government

Organization	Key points from definitions
OECD	The use of information and communication technologies, and particularly the Internet
	Better government
EU	Smaller but smarter back-office operations and bigger and better front-offices
UN	Commitment by government
	Practical realization of the best that government has to offer
	Enhanced, cost-effective and efficient delivery of services, information and knowledge.
	Improve the relationship between the private citizen and the public sector
The World Bank	Use by government agencies of information technologies (such as Wide Area Networks, the Internet, and mobile computing) to transform relations with citizens, businesses, and other arms of government
	Less corruption, increased transparency, greater convenience, revenue growth, and/or cost reductions
	Better delivery of government services to citizens, improved interactions with business and industry, citizen empowerment through access to information, or more efficient government
CTG Albany	use of information technology to support government operations, engage citizens, and provide government services
	four key dimensions, which reflect the functions of government itself. e-services, e-democracy, e-commerce, e-management
e-buergerdienst.de	Applying and integrating modern information and communication technology
	An organizational form of the state enabling interaction and communication between the state and the citizens, private enterprises, customers and public institutions

Capturing the definitions it is not all about variations in spelling and labels. Below we have captured definitions from the UN, World Bank, OECD, and a German local government association. The list of definitions reveals a variety in objectives, means, and reach for the e-government agenda.

The objectives range from enhanced, cost-effective, and efficient deliveries to objectives of less corruption, increased transparency, greater convenience, revenue growth, and/or cost reductions. In the table we have grouped them as aiming for increased transparency, accessibility, and accountability of government. The World Bank define the ends as "...better delivery of government services to citizens, improved interactions with business and industry, citizen empowerment through access to information, or more efficient government management. The resulting benefits can be less corruption, increased transparency, greater convenience, revenue growth, and/or cost reductions" (2004).

For example, the CTG (UN 2003) emphasizes that "E-government is the use of information technology to support government operations, engage citizens, and provide government services." UN writes that e-government is "...the practical realization of the best that government has to offer" (UN 2003). Accordingly, e-government is not a website with outdated information or half-hearted attempts to implement digital services.

At the application side, various vendors, developers, etc. are offering e-government applications with different approaches to the relations between the users of the public sector and the staff. Government is struggling with conflicting objectives, but that we will see applications being built and implemented focusing on the enduser as a customer relation rather than as citizens or businesses. This may take the focus away from categorizing internal efficiency improvement as e-government application, in favor of the endusers's benefits from the applications.

In Table 5-2 we have depicted examples of e-government applications in a spectra with citizen applications to the left, and business applications to the right side of the spectra. Both enterprises and citizens use the applications centered in the table. For example, it may be of equal relevance to have IT-supported building applications for businesses and private households. For each application area there often will be data interface to various IT-applications and data retrieval from the applications will often be part of decision-making processes.

Table 5-2. The Spectra of Customer Centric Applications

Citizen oriented (required or no payment for the service involvement)				Business oriented (required or no payment for the service involvement)
<←---------------------- e-government application spectra ----------------------→>				
Birth & marriage certificates	Job search	Application for building permission	Registration of a new company	VAT
Income taxes	Public libraries	Car registration	Public procurement and tendering	Corporate tax
Declaration to the police	Social security benefits	Health related services	Environmental permits	Social security contribution for employees
Enrollment in higher education	Personal documents		Custom declaration	
	Announcement of moving		Submission of statistical data	

The *means* highlighted in the four sources are use of IT in its many variations and policy commitment. For example the UN writes that e-government is "a permanent commitment by government to improve the relationship between the private citizen and the public sector through enhanced, cost-effective and efficient delivery of services, information and knowledge." (World-Bank 2003). In regarding the technology dimension, the World Bank Group defines e-government as "... the use by government agencies of information technologies (such as Wide Area Networks, the Internet, and mobile computing) that have the ability to transform relations with citizens, businesses, and other arms of government" (CTG 2004).

The reach and span of the e-government initiatives encompasses services, administrative issues (including e-procurement), and participation and democracy issues. The CTG includes for example e-commerce in their definition as "...the electronic exchange of money for goods and services such as citizens paying taxes and utility bills, renewing vehicle registrations, and paying for recreation programs, or government buying supplies and auctioning surplus equipment" (World-Bank 2003).

We have summarized the reach dimension with four key words: administration, service, policy input, and involvement of users/ citizens. An example of the changed focus of these four areas is stressed by the World Bank. In their report on e-government, The World Bank emphasizes the location and geographical dimension: "Traditionally, the interaction between a citizen or business and a government agency took place in a government office. With emerging information and communication technologies it is possible to locate service centers closer to the clients. Such centers may consist of an unattended kiosk in the government agency, a service kiosk located close to the client, or the use of a personal computer in the home or office" (Arcieri et al. 2002; Doty and Erdelez 2002).

Table 5-3. Objectives, means, and reach of e-government

Dimension	Variable
Objectives	Transparency
	Accessibility
	Accountability
Means	Use of IT
	Permanent policy commitment
Reach	Administration
	Service
	Policy input
	Involvement of customers / citizens

Focusing on the *reach* of dimension of e-government, the largest part of the studies has a governmental administrative focus with tools for improvement and certification of e-service (Hovy 2003) (Lenk 2002), the overall discussion of e-government as driver for modernization (Chen and Gant 2001) and transformation of the service though use of specific technologies such as ASP (Devadoss et al. 2003), e-procurement (Fletcher 2003), paperwork elimination (Sepic and Kase 2002), biological information infrastructure (Lowry et al. 2003), collaborative writing tools (Whitson and Davis 2001), dissemination of R&D through the web (McHenry 2003), criminal procedural codex in the Russian DUMA (Allen et al. 2001), administrative culture & partnerships for successful implementation (Golubchik et al. 2003), technology issues related to scalability and security (Ashbaugh and Miranda 2002), payroll, accounting and personnel administration (Aldrich 1998).

The second largest body of literature we have identified relies on front services, that is public access to the information (Notess 2000; Cresswell and Pardo 2001; Potter 2002; Shi 2002; Gibbs et al. 2003; Tigre 2003; Wong 2003). The New York City case study of the interplay between legal and organizational issues with homeless shelter administration and information sharing in NY (Bellamy 2002).

A large number of the studies have policy input as a key departure of their study of IT in government. These range from the impacts of governmental actions on the diffusions of IS such as e-commerce (Allen et al. 2001; Borins 2002), national-centric studies as the British case study of modernizing government (Strejcek and Theil 2003), and the US & Canada legislative initiatives /deficit (Ciment 2003), the analysis of the e-government legislation in Europe (Koga 2003; McNeal et al. 2003), the NSF digital government program (Koh and Prybutok 2003), and policy oriented studies of general uptake of IT in government (Jaeger 2002; Salem 2003) and considerations on whether government boundaries might be eroding and take over market activities (Chadwick and May 2003).

The least frequently occurring literature on the *reach* dimension, concerns involvement and democracy issues of e-government. This body of the literature addresses such issues as division of power (Carlitz and Gunn 2002), the democracy potential of IT to enhance participatory possibility (Thompson 2002; Parker 2003), configuring e-government to address local needs (Peled 2001), digital divide issues (Snellen 2002), and change of power relationships within bureaucracy (Haque 2002) and between citizens and government (Nolan and Gibson; Nolan 1979; King and Kraemer 1984).

Table 5.6 and Figure 5.2 maps the reach studies on e-government within the domains of impacts (identified in Chapter 3). In Table 5.6 we have compared the findings from review of general IT in the public administration and the political world (1988-1995 and 1995-2000) with the e-government review data. The data show that the areas of impacts reported in the studies are almost identical.

Table 5-4. Domains of impacts: IT in the Public Administration and Political World versus e-government, 1988-2003. Percentage of citations.

Domains of impacts		IT in the Public Administration and Political World		E-government 1998-2003[c]	
		1987-1992[a]	1987-2000[b]		
Capabilities	Effectiveness	15% }	13% } 48%	18% }	
	Efficiency	18% 51%	17%	20% 58%	
	Information Access and data quality	17%	18%	18%	
Interaction		26%	28%	22%	
Orientation		3%	6%	6%	
Values		21%	18%	14%	
Total		99% (N=20)	100% (N=49)	100% (N=112)	

Source. a) Andersen & Danziger (1995) b) Danziger & Andersen (2002) c) Ahmed, Henriksen, Andersen et al. (2004).

The result of this mapping, or correlation, is a triangle that crosses diagonal with the majority of studies in the highlighted area. The e-government triangle covers 50% of the area illustrating a dominance of applications within the domain of capability and interaction for the front-services and governmental administrative functions. Less frequent are studies on IT used for policy input and involvement of users/ citizens and studies that address orientation of the decision-making processes and values.

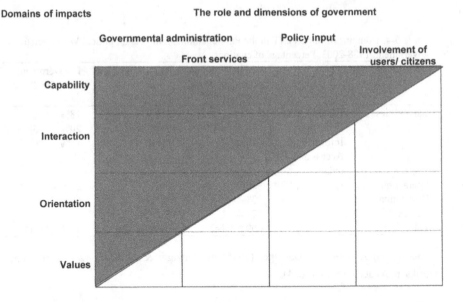

Figure 5-1. Domains of it-applications and the role and functions of government

The e-government triangle displayed in Figure 5.1 illustrates the need for re-building IT-application for government to encompass the dimensions in lower-right triangle. In the move towards this, it is worrying that some of the stage models on e-government primarily deals with the upper-left triangle, and therefore would reinforce the problem for the PPR-approach. Therefore, we will in the next section, outline the stages that e-government could evolve along if PPR is to be agenda setting for application building, implementation, and use.

4.   E-GOVERNMENT STAGE MODELS

Within the IS-community, the debate on stage-model is classical (King and Kraemer 1984), suggesting that as appealing stage models might be, stage models are hard to use as a flag pole and milestones since some governmental operations are one-way services with no interactivity. Also, stage models prescribes an evolution over time and indirectly states that phase IV is better than phase I, II and III. In practice, however, the individual phases will occur simultaneously and be parts of different elements of e-government. Finally, the triggers for moving or entry to one stage rather than another stage are more rewarding to focus on rather than observing whether or not government is at stage I or IV.

Within the e-commerce era, various stage-models occurred, and none of them had the quality to capture the drivers and evolution of e-commerce. Within the e-government field stage-models are in demand although justification may be limited for the models formulated.

The World Bank provides an example of this analogue to the e-commerce stage models by arguing that "E-Commerce has evolved already through four stages: 1) publishing, 2) interactivity, 3) completing transactions, and 4) delivery. To date, most e-government activity has centered on publishing. A study by Anderson Consulting finds vast differences among countries in the maturity of their e-government effort. Perhaps the key finding, however, is that even the most mature countries have tapped less than 20% of the potential" (Layne and Lee 2001).

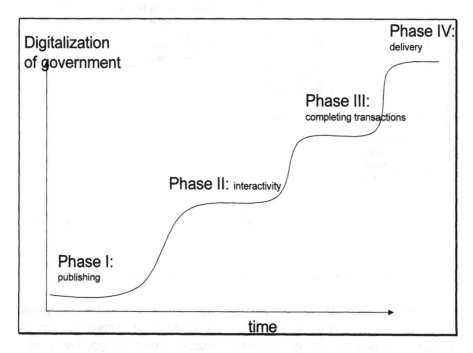

Figure 5-2. A Stage- model of E-government: publishing, interactivity, completing transactions, and delivery - *Source*: Developed after World Bank (2003)

A better and more comprehensive stage-model has emerged from a study of various government websites and related e-government initiative. The proposed model identifies a "...multi-perspective transformation within government structures and functions as they make transitions to e-government through each stage" (Layne and Lee 2001). The issue of integration is profound in the Layne & Lee model. A similar integration focus is demonstrated by a German local government association where e-government is denoting an "...organizational structure where IT enables interaction and integration between the state and the citizens, private companies, customers, and public institutions" (our translation). Although the Layne and Lee model is a functionally oriented model, it is not as activity centric as our PPR-model.

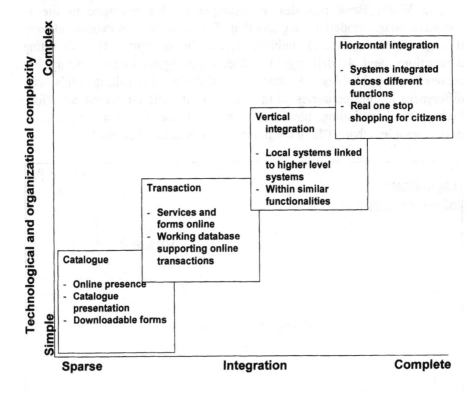

Figure 5-3. Dimensions and stages of e-government development - *Source:*

The problem with the stage model by Layne and Lee is that the adoption of this model could end up reinforcing the findings in chapter 4, namely intragovernmental data integration with a front-end built on top. This could enable integration and will require the solving of various technological and organizational challenges. Online cataloguing and downloadable form is not a wrong or undesired feature of e-government. The problem is that the fundamental challenges to, and progress on, the PPR-approach is not reflected in the Leyne and Lee-model.

The World Bank and Leyne and Lee to a large extent have done little more than replicated the stage models from the e-commerce area. As was evident with the forecasts and typologies for e-commerce progress, most of these failed and did not capture the picture adequately.

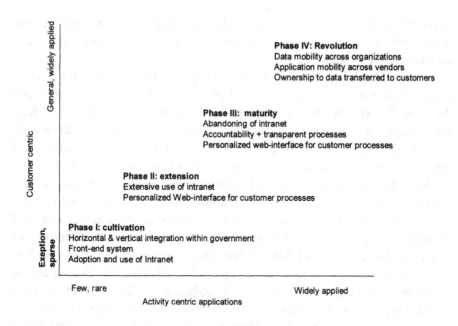

Figure 5-4. The PPR-stage model

We strongly advocate being aware of the shortcomings of stage models. Yet, Figure 5.4 displays how a stage model could materialize if the PPR-approach is taken onboard. The two key dimensions of the PPR-approach – customer centric activities and activity centric applications – are listed along the horizontal and vertical dimensions respectively. Applications developed along these two dimensions can be rare or widespread in the extended organizational room of governmental activities. Rather than being discrete variables, the variables should be used as a *continuum.*

Along the dimensions of activity and customer orientation, the PPR-approach crystallizes four phases for the evolution of e-government: cultivation, extension, maturity, and revolution.

The *cultivation phase (I)* shelters horizontal and vertical integration within government, limits use of front-end systems for customer services, and emphasises the adoption and use of Intranet within government. This is the stage where most governments are now, and worse, it is often considered a strategic goal for most government. We advocate that having the characteristics of this phase as a strategic end can be counter productive to the activity and customer focus. *Phase II is the extension stage* with extensive use of intranet and adoption of personalized Web-interface for customer processes. Phase III is the stage where the PPR-approach *matures and abandons the use of intranet*, has accountable and transparent processes, and exclusively offer personalized web-interface for customer processes.

Phase IV is the *revolutionary phase* characterized by data mobility across organizations, application mobility across vendors, and ownership to data transferred to customers.

There indeed is a long push to reach phase IV. The literature on e-government that formed the basis for Figure 5.2 and Table 5.5 has provided the fuel for stating that we are still predominately in phase I where governments are aiming for data and system integrations, but have only limited front-end services, and have essentially still an intra- and intergovernmental view of the development and implementation of IT.

Accordingly, personalized web-interface for customer processes, data mobility across organizations, application mobility across vendors, and transfer of data ownership to the customers is still not implemented and constitute (in light of the PPR-approach) key challenges to be meet. For example, the lack of mobility on the data and application level, lock-in government and their customers to path-dependency, and decreases the competition on IT-enabled services. The in-house and lock-in path has been a convenient road to follow for government, its consultants, and IT-suppliers, since this has in reality created a myriad of e-government solutions that are just as incomparable, in-transparent, and in-accessible for the customers as the previous information and communication channels were. The only difference could be (as quoted by the former UK e-envoy previously), that they are faster and smarter.

5.   CONCLUSIONS

The position taken in the chapter is that most governmental applications and strategies are at a halt in the cultivation phase where horizontal and vertical integration within government, implementation of front-end systems, and adoption and use of the Intranet dominate the landscape of e-government.

In the implementation of e-government applications, governments are more often seeking efficiency, effectiveness, and data quality improvement as compared to improving health and safety and privacy issues. Subsequently, the governmental administrative functions and activities along with general front-end services dominate the application arsenal. Less frequent are IT-applications directed towards policy input and customer involvement. The government centric triangle of applications we illustrated in this chapter can change but are at odds with potential strong institutional practices.

E-government is indeed an example and protein example of IT in government, but in most cases and situations e-government is associated with the use of the Internet rather than the variety of IT-applications that are vital to the PPR-concept. As such, e-government is in our view more a symbol of crisis than an indicator of change. The "e" reflects what the late Rob Kling labeled *utopian optimism and. technological centric beliefs* stipulating that a digital front-end is a mechanism of change. We advocate throughout this book that a more reflective and critical use of IT is desired. Rather than focus on the front-end, we argue that the core processes and the activities involved are a prosperous road to follow.

This observation is oiled by the literature findings on the terms e-government, e-governance, online government, digital government, one-stop government, and electronic government. Of these six concepts, e-government is the most frequently cited term. This occurrence is interpreted as indicating a *high reliance on formal government* rather than on the activities performed by government. E-government were captured along the dimensions of objectives (transparency, accessibility, accountability), means (use of IT and permanent policy commitment), and reach (governmental administration, front services, policy input, and involvement of users/ citizens).

Departing from the reach dimension of e-government and impacts of IT, the chapter introduced a four phase stage model of e-government evolution along the key dimensions of PPR: activity centric applications and customer oriented activities. Regardless of the findings in the literature review reported earlier in this chapter and the findings on IT impacts in chapter 3, the current stage of evaluation is a far cry from the levels of maturity and revolution.

In the subsequent chapter we will address how mobile technologies may help the process of moving to the next stages of the PPR stage model. Mobile technologies can be a vital group of technologies re-focusing the implementation challenges to the activity level, and accentuating the necessities of abandoning the prevalent division between inside and outside the governmental organization, pushing for data and application mobility across vendors, and transferring data ownership to the customers.

Chapter 6

THE ORGANIZATIONAL MEMBRANE
PENETRATED BY MOBILE TECHNOLOGIES

1.   INTRODUCTION

The PPR-approach is advocating an activity and customer centric approach. This involves a realignment of the IT infrastructure and require mobility at the activity level for the customers in the public sector. Customers will be in demand of not only accessible services, but will want to set the agenda for the type of technologies mediating the communication. This is a challenging agenda for the employees in the public sector merging from defining the needs to responding to the demands for technologies.

In this chapter we introduce the concept of the *organizational membrane.* The aim is to capture the change from the formal organization with widespread use of formal gate-keeping mechanisms, and predictable and controllable communication patterns, to the organizational membrane. The shift to the organizational membrane is accompanied by employees' random pattern of IT-use, by fuzzy logic on how demand will penetrate the organizational membrane of the public sector, and formal regulation on entry and exit from the public services will be replaced by informal communication patterns.

Governments being in, operating through, and exploiting the digital opportunities is a key concern for this chapter – a concern that has many parallels in the literature (Negroponte 1995; Earl 1998; Tapscott 1999). Throughout the 1990s, virtual organizations became one of the most important management IT-issues (Davidow and Malone 1992; Hedberg et al.

1997; Mowshowitz 1997). We are taking this one step further and argue that rather than paying all attention to an organization being transformed from being physical to having virtual components, the attention for the generation of technologies spreading should be concentrated on organizing the activities. We suggest this should be done through the organizational membrane that enables the seamless communication and customer centric activities. The organisational membrane also has room for excitement at work and encourages a cluster of activities that excel in innovation.

2.   IT IN ORGANIZATIONS

IT can be viewed as an aid to build barriers to entry, build in switching costs, change the basis of competition, alter the balance of power, and generate new products (McFarlan 1991). This view is challenged by various scholars that argue that IT can help reduce barriers to entry, collaborate (even with competitors), eliminate various existing modes of power, and to enable production at low marginal and transaction costs (Shapiro and Varian 1999; Smith et al.; Brynjolfsson and Kahin 2000; Choi and Whinston 2000). Although these two views originate in the private sector, it is striking to note how prevalent the two views have been impacting on the roll-out of IT in the public sector.

Yet, in this chapter we turn the attention more towards the customers and the relations with the employees. Incorporating digital components in the organizational routines and structures has been a key concern for a vast amount of literature (Willcocks et al. 1997; Laudon and Laudon 2000). Equally there is an intense debate and concern on the level of capabilities required by the staff to enter the networked economy, and as part of this, to use the applications in a way consistent with the networked economy. Drucker argues for transferring attention from the chief information office to the tool-user:

> "You must accept the fact that if the computer is a tool, it is the job of the tool-user to know what to use it for. So the first thing practically everyone must learn is to take information responsibly....Unfortunately, most of us still expect the chief information officer or some other technologist to do that. It won't do" (Drucker 1994).

In the light of the current spread of technologies that could enable the networked organizations and in turn penetrate the organizations, it is important to raise the discussion of users capabilities. Our strong impression is that the user within and outside government is not ready to use the technologies in any way that is substantially different from the way they use IT five years ago.

We propose that the information strategist need to rethink the balance of overall organizational choices/ strategies to the environment (the external domain) and the strategies for adoption of IT (Earl 1998). The adaptation strategies are in the PPR-approach are highly demand oriented, in the sense that it is the customers that direct the activities and the way technologies are used in the organizational membrane. We do acknowledge that various in-house and institutional factors guide the IT-strategy. However, with the increased transparency and global competition market, we also subscribe to the view that the relative weight of institutional explanatory variables will diminish.

Various authors have pointed out that technology does not have any impact per se, it is all a matter of choices, power and situated change - the e-government is not evolving by it itself; it is all about decisions on how to adopt IT at the societal, company, and individual level (Marcus 1983; Orlikowsky 1996; Orlikowski and Iacono 2000; Piccoli and Ives 2000). "With today's modern information technology, the transaction costs of organizational coordination drop so sharply that at a number of new points hierarchy can be replaced by the market" (Hedberg et al. 1997) suggesting a move towards the markets and away form the hierarchies (Malone et al. 1987).

In developing the organizational membrane concept, we rely on "classical" studies on technology organizing (Weick 1969, 1990, 1995). Also, we are indebted to the *information strategy triangle* (Earl 1998) and the studies on digital/ analog distinction of the work processes, the interaction among the actors, and the product/ service content (Bolman and Deal 1997).

The ambition expressed by government to impede collaboration, innovation, creativity, and accumulation of knowledge (Faucheux 1997) conflicts in our view a closed, organization view. Addressing the role of IT in organizations, we bring attention to the old-timer insight on *organizing* (Weick 1969). Various studies have suggested that existing organizations and virtual entities benefit from using IT to support teamwork (Kock 2000). The marginal and value added changes are at the team level inside, across, outside and between organizations (Lipnack and Stamps 1997).

At the organizational level, we find various indicators of blurring organizational boundaries (Weick 1995; Bolman and Deal 1997; Maira and Scott-Morgan 1997). The move from the closed and in-house communication patterns in situation A in Figure 6.1, towards penetration of the organizational membrane has already commenced. Situation B in Figure 6.1 illustrates that various IT applications, including mobile technologies, are already part of the process penetrating the organizational membrane of the public sector. Yet, IT follows rather known, predictable, and by most controllable patterns with regards to the access and transparency of the decisions and the service development. The data we presented in Chapter 4 of this book indicate that situation B provides a good description of the current use of IT.

The captivating situation is when organizational actors use IT to support (part of) work processes in rather random ways. Also, the nature of the work processes supported, enabled and created by IT change from following a known and controllable pattern to a diverse, chaotic, and uncontrollable pattern, and that the demand side is communicating in incremental and ad hoc fashion rather than a constant and planned matter. This development is illustrated in situation C in Figure 6.1. We underline that mobile technologies are not the only technologies bringing about the change from situation B to C. We argue that situation C represents key characteristics and point to a set of key challenges for the PPR-approach.

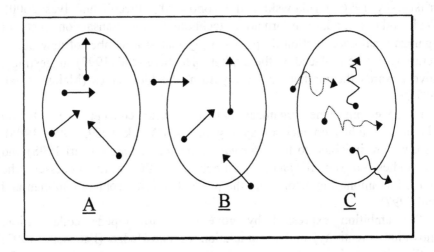

Figure 6-1. Penetration of the organizational membrane

Penetration of the organizational membrane as illustrated in situation C in the above figure, will involve a set of dynamic, integrated, and streamlined activity molecules (see chapter 2) using digital devices for recording, accessing, and exchange of data, information, knowledge across distances, *and* where free entry, exit, and voice for the customers exists, *and* transaction costs approach to zero will also be required.

The membrane has implications not only at the level of the workers, but also at the stock of data and files, the interaction with the front-end partners (customers, citizens, companies, politicians, interest groups etc.) and at the inter- and intraorganizational levels.

We do not claim that the membrane is a valid description of how organizations are structured today or represent a valid picture of how organizations may look like in the near future. Yet, we do claim that the *marginal changes in value generation associated with information technology* will be correlated with the concepts of the organizational membrane and that these changes will be associated with the emergence of the PPR-approach.

A particular group of technologies is associated with the transformation, namely the mobile technologies. The ongoing diffusion of Internet technologies, PDAs and 2.5/ 3G mobile applications along with the innovation in the physical and network layers (ADSL, routers, and switches) and the standard bodies' attempt to smoothen the communication process (XML, EDI, Exchanges), is fueling the penetration of the organizational membrane. This development is not exclusively driven by the infrastructure providers, mobile device industry or the content providers, although each of the three segments indeed is pushing the organizational membrane concept. Instead, this chapter argues that components of our activity molecules are required to be in focus for accessing the drive towards the organizational membrane. Security is a key concern in moving towards this situation, particularly with regards to securing wireless e-mail, preventing loss of data, securing handheld access to the government network, and deploying and managing security policies for many devices. Although we do not want to ignore these issues, they also reflect that in-house concerns can outweigh customer concerns/ demands. Also, the technologies give new opportunities which will be discussed in the next section.

3.   MOBILE TECHNOLOGIES AND THE ORGANIZATIONAL MEMBRANE

Recalling the findings in chapter 5, government is undertaking a variety of tasks such as traffic control, teaching, and health care in a variety of locations. The location of governmental activities might comprise the home care helper visiting the elderly in Trondheim City, Norway, the police officer on patrol in the Nappa Valley, California, and the marine biologist on an expedition to investigate pollution in port outside the capital of Tokyo.

A common activity that is undertaken in all tasks and locations is case handling. The police officer needs to write reports when issuing a ticket for violating speed limits, the nurse has to report status and any changes observed, and the marine biologist needs to write up a report that is filed and can be compared with the reports from the previous years mission to inspect the level of water pollution. It is straight forward to envision that mobile technologies can be used by the governmental officers to help data keying, data retrieval, communication with peers/ experts, and data analysis at the location.

Case handling is, however, more prevalent within the city hall and offices. It is widespread among such processes as citizens' applications for housing subsidy, social security application and renewal, etc. Also, it is within this area that we will illustrate penetration of the organizational membrane using mobile technologies. Within social security, the staff of the Munitown used to spend about one third of the day away from the office having meetings etc. with the customers in the homes, the other part of the day driving, writing reports, and having meetings with people from other governmental offices.

Last year, Munitown digitalized all previous paper based operations and detached all direct physical client-administration contact. Instead internet and in particular the mobile internet, was implemented as the key communication point. There had long been an assumption that the social clients (the customers!) did not have mobile phones and certainly not new ones. A study undertaken by the city found, however, that the penetration rate among the customers were higher and that a significant portion of them had newer mobile phones than the average citizens in Munitown.

Customers and workers are communicating with each other using primarily mobile units, although laptops in the offices are used as well. All PCs and stationary elements have been removed from the offices where a wireless zone enables workers and clients to be connected at any time T and location L to perform application calls, database calls, file operations, and registry operations calls.

One of the key benefits here is the direct transfer of forms and data from client to the administration and vice versa, from one mobile unit to another during the "meeting". They now spend only half a day a week in their offices with all coordination work with other governmental workers being taken care of using a virtual collaboration tool with calendar etc.

Adding mobile components to the *case handling process* raises manifold challenges and benefits other than purely technical issues on integration and interoperability of data and devices, access rights, security check, etc. The mobile applications involves, as pointed to in chapter 2, challenges relating to work and communication content; the division of labor; rules for communication; users tool-capability; and the users themselves. For example, the issue of *synchronization* from remote locations and storage of data in central data bases versus at the mobile unit can involve a reorganization of the entire database structure not only in the adopting unit, but in the entire government. Also, changing user interfaces needs to be balanced with the need for customers right to gain access to their file and not only from a work-efficiency perspective.

At the application level, new mobile applications are emerging, and many existing applications are currently being modified for a mobile environment. With its ability to hide the underlying network's details from applications and yet provide a uniform and easy-to-use interface, middleware is extremely important for developing new mobile applications (Varshney and Vetter 2000). In Table 6.1 below we have listed some of the wireless applications currently emerging. We believe that many of these applications may drive the organizations towards penetration of the organizational membrane. Therefore, we present a brief discussion of some of these mobile applications.

Table 6-1. Classes of mobile applications and penetration of the organizational membrane

Class of mobile applications	Examples
Mobile service management	Tracking the status of services
Service location	Locating services
Proactive service management	Transmitting information about aging and new law / regulation components
Mobile reengineering	Improving customer services, such as claim adjustments or insurance
Mobile office	Providing services for staff, such as traffic jam reports, airport and flight information, vacation reservations, and procurement of products and services
Mobile distance education/ training	Offering classes using streaming audio and video after work hours/ on the spot training/ instructions

4.   THE CHALLENGES FOR THE MEMBRANE

Experiments with mobile technologies progress incrementally and only as an exception will be part of managerial dominated/ controlled organizations. Addressing IT-strategies in organizations has always been cumbersome. Yet, this is escalated by the emergence of the organizational membrane. Strategies on IT might be a set of formulated plans that are written in detail and published at a web page and/ or in a booklet distributed among the various offices and made available to all relevant collaboration bodies in the organization. Conversely, strategies might be a set of norms or even anecdotes of strategies that circulate in the organizational room and not necessarily printed on paper.

Whether, 1) explicitly formulated official and/ or operative goals, 2) consistent or conflicting strategies, and/ or 3) centrally coordinated and/ or circulated in the organizational universe, strategic concerns on whether the digital technologies and associated organizational practices can aid the search for opportunities are even more relevant to address in the information economy. The quandary is, however, that the terminology developed during the 1970s, 1980s and 1990s only to a marginal extent applies to the organizational membrane.

Scholars have pointed to the challenges facing organizations driving towards a T-based organization (Lucas 1996) or the digital organization (Best 1997). These challenges do indeed apply to the organizational membrane:

- How do organizations develop platforms that provides support for productive and efficient collaboration *and* enable self-development, experimenting and innovative behavior among the organizational membrane actors?
- How can companies counterbalance the need for managerial control and action with the privacy rights for the individual workers for transactions and storage of their files (Oravec 1996)?
- How do companies outline strategies for the future work in their business setting? What is pro and contra to business organizations with respect to having workers at home, at a satellite office, or the headquarters in the organizational membrane setting (Grantham 1999)?
- How can the IT-based systems, constituting the core of the organizational membrane, be used for knowledge replication and adaptation and knowledge creation (Maira and Scott-Morgan 1997)?

The IS-community is struggling to find answers or methodologies to unearth the answers to the questions outlined above. In finding the answers, we propose that we need to take a solid look at some of the fundamentals that have guided the IS-community research during the 1970s, 1980s and particular 1990s. We propose the organizational membrane is setting the agenda on the organizational challenges of the PPR-approach.

The organizational membrane will be challenged with regards to: 1) work and communication content; 2) rules for communication; 3) technology. 4) users' tool-capability; 5) the division of labor; and 6) employees. These are the components of the activity molecule described in chapter 2 of this book. In Table 6.2 we have summarized the challenges on traditional approaches to IT in government and the PPR-approach.

Table 6-2. Key challenges for the organizational membrane

Variable	Current approach followed by government	The Organizational Membrane
Work and communication content	Formal description In-house and follows (old) structure Privacy	Formal and informal Customer centric Transparency
Rules for communication	Voice Exit	Entry Voice Exit
Technology	Mediation	Imperatives

	Choices	Short term strategy
	Long term strategy	
Users' tool-capability	External pressures from	Peer and customer
	policy level	interaction and pressure
	Digital divide and inclusive	Elite and exclusive
Division of labor	Interdependencies	Inter-/ intradependencies
	Rationalization	Extension
	Control	Collaboration
Employees	Involvement	Involvement and excluding
	Long term	Short term
	Defining needs	Responding to needs

4.1 Work and communication content

Organizing the activities in the public sector is only a few instances along the lines of the weberian model (Weber 1958). Providing formal description for the activities and with details on what do where and how are done followed a myriad of guidelines. Yet, most of these are formal and follows patterns of routines and structures. Perhaps as a result of this, the formal communication style is a facet of much communication between customers and government, and within government. We point to that we will experience yet more informal communication taking place through media as SMS and chat/ messing program. Certainly this transition is already taking place in the public schools, but will spread to all parts of the public sector. The PPR-approach seeks to reinforce this change since it originates from the customers.

There is also a constant issue regarding privacy and confidentiality within the communications. Regulation of these areas differs substantially among countries, but regardless of the definition and extension of the privacy practice in the country, IT-applications have to consider these carefully in current e-government applications (Dunlop and Kling 1991; Bennett and Raab 1997; Leizerov 2000; Lambrinoudakis et al. 2003; Tillman 2003). In the PPR-approach we envision greater transparency leading the way and privacy issues being scaled down. This will not necessarily be the customers privacy that will be reduced. Rather, the workers in the public sector and their communication will to an increasingly degree of transparency and these will be less sacrifices to their privacy.

4.2 Rules for communication

Organizing the activities is challenging our management thinking regarding promotion of efficiency within organizations with regards to voice and exit (Hirschman 1970) *and* the entry/ access dimension. In the classical writing on virtual organizations, organizational members have been able to pressure management. If critical issues are not fulfilled, there is an increased desire to exit the organization and find other employment (Hedberg et al. 1997).

Allowing customers to access, raise voice, and exit at any given time T and any given location L in situation C of Figure 6.1 (the organizational membrane) is indeed challenging for most government organizations. Although we acknowledge that voice and exit issues are relevant, finding team players and constantly reconfiguring the organization appears to be a much more challenging task. This is fueled by a changing employment pattern where the employees will typically not belong to one, but several organizing units that cross companies and public sector units. Subsequently, the ability to respond to the tacit and explicit needs are making situation C even more challenging to cope with.

4.3   Technology Driver

IT-applications in government are, by good hearted planners, sought to be part of a long term strategy although few can foresee how the need for labor market data will be in five years. Rather than long term strategies for applications, we advocate for short term strategies and rapid prototyping, piloting, and implementation (see Chapter 10 for more on the IT-development issues). The IS community is today quite united in that digitalization is desirable and changes should not only occur in technology. Changes in technical opportunities are mediated by organizations and it is this mediation and the choices, that is transforming the organization (Zuboff 1988). Consequently, various works on the digital economy point to the transformation of the work processes, the products/ services, and the actors (Bolman and Deal 1997; Choi and Whinston 2000).

We acknowledge that the choice of the common available technology is vital, and indeed, is the difference to make a brake when implementing new generations of technologies. Yet, we see the major shift in technology adoption is moving from the choices taken within government with the assistance of the suppliers and consultants (see chapter 10). The government will increasingly be met by rapid shifting and imperative demands from customers regarding technology adoption. Ignoring these demands ("we do not use chat, please send an e-mail") can lead to a reduction in legitimization of the public sector.

4.4   Users' tool-capability

In the PPR-approach, we have previously (chapter 2) advocated for merging intranet and internet interfaces, and in essence proposed abandoning the intranet and all applications that are not targeting the customers. This will imply that the pressure to innovate, maintain and exploit the capabilities to use the IT-enabled tools will no longer be part of the top-down command and productivity game, but will materialize through an interaction (and sometimes as a pressure) from customers and peers. Thus, if a customer uses a newer version of a software package, then it is not the customer who should downgrade, but the governmental worker that should upgrade and learn how to use the new version. Digital interactions with peers in the same office and other offices will also create a group pressure for staying on-top of the applications.

A vital element to building IT for government is the awareness on the controversial issues regarding computerization (Dunlop and Kling 1991). Among these are the issues of privacy (Bennett and Raab 1997), societal issues (Kling 1996) and the digital divide discussion (Dutton and Peltu 1996). These concerns need to be dealt with, and could, (if not addressed properly), impact return on investment as well as create digital cleavages in society making various functional tasks in companies and within the public sector more challenging. Yet, our PPR-approach has a more balanced view on this, advocating that the concerns regarding digital divide are balanced with elite elements.

4.5   The division of labor

The fifth area where the transition to organizational membrane is challenging our approaches to IT in government is with regards to the division of labor and the issues of control, rationalization, and interdependencies.

The overall implications of the proposed transition is that we might need to rethink the managerial focus for organizational configuration outlined in the classical work during the eighties and nineties (Mintzberg 1979, 1998). The pull to standardize the work processes or the output, and the pull to support collaboration, to professionalize or to centralize the supervision were almost revered depending on the specific nature of operations the company/ organization dealt with. Thus, the beauty in the five configurations outlined by Mintzberg during the mid 1980s were the general appeal on managerial issues as interdependencies, rationalization, and control. We propose that each of these is altered substantially.

Also, we have witnessed the move towards the networked organization and the reduced focus on the traditional value chain perspective from both agent and the transaction cost theory (Coase 1937, 1960; Williamson 1975; North 1981). Thus, whereas we in the 1980s and 1990s had the minimization of transaction costs and control of the value chain as overall business goals, there is now a move towards collaboration and extension.

4.6   Employees

Throughout the 1980s and 1990s we have witnessed an increased concern on the role of the culture. This has provided the glue in the organizations to ease the transition towards new communication and production modes. Since the system development process is also compressed substantially, the importance to be aware of the customers' need and the active involvement of the users of the IS in the system development process -- which has been one of the participatory design school main arguments (Bjerknes and Bratteteig 1995) -- are kept in the PPR-universe. Rather than aiming for involvement per se, we advocate for involvement of employees when relevant and for excluding actors that are not part of the activities for which the applications are being build.

The major is however the employees no longer has any needs them selves, rather they will be responding to needs from the customers and will therefore have mediate these into the development phase. Subsequently, we expect a drift away from employees being glued long term to their activity molecule, to a more short term affiliation (due to the existence of the free radicals). Thus, the relevance of employees formulating their needs will make less sense since they on and off will be part of activity molecules defined by customers.

5.   CONCLUSION

The organizational membrane is facing three critical challenges in order to help pave the road for the PPR-approach. First, public sector manager will need to stimulate *instability*, rather than stability. Second, formal learning and bookkeeping of the knowledge stock in the public sector, is being replaced by *informal experimenting and capacity management*. Third, the *concept of time and space* has radically shifted since a) products, processes and actors are accessible and transferable at a larger time span T and b) time lag in communication with customers and decision-makers is significantly different from (all) the settings analyzed during the 1980s and 1990s.

It is our proposition that future research needs to be directed towards yet more technological advanced service provision, more bandwidth, an escalating number of users, and more time independent solutions. This will be setting the scene for marginal revenue and marginal organizational changes in the public sector. Also, we need to address the current technical and strategic opportunities and the choices inherent within the organizational membrane in light of the already embedded technologies in organizations.

Governmental organizations are not an aggregate of digital entities that has abounded analog work processes, services and communication with the employees, customers and business partners. Instead, we face a predominant analog, that is aiming at integrating few and marginal digital components in functions that adds little or rather limited value. Technologies are often implemented in an ad hoc fashion and in political and financial terms as non-issue and low-risk projects. We believe this is highly challenged by the organizational membrane.

Traditional IT-*adaptation and exploitation strategies* are to some degree driven by supply rationality rather than demand oriented rationality. The organizational membrane has the potential to change this. Traditionally, *technology and application strategies* rarely involve radical experiments. Instead IT is often organized along bureaucratic models and routines that are remedies from the past rather than ask fundamental questions such as: are we performing the new functions, mastering the new work processes and managing our organizations in a form and with a content aligned with the economic, technical and democratic restrictions for the organizational membrane.

Finally, overall management of the digitalization is often in control of the functions in the IT-related departments and not in the areas where the bulk of the expenditures are accumulated: in the procurement function, the personnel departments and the ongoing casework. It is within these areas the changing organizational room and changes in organizing the activities that that will be most resistant to working for and with the organizational membrane. Also, it is within these areas that the stakeholders of the public sector will be pushing for changes in the clusters of activities.

Chapter 7

E-PROCUREMENT: THE IMPROVEMENT OF SUPPORTING AND STRATEGIC OPERATIONS

1. INTRODUCTION

Throughout this book it is emphasized that the core of PPR is to focus on the delivery of better, faster, cheaper services and information to citizens, business partners, and decision-makers. After the turn of the millennium, a number of studies related to on-line public service delivery (Hoogwout, 2002) and eHealthcare (Roberts and Alsop, 2002) have emerged addressing degrees of interaction and the requirements for the degrees of integration (Layne & Lee 2001). Other initiatives have focused on providing new digital routines to democratic processes (Grönlund, 2002). Common to the above-mentioned initiatives is the focus on the relationship between government and citizens/ companies.

In the domain of e-procurement the focus is on relations between government and companies solely. E-procurement is part of the PPR-concept although e-procurement focuses on support activities. Although the lion's share of the benefits of the e-procurement applications are within the public sector domain, the private sector can benefit from e-procurement initiatives within the public sector. The benefits include streamlining of data exchange and reduction in access cost to a larger market. Yet, these benefits are highly dependent on how the e-procurement implementation will evolve and could lead to supply risk and negative profit impacts (Kraljic 1983).

The public sector spends between 10 and 20 percent of its earnings on procurement activities (Andersen et al. 2000; Thai and Grimm 2000; Jones

2002; Andersen et al. 2003; Goerdeler 2003). This is a whopping amount when converted to monetary terms. European Union for instance procures for more than 720 billion Euros annually (EU 2004) whereas the US Federal government spends over $250 billion annually in direct purchases and state/local governments spend nearly $400 billion annually in purchases (EPA 2003).

Procurement is part of the supporting activities in government, adding an "e" does not change this. Yet, the "e" could shift and increase the level of interactivity vertically and horizontally in the public sector. Having the potential for a fully fledged market with a range of digital transaction technologies holds great potential implications for the nature of the procurement function and possibly shifts this from a purely transactional to a more strategic task (Carbone 2000) of restructuring supply chains (Croom 2001). A shift to also include a strategic level would suggest that digital procurement became a more integrated part of the public sector strategies. Yet, our research on digital procurement has found that so far governments are only to a limited extent, implementing digital procurement motivated by strategic rationality.

This chapter will open up the black box of e-procurement by *defining e-procurement and the central concepts of e-procurement*. The overall message is to consider three sets of activities as constituting e-procurement: *process* (P), *decision* (D), and *transaction* (T). The chapter progres so address *policy initiatives on e-procurement and the potential gains* with respect to centralization-decentralization, information decision costs, purchasing power, and size. We demonstrate a rather fragmented picture of e-procurement and challenge the view of government optimizing the e-procurement processes. Instead we find a large activity level with e-procurement at the individual level using the internet for seeking information rather than completing the business transaction. Whereas *size is not an issue* when it comes to ordering and paying, seeking information or receiving services and goods through the internet is found to be negatively correlated to the size of the local government. Thus, the *smaller the unit the more likely it is to be an information seeker* at the internet and receive support/ goods through the internet.

2.   DEFINITION OF E-PROCUREMENT

A pure transaction focused definition of e-procurement will define the area as:

".....the process of electronically purchasing the goods and services needed for an organization's operation. It offers a real-time platform for conducting business while providing a significant opportunity to cut costs, increase organizational effectiveness, and improve customer service" (Mitchell 2000).

We define e-procurement as the application of a span of digital technologies (EDI, Internet technologies, and PDAs) to enable the exchanging partners (within companies and the public sector) smoothing and expanding the front-end and back-office integration of contracting, service, transportation and payment of the products and services through processes, decisions, and transactions.

We view the searching, ordering, payment, accounting, transportation, receipt, and keying/ storage of data related to each of these actions as the procurement *process* (P). Whereas the procurement *decision* (D) is the analysis of procurement data and the decision to purchase at a given supplier. In some cases this involves the central procurement officer specifying the exact good, in other cases the good is not specified. The purchasing of a given good by a given supplier we will label the *procurement transaction* (T). The distinction between P, D and T is essential. A municipality might decide that all institutions and all employees have to use certain suppliers for shopping for paper due to a competitive discount of 15%. The contract is then renewed yearly by the municipality. Thus there is no price negotiation during the year, only quantity and time is an issue.

Yet, the variable P gives insight in the complications that might arise when adopting e-procurement. It might be that the goods need to be delivered at a place other than designated by the person who ordered it. Also they might prefer to have it shipped with other goods to reduce transportation and order handling costs. Also, e-procurement might only encompass some of the elements in the P-variable, namely searching for goods and digital invoicing. The variable P also reveals where one of the main benefits from e-procurement might arise, namely in the ability to analyze the procurement and utilize this information in the negotiation with the supplier.

MacManus (2002) calls for recognizing the difference between e-procurement and e-purchasing. Quoting the dictionary of purchasing terms, he explains procurement as "the combined functions of purchasing, inventory control, traffic and transportation, receiving and inspection, storekeeping and salvage and disposal operations" (NIGP 1996). Purchasing on the other hand is narrowly defined as "the act and the function of responsibility for the acquisition of equipments, materials, supplies and services. [Purchasing] describes determining the need, selecting the supplier, arriving at a fair and reasonable price and terms, preparing the contract or purchasing order, and following up to ensure timely delivery" (NIGP 1996).

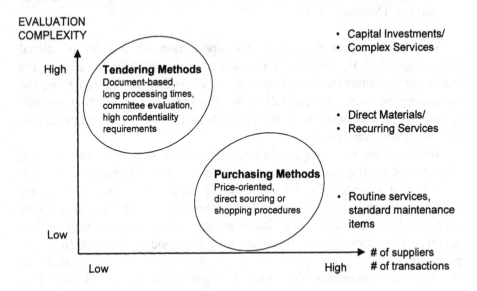

Figure 7-1. Tendering and purchasing methods: Variation in evaluation complexity and number of suppliers/transactions- *Source:* Talero (2001)

Although, the systems developed for the public sector at this time seem to have functionalities similar to that of the narrowly defined "purchasing" rather than to the broadly defined "procurement", we will use the term e-procurement throughout this chapter. The three sets of activities involved in e-procurement -- *process* (P), *decision* (D), and *transaction* (T) -- each hold technical and organizational challenges with respect to transport technology, transport provider, data integration, and choice of standards.

2.1   Transport technology, transport provider, data integration, and standards

E-procurement is not web surfing solely although it indeed encompasses catalog shopping, market places, auctions etc. Also, e-procurement includes 2-tier relations, 3rd party marketplaces and other 3-tier business models such as procurement auctions (Kjerstad and Vagstad 2000; Vagstad 2000) in which the buying decision is automated or created entirely by a piece of software (Wigand 1995). At the one end we have the buyers' deliberate choice/ decision at the time of the transaction. Ordinarily order forms at web sites are examples of this. At a more advanced level, the buying transactions are automated primarily in simple transactions, but with some human choices left using various proprietary standards. In our view e-procurement *can* be aligned with enterprise resource planning systems, data mining, knowledge management, and accounting systems. Yet, we do not require e-procurement to be linked with these other IS-systems to qualify as an e-procurement system.

Digital procurement here is defined as the application of a span of digital technologies (EDI, Internet technologies, and PDAs) to enable the exchanging partners (within companies and the public sector) to smooth and expanding the front-end and back-office integration of contracting, service, transportation and payment of the products and services. To mention a few, Enterprise Resource Planning Systems (ERP), Data mining (DM), knowledge management (KM) and accounting systems (ACC) all need to be aligned with digital procurement efforts. In Figure 1 we have depicted some of the crucial dimensions in digital procurement.

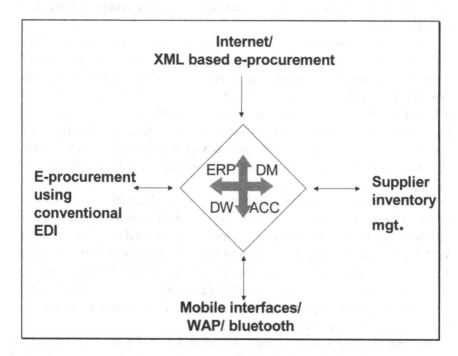

Figure 7-2. Dimensions of digital procurement

At the technology part, it is essential to stress that digital procurement indeed encompasses such "old timers" as EDI. EDI transport between any two parties also requires means for transportation (e.g. VANS) as well as an agreed upon (standardized) message format. XML is not making this statement obsolete. Exchanging messages using XML also requires standards and prearranged agreements among the exchanging parties. Furthermore, to take full advantage of EDI, the information exchanged must be channeled into the existing information systems at both ends, thus providing full integration (Andersen et al. 2000). Besides, to give the full picture of EDI, the technology utilized, including the hardware and software of existing systems and the added EDI-modules, must be taken into account.

For the message format, at least three sub categories are prevalent: Proprietary formats, EDIFACT, and similar definitions like ANSI X.12, and XML-based format. Proprietary format includes all individually negotiated exchange formats and company specific formats such as within the SAP/ R4. Although, one may face difficulties in categorizing for example the STRU-standard developed by the European Articles Numbering Systems Association (EAN) since it enables EDIFACT messages in an XML environment, the three message format types are often competing standards and challenges

For the transport technology, we find proprietary protocols, TCP/IP, e-mail attachments and physical storage to be the dominant dimensions to categorize. Companies might use various protocols although the most predominately used is the TCP/IP protocol. Also, the digital procurement-message might be stored in a file, zipped and sent as an attachment to an ordinary e-mail or stored on a physical device such as a magnetic tape, a disk or the alike. Storage on a physical device has diminished rapidly but is still a method used for storage and transportation of digital procurement messages.

For the transport provider dimension, using third parties (VANS) or direct dial-up are common facilities. Physical transport on a disk or digital transport using the Internet are, however, also prevalent. Several of the VANS-operators are also now offering the web-services to their customers. The web-transport media challenges the VANS-operators' pricing structure and forcing them to seek new sources of income. We have seen various VANS-operators to supplement their earnings from consultancy business rather than from a fee-per-transaction.

A forth dimension reveals the integration into existing systems. Digital procurement messages might be fully integrated in both ends (sender and receiver). However, digital procurement might be integrated in one end only (receiver), typically by using a "forms" interface for data-entry at the sender (EDI-light). In various web-companies we witness this tendency. Also, one can find examples of this with handheld minicomputers that send of orders using a dial-up function. The receiver of the message automatically integrates the message in their ordering system and possibly transmits the message to the accounting and the logistic units.

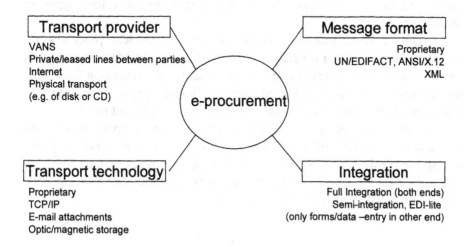

Figure 7-3. Transport technologies, transport provider, integration, and standards - *Source.*
modified after Andersen et al. (2000)

Applying our classification scheme of digital procurement one easily ends up with too many categories. Counting all combinations in a four-space matrix (3 x 4 x 4 x 2), close to a hundred different interpretations of digital procurement emerge. Hence, it is our view that the taxonomy becomes useless to capture the development of digital procurement. Also, the matrix will probably be sparse in reality, as many combinations are mostly artificial. None the less, the matrix does reflect the digital procurement-diversity and suggest why the different digital procurement-players lack a "language" platform for assessing digital procurement and taking actions to increase the digital procurement-use. Adding the specific technologies in mobile technologies adds to the complexity in implementing digital procurement.

2.2   What and how public sector is buying

We distinguish between sources that are recurrent and systematic and those which are directed by business opportunity due to demand being infrequent or difficult to predict. Within the other dimension we distinguish between sourcing indirect products versus procuring for production or manufacturing, i.e. direct materials. Systematic sourcing means to acquire those materials and products that enter directly into producing. For most industries the distinction between indirect and direct materials makes sense where investments can be separated from operations, giving the latter a clear profile within the business. Below, we thus distinguish four types of procurement.

Horizontal Hubs improve efficiencies in procurement processes for operating supplies for a diverse set of industries. Yield Managers work in spot procuring of supplies that are not essential to the production flow. Spot procurement is therefore taking advantage of volatile prices or reflects high fixed cost assets that cannot be liquidated or acquired at short notice.

Exchanges are set up to create spot markets for commodities or near-commodities within industry verticals and may even serve a yield-management role. Vertical Hubs are built on e-catalogues that are industry-specific. They have to work closely with distributors, especially on specialized fulfillment and logistics services.

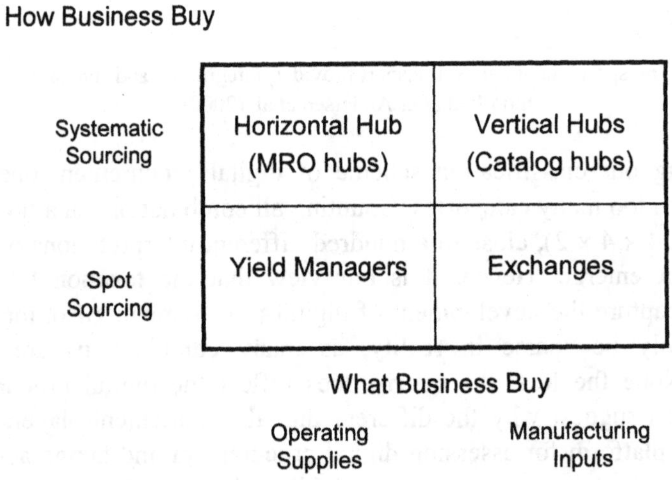

How Business Buy

Systematic Sourcing	Horizontal Hub (MRO hubs)	Vertical Hubs (Catalog hubs)
Spot Sourcing	Yield Managers	Exchanges

What Business Buy

Operating Supplies	Manufacturing Inputs

Figure 7-4. Types of business procurement - *Source*: Kaplan & Sawhney (2000)

In recent years we have seen numerous business initiatives to set up exchanges for business-to-business trading (Kaplan & Sawhney 2000, Aberdeen Group October 2000, Aberdeen Group February 2001). Aggregating demand to create economies of scale and to squeeze margins in upstream supply chains through positioning in the value chain have

motivated the investors. These effects may vary according to ownership;
hence we will analyze the three scenarios according to this factor. Besides
ownership we will also consider the objective of the exchange. We need to
distinguish between types of exchanges to capture how they differ in
achieving competitive advantage. In our sample of three exchanges, the

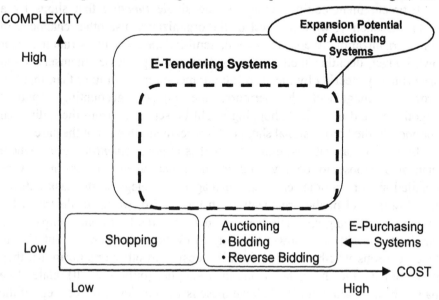

common denominator is indirect procurement though Covisint also conduct
direct. The second common denominator is the technology platform. All
exchanges emerged with the Internet. The open technology platform is
decisive to the advantages postulated by exchange analysts like Kaplan &
Sawhney (2000).

Figure 7-5. The cost and complexity of e-procurement systems: Shopping, auctioning and
tendering – *Source*: Talero (2001)

2.3   The actors and elements involved in e-procurement

In some organizations e-procurement is a *single actor* activity, in other
organizations a formulated *organizational-wide activity* involving one of
more of the following elements:
–   Seeking information
–   Ordering goods/ services
–   Paying goods/ services
–   Receiving goods/ services

– Receiving support/ service

As highlighted earlier, the number of *shopping channels* is quite substantial. Web-based procurement is one shopping channel that might be complementary or supplementary with PDA, EDI, standing orders, catalogues, ads, sales personnel, phone and fax orders and pick-up orders.

E-procurement could encompass one single *function* that shops by a certain frequency, while the rest of the organization use other channels. In some organizations there are several, semi-independent units running their own budget, deciding their content of their work processes themselves and are primarily steering by means of output measurements rather than input or process management. Furthermore, the budget, accounting, contract negotiating and the actual shopping might be separated from the individual shopper. In the "professional shopper" predicament, this is not the case.

In some organizations, e-procurement is a *management-led* event where managers choose to be involved in the procurement process in a very detailed matter. In other cases, the manager has delegated this task entirely to a lower level of the organization. In Figure 7-6, we have illustrated the variety of shopping channels from the demand side D. In one company the employees might have power not only to evaluate the website, but also to take decisions whether to shop at this website. In other organizations, they may not have the choice to change their supplier (only or at all) related to a bad web site evaluation. We believe these issues challenge the concept of the "professional shopper" and are ignored entirely in the literature, yet have the potential to explain the outcome of the procurement process.

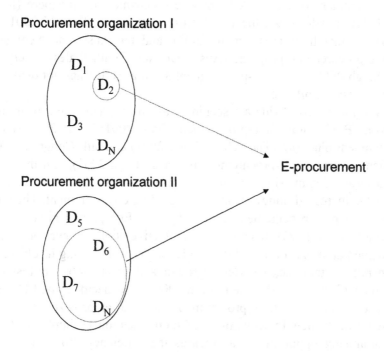

Procurement organization I

Procurement organization II

E-procurement

Figure 7-6. The concept of the "professional shopper"

We have been able to work with KPMG addressing such issues as frequency of orders, number of shoppers, standing orders, and discounts in the physical/ digital value chain (KPMG 2000). The KPMG study demonstrated that accounting system registers only a very general description of the items bought and the sum. This makes it difficult to compare the analog and digital value chain and fuel our challenge of the professional shopper. It can be suggested that whereas we can obtain knowledge of how money must have been spent, and possibly have this distributed to a variety of categories and locations of spending, it would be hard to find anybody in an governmental organization who knows what has been bought, at what prices, and whether better deals could have been achieved. This information is scattered and fragmented and not logged in any standardized matter.

3.   E-PROCUREMENT INITIATIVES

Departing from the overall definition of e-procurement we will in this section address the e-procurement initiatives. Implementations such as the

Irish Government (Ireland 2003), private companies in Singapore (Kheng and Al-Hawamdeh 2002), the US defense contracting (Scacchi 2001) and military organizations (Liao et al. 2003), and the Australian New South Wales e-procurement program (Australian-New-South-Wales-Government 2003; Singh 2003) witness e-procurement as an area that has not died along with the dot.com collapse.

Governments worldwide are seeking ways to implement e-procurement. The World Bank Forum on e-procurement (Bank 2001; Talero 2001), the US E-government blueprint (The-White-House 2001) and bill (Congress. 2001), Brazilian government e-procurement policies (Tigre 2003), and the efforts by European Commission promoting e-procurement (Commission 2002) witness the increased policy awareness regarding e-procurement. The Green Paper on public procurement issued by the European Union in 1996 (European Union, 1996) stated that: "An effective public procurement policy is fundamental to the success of the single market in achieving its objectives: to generate sustainable, long-term growth and create jobs, to foster the development." At the Lisbon summit in 2000 it was decided that EU should pay special attention to e-procurement. It was emphasized that "The emergence of the new Information and Communication Technologies (ICTs) offer promising opportunities as regards the efficiency, transparency and opening-up of public procurement" (European Commision, 2000). Yet, while these policy initiatives aim to push e-procurement, other policies are aiming for shattering employment opportunities in Europe which in turn can be counter productive to e-procurement initiatives by favoring EU produced goods over world market goods (Mann et al. 2000). Also clashing policy concerns can be a potential inhibitor at the local and regional level of government.

Within EU concerns relating nepotism etc have led to a rather formal and lengthy tendering process. The tendering requirement is an example of a EU policy which conflicts with online target goals. Jens Mortensen, the director of applications and industries for Oracle Europe, Middle East and Africa made the following comment concerning an online market place for the public sector procurement, launched in 2002 in one of the EU member countries:

"the system covers all items below the price threshold for open tenders. In 12 months time, however, the plan is to extend e-procurement to higher value goods. There will be possibilities, say, for a local authority to buy its fire engines online. First, however, some European procurement rules must be changed. The EU will have to take another look at the legal side of it with higher value goods. It has already issued a directive saying that, by 2005 25% of EU payments should be online, and if that is going to be achieved legislation will have to change" (Cablenet 2002)

Most, or even all, of the countries are still in the implementation stages. Not all countries diffuse e-procurement similarly; instead there are several diffusion patterns. For instance, the Danish central government has chosen a private e-market as the infrastructure for e-procurement (efokus 2003). The Spanish ministry of public administration has taken the role of defining functional, technical and organizational specifications (Juan 2002). The German government has invested 4.5 million Euro in developing a "flag ship" project e-vergabe, which it touts as the "model for public procurement in Europe" (Goerdeler 2003).

Devadoss et al. (2003) points out that government lacks a holistic and comprehensive view when looking towards digitalization of government. They call for attention to include also structural factors. Within the IS literature, it a classical theme whether institutions can, and with what success, help diffuse IS (King et al. 1994; Lai and Guynes 1997; Saunders 1997; Gregor and Johnston 2001) highlights that procurement in general has been viewed as a back-office function. Perhaps as a result of this back-office setting, procurement has not had a high level of policy saliency and not been part of the political nature of the budgetary process (Wildawsky 1964). Although there has been various plans and rhetoric on e-procurement, there has been a discrepancy between the political rhetoric and the action level (Brunsson 2000).

4.   POTENTIAL GAINS FROM E-PROCUREMENT

In the private sector, there has been a keen awareness of the value chain model described by Porter (1985), and for example Moreton & Chester (1996) have mapped IT for each step in the value chain. Subsequently there have been studies performed that span across the private and public sectors suggesting three sets of conclusions can be drawn in respect to supply chain restructuring (Croom 2001):

- significant potential cost savings in the process of search, order and payment. Thus, the internal procurement process will become "leaner".
- increased information for the customer will lead to an increased incidence of outsourcing for maintenance, repair and operating supply (MRO) requirements. Government will thus focus more on their core competencies.
- the potential to adopt a more strategic approach to MRO procurement will see, inter alia, the restructuring of supply chains, potentially reducing the supply base in some categories (such as stationery) whilst in other

situations eliminating existing links in the supply chain (such as travel agents).

The value chain model gives a very simplified illustration of the public sector both in terms of the "input" and "output" of the administration. Most of the public sector is involved in knowledge work, and the input and support activities are by nature different than activities in an automobile production hall. The model outlined in Figure 3.1 does represent the important split between primary and secondary activities. Although IT is on the move within the primary activities, the overwhelming impression is that the spread is very limited. For the past 30 years the emphasis has been on support.

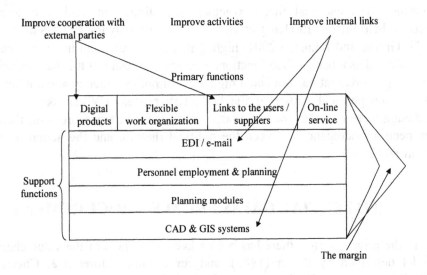

Figure 7-7. Improvement of internal links and supplier relations

Note. Developed after Moreton and Chester (1996), p. 56

The "margin" at the very right end of the figure, which represents the difference between the accumulated costs and the price that the demand side is paying for the goods produced, is challenging to identify in the public sector. The model operates at a formal organizational level, for example a municipality or a department within a ministry. Although this is in line with budget allocation procedures in most countries, the key to boosting IT in government might be to counter-balance the formal organizational view with an activity centric view. This would be more in line with our PPR model.

As stated in the Introduction, e-procurement is referred to as "the public sectors' potential improvement of operations through electronic means in the form of electronic purchase of goods and services." When referring to "electronic means" these can be related to a span of digital technologies such as EDI, Internet, and PDAs. The term "improvement of operations" is less clear to define. Timmers (2000) suggested that the benefits derived from e-procurement include a wider choice of suppliers, lower cost, better quality, improved delivery, and reduced cost of procurement. Mitchell (2000) referred to e-procurement, as the process of electronically purchasing goods and services needed for organizations' operation, where a real-time platform for conducting business is offered. He suggested that the real-time platform provides a significant opportunity to cut costs, increase organizational effectiveness, and improve customer service.

Yet, there are many obstacles to reaching these ends. Most purchases in public sector institutions require a bureaucratic procedure to be followed due to a variety of reasons. One reason is that the majority of items are bought on requisition. This means that an enormous amount of effort is spent on sending forms back and forth within the system.

Another reason for the bureaucratic procedures of public procurement is related to the tendering process. The public sector institutions in the European Union countries do, unlike private businesses, have to follow a procurement process, which is highly regulated. In the EU it is illegal to favor domestic over foreign firms. For purchases exceeding EUR 160,000 and 248,000 for state institution contracts and county/municipality contracts respectively (EU 1993), a publicly advertised tender in the Supplement to the Official Journal of the European Communities is mandatory.

One consequence of these conditions an increasing complex technical solution of a given e-procurement system for public sector institutions. Another issue, which may be even more significant, is that of e-procurement adoption. This involves a change to organizational routines, which go beyond mere rationality.

Four major issues relating to the benefits of e-procurement involve 1) centralization versus decentralization, 2) information decision costs, 3) the use of the shared purchasing power in government, and 4) the consideration of whether size is a positive correlated to e-procurement initiatives and benefits.

4.1   Centralization versus decentralization

The centralization versus decentralization debate at an organizational level is about who in the organization will decide on the goods and services that an organization requires and from which supplier should they be procured from. McCue and Pitzer (2000) explain the various combinations along which purchasing can be centralized. In one extreme, there is a centralized purchasing authority to whom end users send their requests. The centralized authority authorizes the requests, identifies the suppliers, negotiates prices and makes the purchasing decision. In the decentralized extreme, end users make their own purchasing decision.

Procurement authority is both centralized and decentralized among the Danish governmental organizations. Procurement is a centralized activity in the Danish tax office and it has remained that way for the last 40 years (source: interview with a purchasing officer in Aarhus tax office). In contrast, procurement is a highly decentralized activity in the Danish universities. It however used to be centralized like a decade back but since then it has gradually become decentralized. A secretary in a Danish university explains procurement practice as follows;

> "We thought that agreements made by a central purchasing body would be cheaper. But after a couple of years, we started checking on the prices ourselves. If we buy furniture directly from furniture stores, we can get them a lot cheaper than if we buy from the university because her salary needs to be paid. If they get a 500 DKK table and sell it for 550 DKK. Then the 50 is for her salary... It is what they give and what they take... We would not allow that. So we buy it ourselves." (*Our translation*).

The initiatives have progressed from defining standards and implementation to focus on innovation of government. Yet, there is a lack of comprehensive initiatives for e-procurement in local government. There have been attempts by the Ministry of Finance to cut the budgets by a sum that corresponds to the estimated amount of savings. However this has resulted in a massive critique from the chairman of the association of procurement managers:

> "The Ministry of Finance has based its analysis on one item in twenty different groups such as pens and envelopes. All goods are marginal. We do not agree that this can be generalized to other groups of goods... Through a very professional procurement behavior in the majority of the municipalities through many years, savings by the billions have been made. Also, tendering processes have been launched for both goods and service; competition has been a key area and as has use of bargaining power in the tendering process. Thus, public procurement is already in extreme competition through centralized procurement systems. Procurement is already to a large extend professionalized both quantitatively and qualitatively enabling attractive and broad assortments." (Jensen 2000) (*Our translation*).

4.2   The decision information costs

Both the centralized and the decentralized structures have their respective advantages and disadvantages. An organization is able to accumulate its purchase and negotiate volume discounts involving professional expertise when the decision authority is centralized. However, the central authority can make a good decision only when it is well aware of the end user's requirements. Gurbaxani and Whang (1991) term the cost of informing the central authority and the lack of it as *decision information costs*. Decision information costs tend to be high when the purchasing authority is centralized and low when decentralized. Organizations are not able to obtain volume discounts when purchasing authority is decentralized. The end users when given the responsibility can act in a self serving manner instead of serving the organization, the risk of which is termed as the *agency costs*. The agency costs can be minimized through *monitoring,* which costs as well.

The use of IT for automating procurement procedures alters the arguments for centralization and decentralization. Those arguing for centralization can cite the role of IT in reducing the decision information costs. The end users can request their requirements via a workflow system based on which the central purchasing authority can negotiate frame agreements. The end users can access negotiated frame agreements posted in the intranet or in an e-market simply via a desktop. The central purchasing authority can use business intelligence tools for learning about the needs of an organization and thereby is in a position to negotiate better frame agreements. It is thus the implementation of e-procurement system that supports the centralization. Those arguing for decentralization can cite the role of IT in minimizing the cost of monitoring and thereby reducing the agency costs.

The effect of IT in centralization versus decentralization of organizational structures has been a lengthy one. Gurbaxani and Whang provide a seemingly good solution to the debate. They recommend choosing the organizational structure in which the internal co-ordination costs, which is a sum of agency and decision information costs, are at a minimum. The centralization of decision making at the organizational level is recommended in this paper and, is expected to reduce decision information costs much more than it would the agency costs. Such a claim is made despite Denmark being one of the least corrupt countries in the world. Centralization however is a challenging task for power when let gone is difficult to get back (King 1983).

4.3   Purchasing power

Government organizations can negotiate better frame agreements when they accumulate their purchasing volumes via joint ventures. Such a trend is prevalent. Thirty three states in the US formed an alliance ("Western State Contracting Alliance") whose motto is "every body benefits from the use of cumulative volume discount contracts". Bartle and Korosec (2003) identify several such efforts made by the US states. In the Danish context, Kubus embarked on building the trade builder system when two local bodies that procure as one entity sought its assistance for developing a catalogue management system. SKI was formed to negotiate agreements on behalf of the whole Danish government.

The science behind this debate is quite similar to that of the previous debate. It is just the level of analysis that changes. Those arguing for centralization cite the advantages of reduced decision information costs. Those arguing for decentralization have a much stronger argument. Firstly, the local bodies would like to support their local economy by awarding government contracts to organizations based in their area. To remind the reader, local bodies obtain as much as 66% of their revenues from local taxes and the Danish government's expenditure accounts for 25% of the GDP. The local bodies thus would want to maintain their autonomy or enhance it. Secondly, only the large suppliers have the ability to provide for the requirements of a large buyer such as that of a government. Small suppliers when unable to compete with the large might not survive especially when they are highly dependent on government orders. Government traditionally has taken efforts to encourage small and medium sized companies and not discourage their existence. Thirdly, adopting new public management (Ferlie et al. 1996; Lane 2000), authority has been decentralized during the last decade to local governments such that service is generated as close to the citizens (Andersen et al. 2003). An attempt to centralize procurement is against this ideology. Finally, the local bodies query the notion of being monitored at the governance level.

This debate is much more complex than the previous one. It is difficult to apply the solution that Gurbaxani and Whang (1991) suggest for resolving this debate. Local bodies for instance query if they should be monitored at all. The issue is not just about efficiency but also about effectiveness. Governance is not just about making economically rational decisions as the Cybernetic theory explains. There are also the adverse effects associated with rationalization that need to be taken into consideration (Stepney 2000).

The debate about whether to centralize or decentralize the computing infrastructure is a traditional one. King's (1983) summary of the debate is very representative of the topic. The debate has originated in the e-procurement context as well. In the Danish context, should all governmental organizations adopt the centralized Gatetrade infrastructure or should they all develop custom solutions? The two sides of the debate are hereby presented;

Those supporting Gatetrade as the standard argue as follows; we should regard government as a single entity. Applications required for e-procurement are quite similar. Why then should multiple infrastructures for the same purpose be developed by the same entity? E-procurement infrastructure is not only costly to develop but also to maintain and further advance. It is prudent that investments are made in one sophisticated system that seamlessly connects with all of the government. This view assumes that all involved actors are rational and that they all share the same ideas on improving government performance.

The other side supporting decentralized computing has the following arguments; unlike private enterprises for which efficiency is the sole evaluation criteria, governments as well have to take effectiveness into consideration. Government is such a complex entity that one system cannot possibly satisfy all of its requirements. As an end user in a large Danish university puts it:

"There are 22 departments. It is like 22 different firms. Some are old fashioned. We have a lot of responsibilities here. We can buy all our things. In some departments it is department heads like Peter who is buying but not here. There are different rules dependent on where you are hired."

King (1983) explains that the extent to which the computing infrastructure is centralized or decentralized is not about *"which way is best?"* It usually is *"whose way is it going to be?"*

5.   SIZE AS AN INHIBITOR RATHER THAN DRIVER

One of the expectations held by government is that the greater the government is in terms of size, the more likely e-procurement is to spiral and materialize in measurable benefits. In a survey we did, we found the opposite to be true. In the subsequent sections we will examine the case as this will help further stimulate our adoption of the PPR approach suggesting that we redirect our initiatives to target individuals and sub-processes of procurement, rather than viewing procurement as a unified and necessary interlinked phenomenon.

The survey data is from a study on Danish local government. The total Danish GDP is 986 Billion DKK at factors costs (about 140 Billion EURO). The public sector spends about 288 Billion DKK and redistributes about 70% of the GDP, covering a variety of expenditures (unemployment insurance, housing subsidies, health care, elder care) and income sources (income taxation, corporate tax, consumer tax, import tax, etc.). About two-thirds of the total public expenditures are allocated through the local government (Knudsen et al. 2002).

Local governments in charge of the health sector, school, road construction, and elder care are seeing electronic commerce as vital in the area of the procurement and as a means to get electronic documents from citizens and companies. Central government and semi-governmental units such as the postal service and train service are seeing electronic commerce as a means to achieve strategic advances, cost and time reductions and smoothing the communication. The estimate is that goods and services (procurement) amounts to about 100 billion DKK in government budget of which the 275 municipalities spends about 48 billion on procurement annually.

Within the Danish scene there has been a development toward horizontal and vertical e-procurement solution and a mixture of integration modes. Based on the annual turnover, however, they are all either troubled or having a very marginal market share. The portfolio of e-procurement solutions encompass:

- SKI (www.ski.dk)
- DOIP – Gatetrade (www.doip.dk)
- WebIndkøb (KMD) (www.kmd.dk)
- Purchasing consortia
- E-procurement catalogs
- Digital payments and accounting
- Digital exchange of documents related to e-procurement, for example advance delivery notice
- Tendering sites (www.udbudsportalen.dk)
- Supplier controlled portals (www.lyreco.dk)

At the demand side, 40% used e-procurement either daily or weekly, only 15% never used e-procurement in 2002. This is a substantial increase since 1999. Also we found that 6% shopped using the internet in 1999, whereas in year 2002 14% shopped at the internet.

Table 7-1. Ordering of goods and services via the Internet. 1999 and 2002. Percent (N).

Frequency of ordering goods and services	1999*	2002
Daily	5,7	14,29
Weekly	20,89	27,78
Monthly	23,42	30,95
Annual	8,86	11,11
Never	41,14	15,87
Sum	100%	100%
(N)	(N=158)	(N=126)

Note. *) data from Andersen and Nicolajsen (2000).

Thus, there has been an increase in the number of municipalities shopping on a more frequent basis. Although the figures displayed in Table 7-1 do not reveal data on the number of transactions or share of budget. The type of goods ordered in both 1999 and 2002 are general office supplies, books, IT-products (hardware and software), conference and training, transportation (travel), and inventory. A rather limited number of the respondents reported that they received goods and services in a digital form such as product information, publications, software upgrading, new software programs, and reports.

Secondly, we found that ordering is the least frequent part of the e-procurement process. Seeking information and receiving the goods and services are more important aspects of e-commerce for both our respondents and their knowledge of what is going on in the rest of the municipality.

Table 7-2. Frequency of the five dimensions of e-procurement. Respondent self and others in the municipality. Percent (N)

E-procurement dimensions	Respondent self				Others in the municipality			
	Daily/ weekly	Monthly	Never	Sum (N)	Daily/ weekly	Monthly	Never	Sum (N)
Seeking information	55	29	16	100 (150)	62	32	6	100 (124)
Ordering goods/ services	24	43	34	101 (148)	42	42	16	100 (126)
Paying goods/ services	3	10	87	100 (146)	9	15	76	100 (127)
Receiving goods/ services	31	36	33	100 (145)	40	43	17	100 (123)
Receiving support/ service	31	33	35	99 (147)	43	48	9	100 (120)

We tested whether the number of citizens, total budget or budget relative to number of citizens could explain any variation in the respondents' use of e-procurement. The outcome of the test did not support any correlation except in seeking information and in receiving support / service and in the ordering process. Please note that the correlation in these areas is negative, hence suggesting that larger municipalities (measured by number of citizens and budget) are more likely not to seek information through digital channels.

Table 7-3. Gamma test of economics of scale and dimensions of e-procurement

E-procurement dimensions	Number of citizens		Budget		Budget relative to citizens	
	Respond ent self	Others in the municipality	Respond ent self	Others in the municipalit y	Respond ent self	Others in the municip ality
Seeking information	-0.31*	-0.15	-0.35*	-0.26*	-0.27*	-0.36*
Ordering goods/ services	-0.06	-0.12	-0.16	-0.14	-0.20*	0.10
Paying goods/ services	0.14	0.08	0.14	0.14	0.11	0.06
Receiving goods/ services	-0.16	-0.14	-0.12	-0.04	-0.06	-0.03
Receiving support/ service	-0.16	-0.15	-0.22*	-0.14	-0.20*	-0.17

Note. A strong significance is indicated by a p-value less than 0.001 marked bold face and with *

We asked the respondents to address the impacts of e-procurement on six dimensions: financial savings, administrative savings, lower distribution costs, improved collaboration with suppliers, improved work flow routines and improved image. If we add the respondents that answered 1-3 on the Lickert scale, the improved work flow routines got more than half of the responses (55%). Financial savings had been viewed favorably from 34%, whereas 45% of the respondents found administrative savings to be an impact on e-procurement. Yet, as is revealed in Figure 7-8 below, the distribution is centered in the middle.

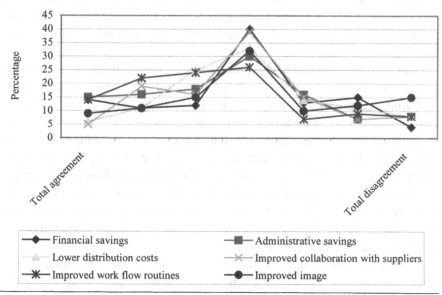

Figure 7-8. Impacts of e-procurement. Percentage

There are only few strong positive or negative evaluations of the outcome of the e-procurement. In statistical runs, we have tested whether the evaluation of outcome is correlated with whether the respondent himself or others in the municipalities perform the e-commerce. We did not identify any correlations on these accounts. Nor did we find any correlation on whether the type of e-procurement is just information seeking or actual ordering. Finally there is no correlation between number of suppliers that the municipalities exchange data with and the outcome.

6. CONCLUSIONS

This chapter has opened up the black box of e-procurement by *defining e-procurement and the central concepts of e-procurement.* We then addressed some of the *policy initiatives on e-procurement and the potential gains* with respect to centralization versus decentralization, information decision costs, purchasing power, and the issue of size.

The chapter has painted a rather fragmented picture of e-procurement thereby challenging the view of government optimizing the e-procurement processes. Instead we find a large activity level with e-procurement at the individual level using the internet for seeking information rather than completing the business transaction. Our interpretation of the findings reported in this chapter is encouraging for the adoption of the PPR approach, and suggests that we redirect our initiatives to target individuals and sub-processes of procurement, rather than viewing procurement as a unified and necessary interlinked set of activities.

We also have to emphasize that e-*procurement cannot be an end but should be considered a mean to reach operational and strategic goals.* Accordingly, various e-procurement sites are facing fierce competition from well-trimmed and well-established analog procurement processes. An example of this is the procurement of office supplies, where navigation between product information and meetings with the sales representatives are factors that can be serious competitors to any business-to-business website.

The chapter also highlighted that legislative issues clearly are equally relevant to address. The most critical dimension where legislation plays an important role is requirements on tendering and implementation of legislation on digital signatures.

Our data presented here suggests that the bigger the municipality (measured by number of citizens and budget), the more likely the municipality is *not to seek* information through digital channels. This might be explained by considering that the manager in the smaller municipality has more *information about and control of the procurement process and the actual goods* bought whereas in the larger municipalities the procurement is more decentralized.

Our analysis also revealed that there are *no clear positive or negative outcomes* of e-procurement on the six measurements of outcome: financial savings, administrative savings, lower distribution costs, improved collaboration with suppliers, improved work flow routines and improved image.

This could be due to, for example, supply-side setting the prices listed in the electronic catalogs so high that there is no room for negotiation in the non-digital procurement channel. E-procurement could encompass a variety of strategic and dynamic items, but there seems to be limited or no supply of these goods and services. Yet, we did not investigate this issue as we did not incorporate a supply-side perspective in our research for this chapter but can only encourage research to understand the *highly dynamic relations between demand and supply side.*

Various launches of portals, market places, etc. experience a *lack of demand* from B2B e-procurement offices in government. One possible explanation could be a fundamental misunderstanding of the demand side in government. Our line of argument would be that there is not a unified, single government demand side and few procurement offices with control of all three aspects of procurement: *process* (P), *decision* (D), and *transaction* (T). Instead, there are a variety of people in a variety of governments' locations.

Although e-procurement amounts to a large sum, procurement is only a fraction of governments' overall budget. Thus, although e-procurement is a potential vehicle for cost-saving etc., the *relative policy importance e-procurement is limited.* Salary and construction activities make up the major part of government budget, leaving e-procurement with a much lower level of policy saliency. In turn, governments are *not pushing e-procurement in strategic operations* such as the social services, education, etc. and appear to have yet to find their way to become an active player in the use of e-procurement in strategic management of their supply chain.

Chapter 8

INSTRUMENTAL DIGITAL CUSTOMER INVOLVEMENT

1. INTRODUCTION

This chapter turns the table from the attempts to streamline the procurement processes to the customer involvement in core activities as childcare, education, eldercare, and council meetings. We focus on availability of digital channels for the involvement of customers of the public services in the decisions at the *institutional level*.

Customer involvement is part of an overall democratic debate within government on what, how, and when to involve customers. The challenge with studying IT from a democracy point of view is that "....both democracy and good governance remain 'essentially contested concepts' (Gallie 1956), since there is not now, nor will there likely be, a final consensus on their definition or content." (Landman 2002). We encourage the flourishing of this vital debate when government designs the new generation of IT-application. Competing views concerning involvement principles can result in lack of understanding of initial arguments when building, implementing and exploiting information systems for customer involvement.

One of the key issues that government faces is the type, extent, and timing of interaction between government institutions and the customers. Also, governments are challenged by balancing open responses, facilitating the gathering of disparate information, and running a cost-effective organization. Although customer involvement is a positive good and something everybody in principle would want, there is a cost of involvement. In this chapter we point out that the costs of customer involvement are even more apparent at the institutional level of government where the competition of resources is apparent. The dilemma is to divide time between customer involvement and core services.

Recalling the core focus of PPR being a customer and activity centric approach, involvement is in this chapter explored through this lens. Looking at the spectra of involvement modes, we take a rather *instrumentalistic angle* to customer involvement, by focusing on involvement channels through the Internet.

The illustration of customer involvement through the net is taken from three Danish municipalities. During the last 30 years, municipalities have chosen to digitalize primarily internal administration and have been quite successful in transactions using their digital wheelbarrows (see Chapter 4). Digitalization of the municipalities progressed uniformly and simultaneously in supporting administrative functions. Yet, this chapter proposes to that there is still a major task to address in providing digital channels enabling customer involvement.

2.   INSTITUTIONAL CONTROL VERSUS CUSTOMER CONTROL

Customer involvement is occurring in a variety of settings and situations rather than in stereotype and unified pattern. In some instances, participation requires high levels of security technologies, as in the case of elections. In other cases, there is less demand on security and more emphasis on flow of information and open dialogue (as in public hearings). Most of the participation and involvement media that has been implemented is text based, rather than being voice and visualization enabled and in general is not an active part of the dynamics of multimedia. Instead the government is a lagging uptake of media for supporting involvement. On top, most of the applications deigned for involvement is done half-hearted in the sense that critical parameters as scalability, logs, and software transparency/ update are left unexplored at the time of the first round implementation of the application. Stephen Coleman commented this at a seminar at EU premises in February 2004 as the experiments could end up doing more harm than good.

Most applications for user involvement seem to be top-down driven and supporting formal communication, use of traditional technologies, and institutional values. Few applications are at the left hand of Figure 8.1

enabling informal communication and non-institutional values using experimental technologies.

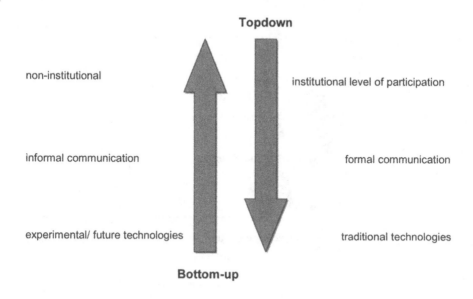

Figure 8-2. Top-down and bottom-up approaches to user involvement

Picturing the applications for customer involvement in a three dimensional diagram with communication, technology, and institutional values along the axises, there is a congested areas in the south-west corner of the diagram, whereas the northeast part of the diagram is close to empty. Government lacks the experimental stage of involvement. This is in part due to budget regulation and law requirements, but also can be subscribed to what we in chapter 3, 4 and 5 identified as a transactional and capability oriented government. Recalling the triangle from chapter 5 (please consult Figure 5.4 at page ?), few e-government applications are targeted at improving the areas of values-interaction-democracy.

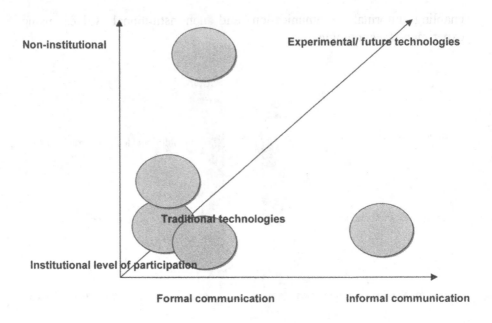

Figure 8-3. Three-dimensional user involvement

3.   DILEMMAS OF CUSTOMER INVOLVEMENT: COST AND GAINS

Countries differ substantially with respect to the extent of public services and the way they traditionally undertake customer involvement in decisions on the contents of the services, their finance, and on running the daily operations. In some countries there are few governmental services within areas such as childcare schools, and eldercare. This group of countries tends to rely more of private institutions. Other countries have largely exclusively run public childcare, schools, and elder care institutions. Often the Scandinavian countries are associated with this group, whereas the US is used as illustrative example for the first group of countries.

Despite the divergence in the extent of government and their service packages, governments are united in their implementation of technologies that aim at penetrating the organizational membrane and giving the customers more (sense of) being informed and being involved in decisions that relately their specific service. Yet, the institutional level has been rather ignored in the studies so far. By contrast the studies have concentrated on election, voting, transparency etc. (Grossman 1995; Holmes 1997; Bellamy and Taylor 1998; Hoff et al. 1999; Grönlund 2000; Holmes 2001; Grönlund 2003).

Parliaments on-line, voting, and digital divide issues are not a core part of what PPR is aimed at – despite the acknowledgement of both the relevance of each of these concerns and considering that each of these areas are drivers of e-government and e-governance initiatives. We are not, in this chapter, or elsewhere in this book, covering the important question of the fundamental relationship between IT and democracy (Heptinstal 2001; Bellamy 2002; Snellen 2002; Chadwick and May 2003). Also the limitations to user involvement (SOS 2000) and specific concerns relating to the policy domain are not discussed here (Champy 2002).

One of the single most critical features of PPR is its ability to direct new IS application towards the customer. Champy argues in his 2002-book that connectivity between a company and their customers should be kept in focus and that the principal benefits of using IT should be to create benefits for the customer (Browning and Powel 2002). We explore here whether and how this is being pursued in the governmental setting beyond e-voting implementations (Olson 1965; Downs 1967).

Governmental institution needs to balance how much they want to spend on IT enabling customer involvement relative to spending resources on a) *other activities for customer involvement* and b) *other activities than customer involvement*. The preference for A and B will reflect the underlying model of democracy as being either a service oriented democracy, elite model, neo-republican model, or a cyber-democratic model. The PPR-approach is a mixture of the four models rather than clearly following one of them. Most divergent is the elite model that often will be the preferred model taken by the government staff seeking to legitimize existing structure and innovate only the service content through consensus oriented mechanism. Of the four models the service and customer orientation is closest to the PPR-model with delivery of service, data security, and protection of the privacy sphere as key IT-policy issues in giving the customer more information, more choice, and more power in dealing with the public sector.

Yet, the PPR model is not accepting of the view that the only political action of importance is to cast a vote (Hoff 2002). The decision and involvement forums analyzed in this chapter illustrate that the PPR-model does not necessarily try to bypass the political institutions or replace exiting ones. Yet, it does echo the consumer models by giving the customers choice, access, redress, voice, and possibilities to exit as well.

Table 8-3. Preferences for Customer Involvement: Four Models

Preference variable	Service and customer orientation	Elite model	Neo-republican model	Cyber-democratic model
Dominant democratic rationality	Customer choice	Effectiveness	Discussion and participation	Communities and acceptance of different agendas
Key information policy media	Producer-customer relation data	Expert discourse, reports, etc	The public sphere, media	Internet, URL, chat, SMS
Political participation	Choice of public service	Consensus, lobby	Public debate, membership of organizations	Virtual debates and actions
Key political institution	Service institutions	Negotiations and campaign institutions	Meetings with citizens, public hearings	Digital network and communities
Dominant applications	Digital services to customers, self-services	Homepages, personalize mail/ messaging	Moderation of discussion forum, organized chat	Self-organized discussion groups
Key IT-policy issue	Delivery of service Data security Protection of the privacy sphere	Legitimization and innovation of institutions	Political participation Quality of the political discussions	Political reflections and competencies
Key democratic challenge	'Big brother' versus 'soft sister'	Centralization versus autonomy	New public spheres versus new possibilities for control	Atomizing versus communities

Source. Translated from Hoff (2002)

Dilemma A and B (spending the resources on other activities for others than customer involvement) are united in the challenge on aggregating demand preferences and identifying costs of the IT-application that are considered necessary for improving customer involvement. The demand side preferences will be the customers in the PPR-approach, but institutional powers will push employees preference curves. Although there are various examples of government not being the price taker but price setter, for most government institutions the price of hardware, integration modules, web solutions etc. is very much dictated by the market. Thus, the public sector is rarely in a situation where they negotiate the price but will have to decide *how much and what kind of IT they can afford given a certain budget.* Although the budgeting process is political and involves various departmental fights on who gets increases and who get budget costs (Intel

2003), government budget is mostly influenced by the tax base and the associated tax revenue during the fiscal year and following budget years.

In Figure 8.3, the budget line represented by X_1Y_1 reflects the prioritization of digital development relative to other areas. If the municipality budget situation improves following a rise in tax revenues, as a result of increased income tax or economic activity, the budget line can move up to the upper right hand corner to the X_2Y_2 line. A decrease in tax revenues will have the opposite effect. Within the IS-community this is rarely acknowledged, but particularly within local government and institutions, variations in tax revenue during the year can be substantial. Thus, given that preferences for IT remain intact relative to other expenditure areas, increases in tax revenue will imply that more resources can be applied to IT for customer involvement.

The aggregation and the slope of the demand curves for digitalization of user involvement is demonstrated reflecting the preferences for spending resources on a) *other activities for customer involvement* and b) *other activities than customer involvement*.

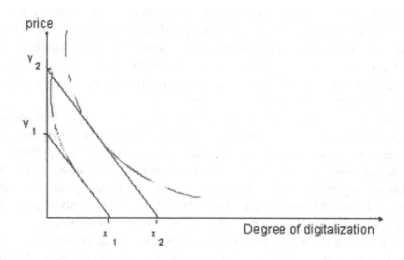

Figure 8-4. Budget restriction and preference curves for digitalization of customer involvement

3.1   The marginal customer involvement costs

The costs connected with involving yet one more player to the democratic decision processes is called *the marginal customer involvement costs*. Customer involvement costs money and other resources, and may not pay off in terms of overall lower expenses for the public sector. Nowhere is this truer than in the consumer democracy model as illustrated in the PPR-approach.

Assuming that the time staff spends on activities in their work time can be split into two main groups: core processes (COR) and administrative processes (ADP), COR + ADP will be their total work time. Introducing customer involvement will imply that either COR or ADP will be reduced, unless the staff will do their part of the involvement for free. Staff will typically have to host some of the forums and will as part of this have to do some preparations. The preparation time necessary to generate proposals for public hearings, customer management committees, process digital user referrals and participate in customer discussion groups must be taken from other areas, possibly from another administrative task or from a core function.

One hypothesis is that the time the local governmental institution must use for customer involvement through digital channels such as the Internet might not reduce other administrative costs within the same institution and might even increase administrative costs within the unit or in other units of the government through increased demands from customers relating to alternative scenarios for running the service.

Also, the costs associated with customer involvement most often needs to be taken from the current expenditure budget. Although the marginal costs for customer involvement might approach zero over time, there are substantial high sunken costs for governmental institutions. The real challenge regarding costs, however, is that if focusing on the costs associated with the involvement, (and for the argument), ignores gains that come from the involvements, government easily can experience a cost paradox as illustrated in Figure 8.5. The figure shows decreases in marginal costs for involvement, but due to the higher number of customers that will use the increasingly efficient channels for involvement, the total costs will increase. This situation captures a key challenge for government, namely that better and more use of their product is a budget challenge and that they cannot charge for involvement per se.

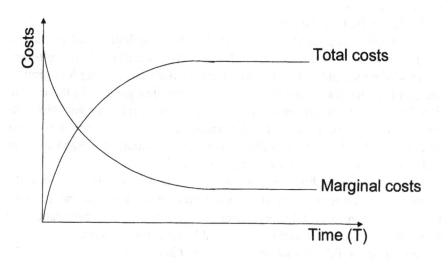

Figure 8-5. The cost paradox for customer involvement: decreasing marginal costs and increasing total costs

3.2   Cost for involvement through digital channels versus other channels

It is assumed that although the costs of digitally producing municipality services are higher than analogue production, the digital way is quicker. Production can mean either the execution of a public service or communication with citizens.

It can also be assumed that with a relatively small number of participants, both analogue and digital production can be maintained while democracy at the same time is preserved. However, there are also substantial extra costs involved with realizing these democratic ideals, which can mean the shift towards either smaller or larger units. In the case of larger units it is generally argued that the digital channels are superior to analogue channels as they are less cost intensive and at the same time intersect the democratic cost curve at a lower point.

However the following is a list of factors that can affect the solidity of this conclusion:
-   Processor and transportation technologies/media
-   Building a technical infrastructure
-   Standards and integration

- Insourcing, outsourcing and collective sourcing
- New work processes
- Affect/process goals
- Analogue/digital channels

The development of digital transportation technologies and media are developing steadily and therefore shift the curve towards the lower left-hand corner of the diagram, while the analogue methods are gaining less ground. The gap between these two curves is only becoming greater. In the case of digital transportation, processor speed has doubled every five years since the 1960's. This development is illustrated below in Figure 8.6. This development has been vital in the areas of mathematics, and graphic art, as well as in technologies such as speech reproduction.

The curve is also shifted inward in the diagram (lower left) because the digital infrastructure is exemplified by the number of mobile phone accounts that are relative to stationary phone accounts, steady penetration of broadband connections (ADSL, FWA, Cable Modem) and a marked increase in usage areas for PDA's such as in the area of healthcare.

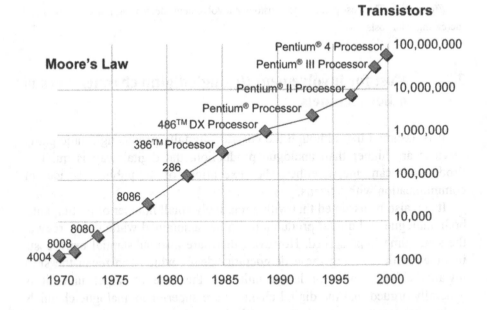

Figure 8-6. Number of transistors per integrated circuit 1970-2000
Source: (Statistics-Denmark 2003)

Outsourcing and collective sourcing are clearly an advantage of digitalization, as standardization of digital tasks can have a very positive effect on the rules of customer involvement. If nothing else, it will indicate that these digital media be used to measure and weigh all the points of the work process.

The search for new and renewed work processes takes place using both digital as well as more traditional work processes. The hypothesis is that there is a) inferior coordination between the different renewal methods; b) inferior success criteria for the new digital platforms for democracy input, process, and output; and c) lack of motivation for investing resources in customer involvement.

Furthermore it should be noted that introducing new public management in the form of effect and process goals analysis could shift the placement of the individual curves. An example of the expected increase in the attention that is paid to the individual institution's productivity and best practice, is grade point averages of graduating high school students be correlated with the use of the digital media, which will give insight into the institutional processes. This tends towards user democracy and further away from the indirect forms of management. It must also be noted that there are significant costs associated with this, as digital representation and the documentation of processing time, teaching and the provision of childcare etc. do not automatically reduce costs.

Furthermore, the placement of the curve is difficult to pin down, as more often than not work processes take place between both analogue and digital channels. The product of these tasks has often both digital and physical elements.

The public sector's use of the Internet to support business processes is the cornerstone of growth for the services offered by this sector. It is however an oversimplification to discuss these democratic challenges isolated from the technology and the costs of implementing public service.

In an imaginary framework, costs are connected with involving the user of these public services transversely proportional with the number of actors. This means that where there is one actor the costs of involving users is less than if there are two actors and so on. One hypothesis is that user involvement requires a high number of actors (N) because the democratic perception changes. The question then is whether this argument changes when digital technologies are utilized.

Figure 8.7 captures how customer involvement might be changed with regards to marginal costs and number of actors involved. Along the horizontal axis we have the number of decision makers, customers, and institutions involved in the decision-making process. The vertical axis show the marginal costs associated with customer involvement through physical and analog channels respectively.

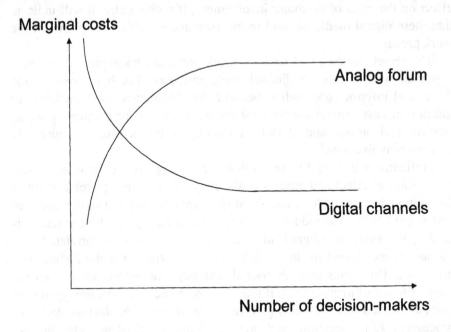

Figure 8-7. Marginal costs for customer involvement through analog and digital channels

The curve representing decision processes illustrates the hypothesis that the marginal costs of involving more decision makers in the decision process rises to a distinct point, then due to the economies of scale and scope and other organizational advantages, the marginal costs fall drastically.

4.   DIGITAL CHANNELS FOR CUSTOMER INVOLVEMENT

In analyzing the status for customer involvement we have examined channels in three Danish municipalities. The Danish municipalities are all by law required to have customer involvement forums. At the demand side, (the customers), the Danes adopt new technologies very rapidly. There is, for example, greater cable television coverage in Denmark than in the US. Technologies such as FWA and ADSL are offered to a much broader audience by companies such as Sonofon (FWA), Cybercity, TDC Internet, and Tiscali and Orange (ADSL). Furthermore, it is to the digital curves advantage that the standards and data integration possibilities are developing steadily at an extremely fast pace. Yet, there is an apparent gap between access to the Internet and the use of the Internet. For example, 81% of citizens have access to the internet (ITU 2001), but at a comparative level a substantially less number are users. Thus, there are reasons to believe that customer involvement would be very high and mature in Denmark.

Table 8-4. PC, Internet users, internet hosts, Cable TV, and Cellphone users: Denmark, Scandinavia, EU, and the US (2000)

	Denmark	Scandinavia	EU	USA
PC	415	422	248	517
Internet Users	282	391	159	272
Cable TV	251	130	111	251
Cellphone users	495	584	400	316

Source. OECD (2000) ; ITU (2001)

It is important to think back to the historical development in order to explain why the various digitalization strategies succeed best when they are internal administrative routines that are being digitalized, and why digital democracy growth is so under developed and is implemented using ad hoc strategies.

Denmark possesses a good 40 years experience with digitalization of work processes using tools other than the Internet. The assertion is therefore that the development of the Internet as a transport media is least interesting from an historical perspective. It is more relevant to look forward to what the Internet will mean for the User Democracy in the future, as it will break down barriers.

Digitalization did not begin in Denmark with the advent of PCs. Computer technology in Denmark actually began with the Marshall Aid, which donated the first computer to Denmark. This unique contribution facilitated the establishment of Kommunedata and Datacentralen who integrated local and state internal IT administration. This has allowed the public sector, from an international perspective, remarkable digitalization. Digitalization, is in itself, not necessarily unique in the sense that Danish administration is in the lead. It is unique however that digital development in Denmark happened uniformly and simultaneously in the broad administrative field. It is in the area of the complicated administrative tasks where digitalization has penetrated the most. Where digital development has happened in a more segmented way is apparent between data centers and the municipalities, rather than between the municipal institutions themselves.

It is also important to keep in mind the historical perspective, as the collective sourcing and outsourcing methods utilized by the municipalities for IT development, implementation, and maintenance has meant that there is a limited amount of IT competency development within the municipalities in the digital field. IT has in the past been seen only as an auxiliary work tool and rarely as a central task. There was therefore good reason to outsource many IT functions. The present shift in the use of IT is increasingly becoming a part of the central operations but without the acquisition of long-term or local experience. These municipalities are thus only to a small degree able to complete this task. The risk of unsuccessful projects is therefore much higher depending on the amount that the municipality itself does on its own.

The combination of years of experience with externally initiated digitalization of administrative processes, the lack of local development of IT competencies, and the perception of IT as a auxiliary administrative tool instead of part of central processes or democratic channels plays a large role when the choice is to be made between digital and analogue channels.

We have analyzed the availability of digital channels for customer involvement in four areas: city councils and committees, education/schools, services for the elderly, and day-care centers for children (kindergarten). By simultaneously looking at institutions on the Internet within the same period, we have investigated the 14 variables for the schools, eldercare and daycare area. The variables address whether there is a digital route (a hompage) and whether the information is found only at a general homepage for the municipality. Also, we investigated whether there is information on how to contact the manager/ director and the availability of forums for customer involvement. The forums for customer involvement were investigated in detail with regards to information about future and past meetings, election process, and their role / function relative to the director/ manager of the institution. Finally, we investigated whether information is available regarding complaints on the institution, waiting lists, and number of transfer request. The variables analyzed are:

– Own homepage for the institution
– Homepage as part of the municipality's website
– Available contact information for the director
– Number of customers represented in the governing body
– Management structure
– Method of choosing management
– How often new members for the governing body are voted on
– Appointment process for the governing body
– Agendas for future meetings
– Minutes taken of earlier meetings
– Handling of complaints
– Information about earlier complaints
– Number of people on the waiting list
– Number of transfer requests

In the case of the city councils we have investigated the following variables in the three municipalities:

– List of city council members
– Committee structure

- Represented political parties
- Previous meeting agendas
- Future meeting agendas
- Council meeting minutes
- Office hours for committee chair people, as well as contact information
- Overview of committees, mandates, councils and boards
- Information about the work of the city council and committees
- Rules for question time

4.1   Educational sector

All three municipalities use the Internet to inform its inhabitants about general school issues but not in detail and with very little consideration for user input. By simultaneously analyzing schools, pre-schools, after school clubs, and special needs schools, in these three municipalities within the same period, there seems to be a correlation between the size of the municipality and information about the user management but no connection between school size (number of students) and digital information about user management is evident. In the case of five schools in the MuniLarge school system, there is, for example, all information with regard to school board members and elections. In MuniMedium there is only information available for a few schools, while no school in MuniSmall offer any school information on the Web.

Table 8-5. Primary and secondary education statistics: Number of students enrolled, number of institutions with a webpage, and information about the school board

	MuniSmall	MuniMedium	MuniLarge
No. of students	1,615	2,652	11,984
No. of schools on the Internet	2 out of 6	8 out of 10	37 out of 37
Information about the school board:			
— Composition	1 out of 6	5 out of 10	14 out of 37
— Competencies	0 out of 6	3 out of 10	10 out of 37
— Election System	0 out of 6	2 out of 10	15 out of 37
— Goals	1 out of 6	5 out of 10	25 out of 37
Minutes and agendas	1 out of 6	1 out of 10	5 out of 37
Digital contact to school	3 out of 6	7 out of 10	19 out of 37

Digital contact to school board	0 out of 6	2 out of 10	3 out of 37
School schedule & operational plans	1 out of 6	6 out of 10	33 out of 37

4.2   Day care centers

The area of day care centers is clearly the worst represented on the Web. There is no transparency as to the decision processes here. There are no budgets for the individual institutions, and no information regarding transfers, waiting lists, etc. There is generally so little digital information and so few influencing channels that the general conclusion to be drawn is that there are no or very negative indicators for digitalization in the area. There are only a few day care centers on the Web, but apart from the much-needed user influence there is also a lack of information with regard to waiting lists and prioritization criteria, budgets or the number of users who reject the institution. In this area there are no indicators in the direction of cyber or user democracy.

Table 8-6. Day Care Center Statistics

	MuniSmall	MuniMedium	MuniLarge
No. of users/places	850	4.501	7.063
No. of institutions with own homepage	0 out of 12	8 out of 69	2 out of 161
Presentation on municipality site	12 out of 12	0 out of 69	2 out of 161
Information about management			
Composition	0 out of 12	4 out of 69	2 out of 161
Election System	0 out of 12	1 out of 69	0 out of 161
Goals for Institution	0 out of 12	7 out of 69	13 out of 161
Minutes and agenda	0 out of 12	0 out of 69	0 out of 161
Digital contact with institution	0 out of 12	6 out of 69	0 out of 161
Digital contact with management	1 out of 12	0 out of 69	0 out of 161

4.3   Eldercare

The top scorer for available digital information channels in the area of elderly and handicapped care is MuniLarge who offers comprehensive information on the following subjects:
–   User influence for younger handicapped people and the elderly
–   Preventative home visits
–   Handicapped citizen's council
–   Fielding of complaints
–   Instructions on how to complain

Besides MuniLarge, the other two municipalities now offer digital information with regard to the fielding of complaints. In MuniMedium there are 6,726 inhabitants over the age of 60 where 4,720 of them are retired. Other than that, there are 1,516 inhabitants under the age of 60 that for one reason or another are in need of temporary homecare or to stay in a convalescent home. There are over 8,300 people that are without any form of digital user information in MuniMedium.

Table 8-7. Councils for the Elderly on the Internet

Municipality/Elderly Council	Description of goals	Committee Composition/ (possible) user representation.	Meeting Minutes and Agendas	Information About the presented initiatives	Information About election methods
MuniSmall					
Counseling the Elderly	Yes	No	No	No	No
MuniMedium					
The handicap advice council	Yes	Yes/Yes	No	No	No
Complaint council	Yes	Yes/No	No	No	No
Elderly council	Yes	Yes/No	No	No	No
Elderly & handicap committee	Yes	Yes	No	No	No
MuniLarge					
Elderly council in each of the 13 local areas	Yes	Yes/Yes	No	Yes	Yes
Elderly and handicap	Yes	Yes/Yes	No	Yes	Yes
Handicap Council	Yes	Yes/Yes	No	Yes	Yes
Complaint Council	Yes	Yes/Yes	No	n.a.	n.a.
Committee for Retirees	No	No	No	No	No
Central Council	Yes	Yes	No	(Yes)	Yes

Table 8-8. Elder Councils at the Internet

Municipality/Elderly Council	Electronic contact with committee members	Fielding of complaints
MuniSmall		
Elder counsel	E-mail	Yes
MuniMedium		
Handicap council	No	Yes
Complaint council	No	Yes
Elderly council	No	Yes
Elderly and handicap committee	No	Yes
MuniLarge		
Elderly council in each of the 13 local areas	(Yes)	Yes
Elderly and handicapped Forums	No	Yes
Handicapped council	No	Yes
Complaint council	No	Yes
Committee for retirees	No	No
Central council	No	No

4.4   City Council

The greatest contributor to this digitalization is the city council of these three municipalities. Each is considering a one-way communication channel, yet none of them are considering developing the capacity for two-way real time communication. Functions such as chat, news groups and mail services are not implemented. Nor has voice recognition or other technologies to aid the visually impaired as well as interface with mobile Internet devices and PDA's been implemented.

Two of the municipalities do not have the technology to support an email service to send out new meeting agendas or minutes. Citizens must download them off of the website each time. Office hours or contact information for committee chair people is not given.

Table 8-9. Meeting schedules, news and office hours

		MuniSmall	MuniMedium	MuniLarge
Possibility for registering for email newsletters				
• With new agendas and minutes		No	No	Yes
• Long term meeting schedules		Yes	Yes	No
Contact information for city council members	E-mail	Yes	Yes	Yes
	Phone #	Yes	Yes	Yes
	Address	Yes	Yes	Yes

Office hours for committee chair people		No	No	No
As well as contact information	E-mail	Yes	No	Yes
	Phone #	Yes	No	Yes
	Address	Yes	No	Yes
Committee members contact information	E-mail	Yes	No	Yes
	Phone #	Yes	No	Yes
	Address	Yes	No	Yes
Overview of committee mandates, councils and initiatives	General information	Yes	Yes	Yes
	Activity Description	Yes	Yes	Yes
	Work description	Yes	Yes	No
Rules for question time		Yes	Yes	Yes

5. CONCLUSION

Customer involvement is from the PPR-approach a functional imperative for government. In this chapter we have focused on customer involvement through digital channels illuminated in a large, a medium, and a small Danish municipality. Within the three municipalities, we accessed the webpages for the institutions within childcare, primary/secondary education, and eldercare as well as municipality councils. We did not address the effects or suitability of digitalization.

One point made was whether citizens have democratic communication channels that already function satisfactorily excluding the need for complementing digital channels does not exist. The innovation of cyber-democracy indicates a shift towards self-administration.

We have suggested that it is worth considering if there is the advantage of economies of scale and scope with regards to involvement. We suggest that it is a rather hasty conclusion that larger municipalities are better prepared to support democratic decision channels in an information society.

The third point relates to the cost function. The point of view of this chapter is that democracy is costly. Implementing web-based user involvement (governance) channels, results in extra workload to administrative and core function employees in order to help to facilitate the frictionless uptake of these democratic channels.

We have taken the point of view that in order to make the institutions ready for customer involvement, support for the new digital democratic influence channels can be challenging for the simple reason that it utilizes a great many resources. This is not an argument to abandon the process of democratic information, discussion and decision channels. But it highlights the need for a resource prioritization strategy discussion. Most IT resources come from each individual municipality's operations budget. Yet with more budget decentralization within more and more areas of the institutional task inventory, institutional digitalization has become apolitical. It is surprising that in this field there seems to be the seeds of change of content for user involvement and self-administration. At the same time, IT politics will become a more central part of the municipal political debate, as IT will require a still larger part of the budget.

The area of day care centers is clearly the worst represented on the Web. There is no transparency as to the decision processes here. There are no budgets for the individual institutions, no information with regard to transfers, waiting lists, etc. There is generally little digital information and few channels of influence that the general conclusion to be drawn is that there are no or very negative indicators for digitalization in the area. There are only a few day care centers on the Internet, but apart from the much-needed user influence there is also a lack of information with regard to waiting lists and prioritization criteria, budgets or the number of users who reject the institution. In this area there are no indicators in the direction of cyber or user democracy.

Our earlier studies show that there is a lack of planned strategy with regard to digitalization of the public sector, which at this time concerns mainly the Internet. In 2000, only a third of the municipalities had a strategy for utilizing the Internet. Our interpretation of these findings is that the development of digital media takes place piecemeal or ad hoc with a great amount of flexibility with regard to implementation methods. The municipal sector has increased its presence on the Internet but their approach is neither coherent nor long-term. As pointed out in chapter 4 of this book, government has been obsessed with internal data transport and efficiency and effectiveness gains. Although this chapter has found examples of customer involvement digital paths, the examples are few and apparent without strong policy commitment.

Chapter 9

EVALUATION OF IT APPLICATIONS

1. INTRODUCTION

Evaluation analysis of IT is not a new focus area. Researchers, consultants, companies, and the public sector have undertaken evaluation studies of IT throughout the 1970s, 1980s, and 1990s (Hamilton and Chervany 1981; Willcocks 1994; Farbey et al. 1999). It is nevertheless an area in constant development where the methods for evaluation of investments are becoming more varied and the technology evaluated is developing at a rapid pace.

IT is the cornerstone of PPR and constitutes an instantaneously appealing object for evaluation. In turn, "do we get value or money?" is a vital question that all organizations are facing in their exploitation of IT. Regardless whether the exploitation of IT focuses on internal efficiency or external effectiveness, public organizations are being confronted and prompted for answers regarding the outcome of the use of IT by questions such as; Did IT exceed the estimated costs? Did IT match the expectations?

Demand on cost-effectiveness can be more severe in government as compared to the private sector since government in general are not able to use IT as a competitive instrument to gain bigger market share and improve profit margin but are using IT to help shrink current expenditures. Thus government are prompted to beware of the resources applied are spend *according to preferences* and whether the same resources could have been *saved or spend elsewhere with overall increased optimization of preferences.* Acknowledging these motives, this chapter points to the challenges in identifying the goals, separating cause and impacts, measuring and counting the variables, and using the results of the evaluation efforts.

Evaluations are in fact done daily when each actor in the public sector value chains experience and access their use of the government IT applications. This chapter underlines that evaluation of IT investments add overhead costs to the IT application and should as such be avoided unless the evaluation exercise contribute constructively to the planning and implementation of the planned or future IT applications in government. Onwards, the IT application evaluated needs to be of a certain size before it makes sense to engage in a formal and extensive evaluation. Thus, our argument is that there is no need to perform an evaluation exercise for the sake of the evaluation per se.

The proposed evaluation framework can help bringing the IT-applications more in line with the PPR-approach. In this chapter we provide two examples of how evaluations of an e-procurement and a web-service application could be undertaken with respect to simple cost benefit analysis (CBA) and also addressing the content and processes the applications are intended to improve. The example of the CBA evaluation is a very simple and straight forward example and no indirect impacts and costs have been taken into consideration. The content variables derive from the domains of impacts described in chapter 3 (capabilities, interaction, orientation, and values), whereas the process variables (volume, data integration, diversity and span) have been incorporated from the Massetti and Zmud (1996) study.

2.   OBJECTIVES OF THE IT INVESTMENT

Conflicting reasons for investing in IT can easily, and do frequently, occur when government acquire and implement IT. Putting this aside, a rational framework would argue that arguments and objectives for IT may range from operational or tactical issues to strategic statements, or they may represent a combination:
- Strategic vital reasons, as if e.g. it is vital to the organization's core areas or in connection with a project activity.
- Overall process improvement
- Cost saving and/or profit earning motives.
- Compensation reasons, as e.g. after a burglary or a damaging virus attack.

In order to conduct evaluation studies along these motives it is crucial to know the owner of the investment and the objectives that the owner, i.e. person, department or private/public organization, wants to achieve with the IT investment. Along this rationality, a CBA can be performed along the action lines in Table 9.1.

Table 9-1. Classical steps in conducting CBA

No.	Recommendations
1	Identify the owner of the planned investment
2	Identify investment objectives
3	Choose perspective (additional earning capacity, cost reduction, development of communication/relations and/or learning/knowledge management)
4	Choose method (financial and/or non-financial)
5	Identify the variables in CBA
6	Collect data and calculate the CBA

A number of studies show that IT investments are not always based on or are part of a strategy, hence do not question whether for example CBA are beneficial (Clarke 1995). Even when the objectives are clearly stated, it is paramount to know where and how to achieve and measure the benefits. In other words, it is necessary – but most often challenging to get - to have general strategic objectives that can be decomposed into measurable and localized benefits.

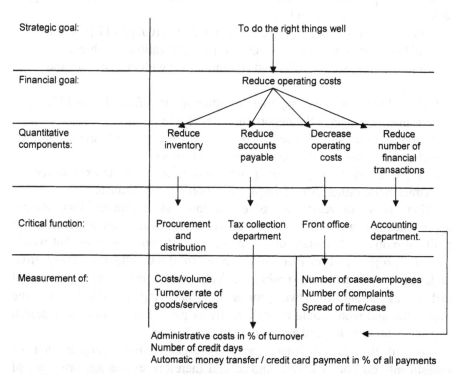

Figure 9-1. IT, Strategy and Measuring - *Source*: Developed after Willcocks, Feeny and Islei (1997)

In Figure 9.1 we have illustrated the complexity in evaluating strategic goals (to do the right things as well as possible) assuming that these exist and how these are fulfilled by applying IT. In this example, inspired by Willcocks et al. (1997), the municipality has two overall goals: to reduce the operating costs and increase the customer satisfaction of the cases handled.

For the operating costs, this can be decomposed in quantitative components (reduction in inventory and accountants payable) within four critical functions of the municipality; 1) the procurement and distribution function and the tax collection department. IT applications in these functions can be measured by cost/ volume variables and the turnover of goods/ services; 2) the reduction in outstanding taxes, the ratio of automated money transfers, and the administrative cost related to tax collection as percent of the total tax collection; 3) the front offices handling of cases/ employees, number of complaints, and the distribution of time spend on cases; and 4) the number of financial transactions.

Although the above example gives the government useful information along the conventional lines of governmental concerns, the example indirectly assumes that there is a linkage between strategy and goals and the required IT applications. Evaluating the above motives is a very challenging task complicated further on by:

– Distraction motives by creating the image that solving an IT problem would help solve fundamental societal or organizational problem
– Competing project activities and collaborations with other actors and companies
– Enforced reasons, if e.g. suppliers or other public offices demand IT investments and have the negotiating capacity to do so.
– Routine activity, e.g. an exercise performed with a given frequency due to budget allocations or the need for proving activity
– IT is part of an ongoing learning curve and process with an explorative characteristic rather than IT implementation and skill transfer

There is no universal law of evaluation that legitimizes that rational approaches and motives are better or more legitimate than incremental or political motives. A variant of this could be *distraction motives* that would start IT project and evaluation of these to direct attention away from underlying organizational problems. Yet, there clearly are fundamental differences among the two groups in identifying the targets for the evaluation and who should act differently as part of the evaluation research and also who will demand and initiate the evaluation.

One of the bullets listed above, *enforced reasons,* argues that IT investments do not involve a choice and therefore evaluation tasks are of little value. Investments can lead to an almost unavoidable spiral with very few options. When a software company announces that their company will not support earlier versions of a piece of software, the user can still run earlier versions of the software. Yet, the users cannot expect new gadgets, software and different kinds of hardware to function together with earlier versions of that particular software. It is possible e.g. to purchase a printer, but you might have to upgrade to for example a new operating system to make it function. In this way, the company has achieved a lock-in effect of the customer (Hax and Wilde II 1999).

Another approach to evaluating IT investments is to regard IT primarily as part of a *learning process*. This position argues that it is more important to allow room for experiments with the technology than to settle on one single solution. Correspondingly, attention may be focused on knowledge sharing and exchange, or establishing of IT and Internet competence in the organization, which will not necessarily give measurable results in pounds and pence, and especially not in the short term.

Evaluation of IT projects in the public sector can take various modes (ex ante, process, or ex post) and use a variety of epistemological approaches. It makes a big difference whether the approach favors an extension of the ideas in the waterfall model relating to IT systems development separating pilot and prototype studies, implementation and utilization or the phases are regarded as an integrated and repetitive process (Earl 1999; Bødker et al. 2000; Earl 2004).

In Figure 9.2 we have displayed three competing views of the interplay between IT-applications and government. IT applications can be assumed to have direct or indirect impacts on for example cost saving, and whether the strength of the impact is expedient and feasible to determine (situation 1). This is a widespread, and in our view, a wrong assumption that acquiring new IT equipment lead to impacts in a direct matter. Certainly the bulk of the IS-literature would oppose any simple cause and impact approaches. Yet, this view is held by many practitioners and in particular by the financial departments allocating the money to new IT.

Many IS scholars argue that the relation between the organization and IT is an interactive and integrative issue that makes it futile to address impacts of IT per se. This view is illustrated in situation 2 in Figure 9.2. The implication of this view is that any evaluation exercise will have to address impacts over time to identify the drivers and inhibitors within both the organizational and the IT domain and the interaction between the two domains.

Other scholars within the IS community would argue that there is only limited value to focus on the domains and the interaction between these. Instead, we ought to focus on dynamics within the domains along with the interaction between the domains. This view, captured in situation 3 in Figure 9.2, could imply that we in the evaluating of IT incorporate variables regarding learning cycles and viewing IT development and implementation processes as an iterative and cyclic view, either within the same project or in a longitudinal view (see chapter 10). The closer we move to adopt the view displayed in situation 3, the more complicated, time consuming, but also more relevant the evaluation is for the PPR-approach.

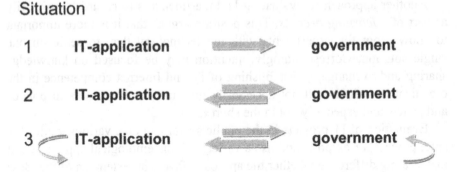

Figure 9-2. Fundamental cause and impact situations

There is an implicit notion in most evaluation literature on IT that the duration of the IT-application is long term and that there are internal fix points for the evaluation. In the PPR-terminology we do recognize that there exist such applications but we essentially argue that we move towards shorter term and external/ open application interfaces abandoning the intranet and internal applications (see chapter 4). Clearly the possibility and relevance of performing the evaluation along with the ability to identify and hold any variables constantly diminish as applications move towards the South-East corner of Figure 9.3, picturing the life-span and duration of the IT project, and its development along the vertical dimension and the customer orientation along the horizontal dimension.

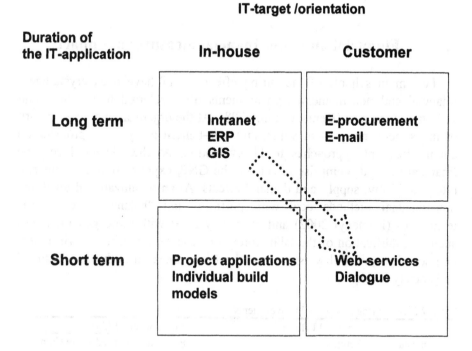

Figure 9-3. Duration and customer focus of IT applications - *Source*: Developed after Lamb (2002)

One of the key observations in the PPR-concept is the drift from the formal organizational view of evaluations to the individual level which clearly do not make evaluations an easier task. For example, it is doubtful challenging to assume that we can identify the right person in an organization to ask the questions regarding the impact of IT. This is a classical concern when performing evaluation but the drift pictured in Figure 9.3 accentuates this concern. Thus evaluations need to take onboard the transactions, projects, and structures that the actors apply IT applications within (Lamb 2002). This need is illustrated by the two cases we pursue in this chapter. Both cases have value for the formal organizational room but also illustrate the shortcomings in excluding evaluations from the actor level within government and from the customers perspective. Before we present the cases, we will give a brief overview of CBA that constitutes one part of our framework for the evaluation of IT.

3.   IMPACT ANALYSIS

3.1   Financial and non-financial measures of impacts

Two main schools of measuring effects of IT have been crystallized: financial and non-financial measurements often referred to as "hard and soft" measurements (Demsey et al. 1998). At the organizational level, return of investment, net present value, and cost-benefit analyses of projects are among frequent approaches to IT evaluation. At the societal level, the financial methods comprise effects on the GNP, export/ import, the interest rate and, if any, supply and demand effects. At an organizational level, the non-financial methods deal with portfolio and "balanced score card" techniques (Remenyi 2002) and at society level with more general issues such as qualification of the labor force. Environment, working environment and social responsibility issues may be focus areas on both organizational and society levels.

Table 9-2. Measuring Effects of IT Investments

	Financial Effects	Non-financial Effects
Organizational Level	Return on investment (ROI), Net Present value (NPV), Cost-benefit analysis (CBA)	Portfolio, Balanced Score Card, Environment, Work Environment, and Social Responsibility
Society Level	Gross National Product (GNP), Export/Import, Interest Rate, Supply and Demand	Environment, Work Environment, and Social Responsibility, Job Content and Quality

In large organizations with several IT projects running simultaneously, portfolio management of the IT projects is often necessary (Solomon 2002) for management to see where the money has been spent, why it is or is not necessary to maintain projects, and which resources are vital to continue the drive. Portfolio management requires *comparable criteria* in cost-benefit analyses making operating profit and ROI (return on investment) key components (King 2002).

The fundamental choices prior to CBA reflect whether the CBA is a single event or a process or group of parallel processes, which take place at different points in time or continuously to search for and make explicit, quantitatively or qualitatively, all the impacts of an IT project, including the program and strategy of which it is part (Farbey et al. 1999).

Irrespective of the positions taken with regards to the directions of impacts, it can be constructive to conduct a feasibility study of resource requirements and expected output/benefits. Just as the reasons may vary, the level of ambition may also be diverse within the organization with respect to how information, communication, transaction and/or integration each are valued.

For example, the interpretative method argues that CBA imposes formalism and functionalism and fails to capture the organizational and human factors (Serafeimidis and Smithsson 2000). We acknowledge that CBA has its limitations and therefore should be used with due respect to its limitations and shortcomings.

Several software programs include very advanced tools to perform CBA's. At several trade associations and consultancy firms, it is possible to download templates with which to perform CBA's; e.g. through the American Office of Risk Assessment and Cost-Benefit (URL: http://usda.gov/agency/oce/oracba). Although there are various software packages that can assist in CBA, there remain serious challenges in determining areas and measurement of benefits.

Figure 9.3 lists a range of factors that can be measured directly such as productivity, production costs, administration costs and IT expenses. The figure's right side shows effects that are more difficult to measure such as increased control of resources and job satisfaction. While the left side illustrates a variety of measures or input reflecting such measures, the right side may be seen as variables explaining why some Internet solutions are not appreciated or fail to get support from employees.

Table 9-3. Measuring Benefits

Measurable Benefits	Benefits difficult to measure
Increased productivity	More efficient use of production facilities
Lower production costs	Improved resource control
Reduction of employees	Improvement of planning function
Lower IT expenses	Increased flexibility
Lower third party supplier costs	Punctual and more information
Lower administrative costs	Improved organizational learning
General cost reduction	Increased job satisfaction
	Improved decision making
	Improvement of routines
	Increased user/customer satisfaction
	Improvement of image

3.2 Objectives, initiator, and owner of the evaluation

A common definition of cost-benefit analysis is that it maximizes a social welfare function that aggregates preferences which are not weighted or restricted. Adler and Posner (1999) argue that constrained cost-benefit analysis is consistent with a broad array of appealing normative commitments and superior to alternative methods of project evaluation.

Cost-benefit analysis operates at various levels (Mishan 1971; Brent 1996) and industrial sectors (Noy 1999; Honig and Lampel 2000; McDonald 2001). Cost-benefit analysis is applied to the evaluation of various phenomena (Fischer 1994; Nolan et al. 1999). In particular, cost-benefit analysis is widely used on micro-level evaluation projects, investments, new businesses, service-loyalty etc. (Lee and Cunningham 2001).

Applications of cost-benefit analysis range from specific and well defined projects to support decision making to "new" management problems within enterprises such as improvement of the quality of working life (De Haan and Terra 1988), advanced manufacturing techniques (De Haan and Peters 1989), and environmental management (Yedla and Parikh 2001).

De Haan & Mol argue that there are two basic principles for CBA at an organizational level (De Haan and Mol 1999). First, any measures to improve performance can be seen as an investment and should be evaluated accordingly. Second, only changes in the relevant items caused by the measures have to be taken into account.

A relevant CBA question to an IT project is: What does it cost and which benefits can we derive? However, after this question it becomes more difficult. A basic piece of advice is to clarify the conditions on which the CBA is based, including the organization's general approach to IT projects and management of IT projects (Cadel and Yeates 2001). The simple CBA comes in three versions:
– Economic efficiency model
– Resource allocation model
– Alternative costs model

The economic efficiency model focuses on the IT project's costs (C) and benefits (B). In allocating resources, e.g. between one department's application of an Internet solution and another department's system application, allocation weights are used to ensure that department 2's benefits are larger than department 1's costs (disadvantages) in e.g. presentation of an Internet solution. Finally, the alternative costs can be evaluated, i.e. do department 2's benefits from the Internet solution exceed the reallocated resources in the department and the loss, if any, in department 1 as a result of the Internet solution.

Economic efficiency: $\underline{B-C}$
(B: benefits, C: costs)

Allocation politics: $\underline{a_2B-a_1C}$
(a: allocation weights)

Alternative costs: $\underline{a_2B-a_2R-a_1L}$
(L: loss, R: re-allocation)

Figure 9-2. The Simple CBA: Efficiency, allocation, and alternative costs

In the context of the PPR-method, this restriction is hard to meet if we view IT as part of the current, operating costs rather than investment. Yet, for large scale projects the point of focusing the analysis on the relevant items is a challenging but rewarding route. Also, there is a danger that CBA often has an implicit assumption of a stable, top-down managed public sector (Remenyi and Money 1995) which is contrasted by the activity, citizen-centric and organized pattern we paint with the PPR-concept.

4.   OUR EVALUATION FRAMEWORK

There indeed is need for cash-flow analysis of IT investment and financial evaluations of IT. Yet, there is a danger that evaluations reinforce the cementing and closing of the public sector since many of these variables are easier to identify, whereas the citizen/ customer perspective is harder to identify. In the framework we list below, we have aimed at balancing the need for organizational answers to the question "Is IT worth the investment?" and the customers' relevant questions "What's new in this? How do I benefit?"

We propose using the variables identified in chapter 3 as the domains of IT impacts comprising capacity, interaction, values and orientation. The capacity variable deals with the quality of information, efficiency and effectiveness. The interaction variable focuses on control and power, including customer relations. Values comprise issues as stress and violence of privacy and legal rights. Finally, orientation relates to whether the IT application leads to a more digital decision-making process reducing other communication and decision forms. In Figure 9.3 below we have displayed the variables, but we refer the reader back to chapter 3 for a more comprehensive description of the variables.

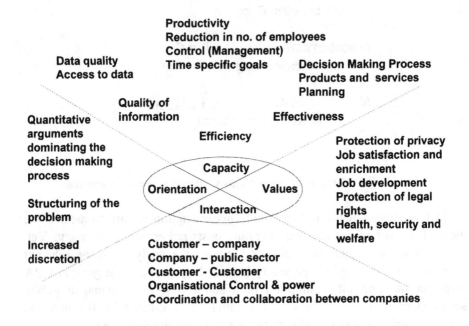

Figure 9-3. Content Variables of the CBA

Complementing the content variable displayed in Figure 9.3, is an awareness on information flow. From an information processing point of view, we suggest to incorporate the variables on volume, data integration, diversity and span suggested by Massetti and Zmud (1996). We label the variables as process variables since they relate to the processing of data.

The variable *volume* denotes the magnitude of digital traffic relative to all structured messages. If the unit receives 10,000 digital documents, but in total receives 100,000 documents, the value of the volume will be 0.1 or 10 per cent. The *Integration* measures whether the internet application is "genuine" or whether it is just applied by one level within the organization. To achieve the full benefit of internet applications requires back office integration. If 10,000 documents are receiving in digital format but only 100 of these remain in digital format through the "value chain" (see chapter 2), the value of integration will be 0.01 or 1 per cent. The variable *span* measures the number of customers and organizations/ people that are the application in the communication with the organization. For example, a local authority receives invoices in digital format from 18 suppliers, but in flat files, e-mail, fax or other formats from 1,011 suppliers. This makes the span value 18/1,011 = 0.02 or 2 per cent. A higher value indicates a higher score on span. Finally, the variable *diversity* measures the number of different types of digital messages that are applied. If a company sends 15 different document types to the public sector, for example, but the application is only used in connection with one type of document, the value will be 1/15 or 7 per cent.

Table 9-4. Process variables (flow) of the CBA

Variable	Description
Volume	What percentage of the total number of documents is exchanged via this solution?
Integration	What percentage of documents received digitally is forwarded digitally?
Diversity	What percentage of the total number of different types of documents is included in the digital solution?
Span	What percentage of business partners (customers and decision-makers) takes part in the digital exchange?

Source. Andersen, Juul and Larsen (2001).

Next, we will present two cases that illustrate the content and flow dimensions of the cost benefit focus. The cases encompass e-procurement and web-based case handling at the central level of government.

5.   EVALUATION EXAMPLES

5.1   E-procurement

A municipality with 36,000 citizens is exploring whether to adopt e-procurement. The municipality is located north of Copenhagen which is the capital of Denmark. The municipality has a solid tax basis with a well over average income population. Public services and environmental issues are high priorities in the municipality. The 21 members of the city council, dominated by the Social Democratic Party, have an annual budget of over 900 million Danish crowns (DKK), equal to about 150 million USD. The left-wing dominance of the city council implies that local employment is a key policy issue.

Eldercare, primary schooling, and childcare constitute the majority of the expenses. Road construction and cultural activities are a minor part of the municipality's budget. All institutions have their own budget. Budget savings will result in a managerial bonus calculated as 50% of the budget savings.

The manager can choose to keep the bonus within the city hall or distribute it to the individual units. A maximum of 50% of the budget savings can be issued as a personal check to the procurement manager only.

Besides computer software, travel arrangements and conference bookings, none of the procurement functions use web-based shopping. It is estimated that about 180 million DKK are spent on procurement annually. This goods purchased include:
– Medical and nursery equipment
– School books and teaching materials
– Furniture, office inventories and stationary
– Travel, transportation, hotel & other accommodation
– Fuels, gas, oil
– IT-products
– Groceries

The municipality has a vibrant business sector but only few outlets that currently provide B2B e-commerce sales. The municipality has a total of 1,800 suppliers. The e-procurement process is expected to reduce the total number of suppliers to 1,000 at the start of the third year. The municipality has access to the web-procurement platform provided by a software company. Through this platform, they have access to suppliers that use pre-negotiated contracts. Currently, 230 suppliers have joined the platform with a total of approximately 700 supplying places, several of which are located close to the municipality.

In the municipality a third of the orders are placed with sales representatives at visits, another third via telephone/fax/e-mail, a sixth via physical purchases in shops and a sixth with suppliers via the Internet. There are 18 locations for delivery of goods provided by 1,800 different suppliers. Annually a total of 35,000 orders are given by 225 individuals, spread within 18 different locations of the municipality (schools, childcare institutions, eldercare home, administration, road construction, etc.).

The administrative costs are estimated to be 80 DKK per order (ordering, invoice processing, payment), for orders through phone, fax and e-mail. On an annual basis, 10,000 orders are processed through this channel. The administrative costs are estimated at 60 DKK when ordering through sales agents that visit the municipality and take orders while being there. The sales agents receive a total of 10,000 different orders annually since they visit each of the institutions in the municipality. 5,000 orders are obtained through staffs physical visits to the stores. This is estimated to cost 120 DKK for each order. The municipality currently has an equal number of orders passing through the Internet at a cost of 40 DKK for each order. Whereas all the internet mediated orders have no faults, the order channels have a frequency of 25% fault orders and have to reorder one or more of the items. When reordering, the total administrative cost is estimated to be DKK 100 per order. Summing up the current expenses, they amount to 2.7 million DKK.

In the e-procurement solution, only ordering, order confirmation, reordering, order status, and delivery notification will be integrated. The order confirmation can involve at least three messages: One confirmation stating that the order is received and understood, confirmation to an order, and notification that the order or parts of the order cannot be executed. Payment however is not integrated which means that individual and multiple payment order, and individual and multiple payment notification, and account information, cannot be provided through the application. In total up to 18 different messages can be included in a procurement process. The internet solution allows only eight of these to be automated.

Table 9-5. Expected impacts on process variables (flow) in the e-procurement case

Variable	Description	The e-procurement case
Volume	What percentage of the total number of documents are exchanged via this solution?	5,000/35,000 (≈14%) ⇒ 24,000/31,200 (≈77%)
Integration	What percentage of documents received digitally are forwarded digitally?	5,000/5,000 (100%) ⇒ 24,000/24,000 (100%)
Diversity	What percentage of the total number of different types of documents are included in the digital solution?	8/18 ≈ 44%
Span	What percentage of business partners takes part in the digital exchange?	300/1,800 (≈17%) ⇒ 650/1,000 (≈65%)

The proposed e-procurement application requires an initial investment of one million DKK, including training. If all purchasers are going to have a PDA, it will cost another three million DKK.

In the solution, the useful life of the investment is estimated to be two years after which the replacement price will be two million DKK. If the austerity model without PDA is chosen, the replacement price after two years will only be 500,000 DKK.

From day one, 300 suppliers are part of the solution, and at the end of the first year another 100 suppliers have joined. At the end of the second year, another 250 have joined. At the end of the first year, 40% of all orders are covered by the solution. At the end of the second year, it is estimated that 80% of all order lines are covered.

At the end of the second year, it is also estimated that the total decline in faulty orders is 50% amongst orders placed via the Internet. The reduction will be linear, thus 25% reduction in faulty order by 25% in year 1. We assume no faulty orders will be made when ordering at the Internet. Of the 18,000 orders (since Internet orders do not result in fault orders) 20% would earlier have to be reordered previously. Due to spin-off impacts of the Internet-solution, this is now reduced to one forth, i.e. 2,700 reorders in year 1 and 1,200 reorders in year 2 where the number of non-internet orders are reduced to 6,000.

The e-procurement results in a net-earning the first year at 390,000 DKK and the second year at 1,100,000 DKK. In the third and forth years the level of cost reductions will be at the level of the second year. If the interest level is at 5% p.a., the project will not give a pay-back till the forth year. Clearly this calculation is restricted and could be favored by lower prices of the goods given access to a bigger supply market through the internet.

Table 9-6. Implementation of e-procurement

Orders mediated through	Cost/ order (DKK)	Year					
		0		1		2	
		Orders (N)	Orders * costs/ order (DKK)	Orders (N)	Orders * costs/ order (DKK)	Orders (N)	Orders * costs/ order (DKK)
Sales agent	60	10,000	600,000	6,000	360,000	2,000	120,000
Phone/ fax/ e-mail	80	10,000	800,000	6,000	480,000	2,000	160,000
Physical shopping	120	5,000	600,000	6,000	720,000	2,000	240,000
Internet	40	5,000	200,000	12,000	480,000	24,000	960,000
Re-ordering	100	5,000	500,000	2,700	270,000	1,200	120,000
Total		35,000	2,700,000	32,700	2,310,000	31,200	1,600,000

Motivated by potential savings, the procurement manager is seeking to balance the following ways to implement the e-procurement solution: a) to team up with existing, local suppliers and ask them to launch a digital sales channel; b) to join a current software development process with invited tendering and value adding services such as back-office integration; c) to run real-time auctions for the overall procurement in the municipality; or d) to leave the role of coordinating the procurement to the individual units letting them shop electronically by (economic) motivation only.

The dilemma faced by the manager is fueled even further by departmental fights over control of the budget. Also, various local businesses must be considered. The local companies are split into a minority that is eager to explore the digital economy and develop a digital marketing, sales and service channel, and a majority that is sticking to their traditional business processes and dislike being front-runners and risk-takers if they are the only benefiting party from the e-procurement solution.

Addressing the content-variables of our evaluation framework, i.e. the capabilities, interaction, orientation, and values, the e-procurement solution has on the positive side the potential to increase the effectiveness by enabling handling of procurement activities with less resources. Also, there is a potential to increase the efficiency of the process as well by reducing the errors and need for re-sending orders due to faults in orders. The erosion of the middle-layers and the direct communication with the fewer supplier companies can improve the interaction variable. Likewise, the availability of digital information of procurement documents holds the potential to increase the instrumental, statistical analysis of what has been bought and at what price. Finally, tracing of orders, order status, and in processing (re-) orders can help reduce the stress-level among the procurement officers.

The flip of coin is, although the procurement process gets digitalized, the lack of standardization and the categorization of items in the municipality's order handling and accounting system prevent the procurement manager to analyze what has been bought and as a result (s)he is unable to know whether there has been a reduction in overall prices for clusters or individual products.

Subsequently, the procurement officers and buyers are feeling monitored and evaluated in an unbalanced matter as compared to their colleagues in the municipality and will seek ways to be transferred to other tasks in the municipality. Yet, they do acknowledge that the e-procurement solution helps reduce the stress and time spend on processing last-minute/ after hours orders and in tracing ordered, but undelivered products.

The procurement officers are challenged by political motives supporting local business and to boost local employments since the reduction in suppliers is mainly local businesses that give in to the regional, national, and global suppliers. For example, the local electricians do all repairs and take orders on cables, washing machines, etc. With the internet orders, the electrician is out of business since the individual machine can be acquired cheaper from the Internet. However, when the school requires repairs they need to acquire a machine from a neighboring city and have to pay extra for the driving and are required to wait longer before the repair is completed. The net result could be that the overall costs on products are not reduced.

Table 9-7. Expected impacts on content variables

Variable	Pro	Contra
Capabilities	Effectiveness and efficiency process gains Information quality increases for the digital documents	No reduction in product prices Comparing prices more challenging due to lack of standard penetration at the internet and the

	Procurement manager gets more timely and more frequent information on purchasing	order handling and accounting IS.
Interaction	Increased digital transactions between companies and public sector align IT systems Fewer suppliers enables stronger linkages Middle-layer eroded/ replaced	Lock-in with digital suppliers Procurement managers control unchanged/ reduced
Orientation	Digital Analysis of what is being bought	Discretion decreased The ability to ask clarifying questions, product demonstration decreases
Values	Stress reduction in processing of orders and in particular tracing orders	Procurement officers feeling threatened Local business give in to regional/ national/ global supplier

5.2   Self-Service: Case-Administration

Our second case illustrates the dilemmas and challenges in evaluation of IT in a government agency that wants to introduce self-service through the Internet. The objective is to reduce the operating costs of the case handling. Also, it is argued by the IT department that the web-based case handling can improve citizen service, transfer resources from administration to case work, and facilitate analyses of work processes. The web-site will have a number of different documents (12 in total) and will be used by both customers (citizens) and staff as well as external evaluators. The web-site will use pre-structured formats and does not allow open-ended comments or document attachments other than the ones specified. The new web-enabled interface will also abandon the existing interface and intranet, and allow the employees to access their cases and all related documents from any location. All case-workers have, due to a pan-governmental program, been equipped with ADSL or higher connections and computers in their homes.

The agency is primarily occupied with case administration and employs 100 full-time staff. The annual payroll costs are DKK 32.5 million (in total 166,000 working hours). 55 employees are directly engaged in casework (in total 91,300 hours). The total operating budget, including payroll costs, amounts to DDK 51 million, out of which 18.5 million is allotted to other operations. This amount is not affected by the Internet solution.

Annually, there are 8,000 completed cases (on average 12.5 hours/case), 17,300 inquiries from citizens about cases (on average 15 minutes are spent directly) and 7,000 inquires from citizens (telephone, letter, fax, e-mail), which are not related to concrete/ non-completed cases (on average ten minutes are spent directly, ten minutes are spent on follow-up activities). In addition, there are 2,000 annual inquiries from other agencies and departments (on average 20 minutes spent directly, 30 minutes follow up). The 2,000 inquiries come from 45 different locations/ people.

They have now adopted an Internet solution that involves complete indexation of cases, IT project management on case, employee, department and management levels and 'open' access to all input, output, content and benchmarks for at least one person other than the relevant caseworker.

The employees communicate with their colleagues within the department and revisit continuously their case handling practices. This is done in informal way in meetings every Thursday morning. This amounts to about 5,000 hours annually. Also, there are a number of planning meetings what amounts to 35,000 work hours. The case workers will often have to communicate with external evaluators considering the cases before they make a final decision on the case. There are 15 external evaluators assigned with the agency. They use digital communication (e-mail) but it still amounts to an annually consumption of 21,207 hours.

There are up to 15 different document types that the case worker and / or customer have to use during the case handling process. After the digitalization, they have managed to reduce this to 12 different documents. The initial investment (development and implementation) including training is estimated to DKK 1½ million and adjustment of existing applications will cost another 4 million. The useful life of the solution is estimated to be one year with an annual replacement price of DKK 750,000.

Table 9-8. before implementation of IT–solution and after implementation of alternatives A and B

		Before implementation of the IT solution	Alternative A	Alternative B
Case-handling	Processing and archiving	10,000 h	5,000 h	5,000 h
	Finding/ revisit cases	15,000 h	4,000 h	21,000 h
	Internal evaluation of cases	5,000 h	5,000 h	23,000 h
	Meetings	35,000 h	25,000 h	37,000 h
	External evaluations of cases	21,207 h	10,000 h	45,000 h
(1)	Total	85,207 h	49,000 h	131,000 h
Inquiries	Case handling	15 min, x 17,300 inq,	5 min, x 10,000 inq,	5 min, x 50,000 inq,

	General inquires	10 min x 7,000 inq,	3 min, x 17,000 inq,	1 min, x 87,000 inq,
	Other agencies/ departments	50 min, x 2,000 inq,	15 min, x 1,700 inq,	10 min, x 31,000 inq,
(2)	Total	7,169 h	2,108 h	7,083 h
(3) Other		72,634 h	72,634 h	72,634 h
Total		166,000 h	123,742 h	210,717 h
Cost reduction			-15,043,848	15,919,252

The challenging issue is, however, how the customers will use the new service and it is their pattern of use that will impact the organizational costs of the website. This demonstrates the ironies of websites in the public sector. In alternative A we expect that the increased level of information and self-service through the Internet will result in less staff-time used on cases. In alternative B we expect a skyrocketing in staff-time spent on intra- and intergovernmental case handling issues and inquiries. Also, we expect a step increase in brief, general inquiries from the customers.

In alternative A, the number of time-consuming direct inquires about specific cases declines. As a result of the Internet solution, citizens can now find an answer to some inquires from the information available at the Internet. There is a small decrease in inquiries regarding the progress of cases from other employees and politicians, but there is a significant decrease in the number of minutes that each inquiry takes. Contrasting this reduction, the number of general inquiries increases from 7,000 to 17,000, now amounting to 3 minutes per inquiry whereas earlier it took 10 minutes per inquiry.

In alternative B, the number of inquiries explodes from all sides: case inquiries increase from 17,300 to 50,000, general inquiries increase from 7,000 to 87,000. The expected time staff will spend on these inquiries is reduced from 10 minutes to 1 minute on average. 'Internal' inquiries increase from 2,000 to 31,000.

Table 9-9. Scenarios for impacts on process variables (flow) in case handling using web-interfaces

Variable	Definition	Before implementation of the IT solution	Scenario A	Scenario B
Volume	What percentage of the total number of documents is exchanged via this solution?	0/ 16,300 (0%)	28,700/28,700 (100%)	168,000/168,000 (100%)

Integration	What percentage of documents received digitally is forwarded digitally?	0/ 16,300 (0%)	28,700/28,700 (100%)	168,000/168,000 (100%)
Diversity	What percentage of the total number of different types of documents is included in the digital solution?	0/15 (0%)	12/12 (100%)	12/12 (100%)
Span	What percentage of business partners takes part in the digital exchange?	60/8,060 (≈%)	8,060/ 8,060 (100%)	8,060/ 8,060 (100%)

The value of interaction from the customer point of view is more tricky. One way to estimate the value is to calculate the time spent accessing the web-service relative to their annual income. Thus, given a person earns 30,000 USD for 1,660 hours of work, we will argue that if that person spends one hour at the public sector website for case handling but previously had to spend two hours, the net benefits for the customer is estimated as 18 USD. Also, general inquiries previously took ½ hour for the citizen, but are no reduced to ¼ hour. The benefit is 4.5 USD per inquiry. This gives the citizens a total benefit of 2,565,000 USD (amounting to 17,955,000 DKK) in scenario A, whereas the benefit to the citizens in alternative B (amounting to 34,055,000 DKK) 4,865,000 USD. By adding these benefits to the calculations in Table 9.8, both alternatives have positive impacts in year 1.

Accessing the content impacts the variables on capability, interaction, orientation, and value, the two scenarios spell out very differently although they are united in an improved effectiveness and efficiency with respect to time reduction and easier archiving. Yet, the increase in number of cases and inquiries in scenario B more than outweighs the benefits of individual cases for the capability variable.

The web-interface allows staff to work at home reporting a 20% higher productivity compared to workers who complete cases from their office. This difference occurs due to the fact that the ones that stay in the office throughout the week attend more internal meetings, they spend longer time at breaks than allowed for in their contracts, and colleagues from other agencies are more eager to contact people in the office than when working at home.

The impacts of the interaction are mixed in both scenarios with scenario A bringing the individual case worker and customer closer, and allowing a more frequent and instant interaction, the scenario B leading to increases in intra-governmental meetings and rapid increases in inquiries and information retrieval from other agencies and departments. The discretion in case handling is reduced which is positive with respect to the speed of the process, but in both scenarios the employees and the customers experience negative impacts regarding instrumentalization since the user interface at the web-site does not allow open-ended comments or document attachments. The overall stress-level is increased particularly in scenario B due to the higher frequency of cases and the expectations of prompt answers to inquiries. The major stress factor is not from customers, but other agencies that send e-mails etc. concerning cases and overall evaluations.

Table 9-10. Scenarios for impacts on content variables in case handling using web-interfaces

Variable	Scenario A		Scenario B	
	Pro	Contra	Pro	Contra
Capabilities	Effectiveness and efficiency process gains Information quality increases for the digital documents Reduction in case processing time and number of cases submitted Archiving time reduced	Productivity of office workers 20% lower than workers who work from home	Reduction in case processing time and number of cases submitted Archiving time reduced	Increases in inquires lead to request for re-evaluation of cases Time consuming general inquires outweigh the efficiency and effectiveness gains Productivity of office workers 20% lower than workers who work from home
Interaction	Increased management control due to work productivity analysis Increased digital transactions between customers and office	Governmental interaction increases	Increased digital transactions between customers and office	Explosion in number of general inquires Governmental interaction increases
Orientation	Digital analysis of cases increases increasing efficiency	Discretion in case handling reduced The ability to ask clarifying questions reduced	Digital analysis of cases increasing efficiency	Inquires: Discretion increases due to irregularities and frequency Cases: discretion

			and ability to ask clarifying questions reduced
Values	Stress reduction in processing of individual cases	Case workers feeling professional work ethics being violated Concerns from citizens on privacy of their files	Stress reduction in processing of individual cases	Stress increases due increases in inquires Case workers' privacy sphere challenged

6.   CONCLUSIONS

In this chapter we have argued that in some instances rational processes and implementation patterns for formal methods as the CBA to be applied. The CBA has its strength and weakness in its simplicity. Moving towards the organizing of activities through application of IT rather than moving toward organization of process through IT, the value of CBA is less obvious for government and should to an increasingly degree reflect activities and the people that work with the activities.

Another challenge for the evaluation research is to carefully consider the independent and dependent variables for the study. Whereas most could agree that there is a short-term, dynamic and interactive relationship between the governmental unit, the customers, and the technology, most evaluations take a more long term, simple and uni-directional view.

The proposed framework with process and flow variables was applied to two cases on e-procurement and web-services respectively. The cases illustrate efforts to acquire evaluation data provide an opportunity to access dimensions of the IT application in ways that we would not have done without the formal evaluation. Therefore the formal evaluation can complement the informal and daily evaluation of IT systems and in situations where the decision to acquire the IT application has not yet been taken.

The content and flow variables that access the impacts can be part of the ongoing dynamics of IT development targeted at lowering overhead costs, eliminate applications that have an internal focus exclusively, and concentrate on activities rather than formal organizations. This is useful and constructive knowledge to have in mind when reading the next chapter that discusses developing IT applications for government.

Chapter 10

DEVELOPMENT OF E-GOVERNMENT APPLICATIONS

1. INTRODUCTION

Large scale government IT projects often fall short on alignment with overall strategy formation, collaborative aspects, and user participation (Currie and Galliers 1999; Danish-Board-of-Technology 2001). Yet, investing more management resources, optimizing software development procedures, involvement of all stakeholders, reporting of both the good news and the less favorable results, incorporating short-term and long-term benefits as project goals, cashing in benefits short term and long term, and cementing IT project changes into daily workflow will not necessary lead to successful IT projects.

Few IT projects in government are developed and implemented in a straight forward matter and perhaps even fewer projects have actors that can cope with the challenges that eventually occur. The main argument pursued in this chapter is that the ability to cope with IT project challenges is equally poorly distributed among consultants, governmental institutions, and suppliers involved in the projects. Particularly in government though, risk aversive and formal check-and-balance techniques are standard reactions facing potential failures. Also, there is a need for investigations seeking underlying cause and impacts relations when the elements and activities in IT projects fail. In the same regard of needs, this chapter calls for establishment of systematical mechanisms for learning from failures. Based on case studies of five major IT projects that all showed divergent process, outcome, and/ or costs from the original bullet plans for the projects, we argue that focus needs to be directed to capability building and have less focus on the formal institutional management of IT development projects.

At the commencement of this chapter we will refine the perception of failure and success proposing a continuum with failure at one end and challenged and impaired projects at the other end of the spectra. The attributes of the continuum are more dependent on the institutionalized practices, interest and norms than it is any time and location independent objective measurements. Thus, awareness needs to paid to the interpretive schemes, the channels for defining and communication in development processes and the norms and organizational rules.

We then proceed in section 3.3 to outline guidelines for how this awareness can materialize in practice in four dimensions: maturation of the organization, the technology and the frameworks for the governmental projects, the organization and management of the projects, and the ongoing interaction with the purveyors and consultants. These guidelines grew from a major study of failed large scale IT projects in the Danish government. Thus the list of the factors is a result of a collaborative work financed and hosted by the National Technology Assessment Board. Acknowledging the support from the Board, we have been able to include recommendations from the report in this chapter. Also, we are clearly in debt to the co-authors of this report (Danish-Board-of-Technology 2001). Despite being indepted to the Danish study, the PPR-perspective and the formal organizational perspective outlined in section 3.3, have been developed for this book. The concluding section sums up the guidelines and discusses implications of following the PPR approach in future development of e-government applications.

2.   DEFINING SUCCESS AND FAILURE

Rather than labeling our IT applications as either success or failure (a discrete variable) it might be useful to consider the terms as a continuum and use the terms success, challenged and impaired (Standishgroup 1994). Let *success* denote that the IT project delivers to the customer everything specified, to the quality agreed, on time and within costs. Let *challenged* projects denote a project that was completed and became operational but at greater cost than the planned project, overran on time and delivered less functionality. Finally, an *impaired project* will denote that the project is cancelled during the development stage.

The real challenge in government is that often success criteria is defined years ahead of the actual development and government procedures are more focused on fulfilling the formulated contracts and criteria than adjusting the project to a new and unforeseen technological context. A second challenge is that government view challenged projects and impaired projects as failures. Yet, it might be a suitable option to halt development along one path and choose another route.

IT management literature focuses on how consultants, the governmental unit and the IT suppliers each can maximize their utility in terms of lower costs, better quality, winning the market battle etc. Yet, we argue that large scale IT projects, over time, are embedded, negotiated and in direct competition with *institutionalized practices, interests and norms*.

Rather than being technical-rational projects, IT projects often progress as *fragile, contingent and highly improvised manners* in which the changing alliances among the actors are forged rather than controlled and straight forward. Yet, the formal mechanisms for securing that IT projects are on the right course in government primarily rely on concepts that have originated in the classical waterfall and spiral models and variations of them (Cadel and Yeates 2001).

Heterogeneous functions, tasks, professions, client groups, and organizational cultures are key features of IT projects, for example in public healthcare services. The heterogeneity is reflected in different organizational principles in simultaneous action. A fragile balance between different interests and values creates dilemmas and contradictions between user involvement, administrative and professional rationalities when building IT applications. Institutional values, such as the right to participate in critical decision issues (a democratic logic), compete with the necessity to manage and control the organization (an administrative logic) and the professionals' claim for autonomy within their domain (a professional logic).

What we argue is that the key is to focus of the customers. On a general level, they represent a shared legitimizing base for all actors in the field, but there is often a hate and love relationship with the customers when building the IT applications. When the employees express their opinion on IT applications, they reflect the values and interests that prevail in their own domain reflecting a mixture of professional, administrative and political judgments. The introduction of IT projects in government can pose challenges to this mixture. The relation is perhaps more prevalent the opposite direction: the personal, professional, administrative and political mixture can undermine the cost, delivery time, and content of the IT projects.

3.   GUIDELINES FOR DEVELOPMENT FOR E-GOVERNMENT APPLICATIONS

OECD formulated in their 2003 report on e-government a checklist comprising four dimensions: visions/ political will, common frameworks/ co-operation, customer focus, and responsibility. The visions and political will addresses leadership and commitment, and strategic integration, whereas common frameworks/ co-operation focuses on the inter-agency collaboration and financing. The urgency to increase customer focus targets accessibility, the customers ability to choose between different providers of e-government services, involvement and engagement, and the mechanism for ensuring privacy. The forth group (responsibility) addresses the accountability and the monitoring and evaluation of the e-government applications.

Table 10-3. OECD E-Government Guidance

Key area	Focus points	Guiding questions
Vision/ political will	1. Leadership and commitment:	— Do you have the necessary leadership and commitment at the political level in order to develop an e-government vision and guide change over the long term?
		— Is there leadership and commitment at the administrative level to implement change?
	2. Integration:	— Has there been a review of barriers to e-government implementation?
		— Is e-government integrated into broader policy and service delivery goals and processes?
		— Is e-government integrated into public management reform goals and processes?
		— Is e-government integrated into broader information society activity?
Common framework /co-operation	3. Inter-agency collaboration:	— Are agencies working together in customer-focused groupings of agencies?
		— Are agency managers operating within common frameworks to ensure interoperability, maximize implementation efficiency and avoid duplication?

		— Does shared infrastructure exist to provide a framework for individual agency initiatives?

— Does shared infrastructure exist to provide a framework for individual agency initiatives?

— Are there incentives to help encourage collaboration and seamless service delivery?

4. Financing:

— Can ICT spending, where appropriate, be treated as an investment with consideration of projected streams of returns?

— Is there a degree of certainty of future funding in order to provide sustainability to projects?

— Are there programs (such as a central funding program) to help foster innovation and allow for key demonstration projects?

Customer focus   **5. Access:**

— Is the government pursuing policies to improve access to online services?

— Harmonization of policies for data sharing across countries (for example regarding security and privacy).

6. Choice:

— Do customers have choice in the method of interacting with government?

— Is there a "no wrong door" principle for accessing the administration?

— Are services driven by an understanding of customer needs?

7. Citizen engagement:

— Does e-government engage citizens in the policy process?

— Are there information quality policies and feedback mechanisms in place to help maximize the usefulness of information provision and strengthen citizen participation?

8. Privacy:

— Are there mechanisms in place to protect individual privacy with regard to e-government?

— Do broad standards for privacy protection allow for information sharing between agencies while preventing abuse?

Responsibility	9. Accountability:	— Do accountability arrangements ensure that it is clear who is responsible for shared projects and initiatives? — Does the use of private sector partnerships maintain levels of accountability?
	10. Monitoring and evaluation:	— Is there a framework in place to identify the demand, costs, benefits and impact of e- government? — Are e-government implementers able to articulate and demonstrate the benefits of e- government in order to raise support for their projects?

Source. OECD (2003).

Although the OECD report has a long and solid list of recommendations we suggest to complement the list of actions by paying attention to:
– Maturation of the organization
– Technology and frameworks for governmental IT projects
– Organization of the development of projects
– Interaction between government and the purveyors and consultants

Whereas the OECD list can be considered to be at the macro and strategic level, the guidelines we propose are at the macro and micro level. The list of practical advice can serve as a useful checklist for management facing the overriding responsibility for a project. The following list can be an aid in setting focus on areas where experiences have otherwise too frequently been overlooked or have been dealt with in an unprofessional way. What is especially relevant is to pay close attention to advice at the beginning of a development project, this means to say, before the contract is signed. Many of these points ought to be checked continuously throughout the entire course of the project.

One of the key challenges that are not included in the OECD is the governmental obsession to contract regulation of relations. The desire for detailed contracts appears to be due to the public authorities' perception of IT projects as demarcated technical plant-assignments. Also, e-government application development and implementation needs a much more diverse arsenal of instruments than normative instruments solely. We have in another study of e-commerce diffusion pointed to the need to apply economic, knowledge diffusion, use the power of government along with normative regulation. Thus applying a combination of sticks, carrots and sermons can help fuel the development process in a dynamic rather than purely contractual based fashion (Andersen et al. 2003).

The detailed contracts have also fostered adverse consequences for the steering of the projects. The detailed juridical contract control and lack of flexible project control damage the development process. It would be a much better idea to hammer out a project plan first and let this serve as the foundation for drawing up the contract.

The regulations concerning offerings contribute toward exacerbates of the problem, because they operate with very short time limits for purveyors. Frequently, because a great deal of time is spent on the demand specification, the governmental unit is operating under immense time pressure. For this reason, the purveyors are asked for a hasty estimate, which they then have difficulty in managing to satisfy in a proper fashion.

Our log of experiences from failed IT projects context show that from the outset, the public sector buyers aim for specifying the system requirements beforehand – and fails. Thus, there is little or room for flexibility and for changes to be made along the way in the course of the project. Our suggestion is that detailed contracts should be replaced by more open contract forms, which can serve to motivate both the buyer and the purveyor into carrying on an ongoing collaboration concerned with finding the optimal solutions.

The public spent an inordinate degree of energy assessing whether there might be a situation that ought to incur a penalty - energy which in many instances would be more wisely spent on getting the projects done. Instead, government could define well-elaborated *principles* for the cooperative process, including making it clear who it is that will be deciding about changes, how the needs can be measured and what process-related demands have to be imposed on the project's control. It also ought to be possible, after the contract has been signed, to draft commonly demanded specifications with the possibility of stopping the collaboration. This would serve to strengthen the common understanding concerning the problems and of what the finished system will be able to do. Moreover, it would strengthen the projects if the contracts did not merely operate with penalties, but also with positive incentives.

Also, increasing the number of *project competitions* could be a way to supplement the detailed requirement specification before the tendering process. The procedure for project competitions could evolve with a number of different purveyors invited to come forth with a total bid on the design of the new IT system. The buyer can then choose between the submitted proposals before the project is dispatched further in the legitimate offering. It is the perception of the work group that the design proposals, in a number of instances, will constitute a valuable tool for qualifying the buyer's wishes with respect to the new system. Also, a project competition can help indicate where the public sector buyer has to mature the organization before the actual work on the system development is set into motion.

The purveyors certainly carry a share of responsibility for problems that e-government projects encounter by their lack of capability, failure to deliver soft competences, and unprofessional contractual bids and performance.

First of all, in several cases, the purveyor was either incapable of supplying the agreed technical solution or has furnished such inadequate project management that this has been a strong contributing factor to the project getting sidetracked.

Secondly, the purveyor part has frequently failed to develop the "soft competences". In several projects, the purveyors have been lacking in the volition to understand the organizational aspects of the IT project, to cooperate with other purveyors, to communicate with non-technical people and to react to problems that are in the offing.

Thirdly, in some cases, the purveyors have performed their work in a manner that can only be described as problematic. The tenders have *deliberately given a bid for the project that was too low.* This has ostensibly been done with the expectation of being able to gain the necessary profits as a result of the buyer's requests for changes in the delivery along the way in the course of the project's development or when the system is implemented. For this reason, the purveyors have also stuck very meticulously to the terms of contract.

The purveyors have affiliated their most proficient project leaders and salesmen in the proposition phase. However, these staff members were replaced later on by *lower ranking employees,* after the contract was signed. The purveyor has not lived up to his/her *ethical responsibility* to say so, in a clear and distinct way, when it is obvious that the technical demands from the buyer's side are inexpedient. Among other things, this can be due to the fact that unfortunately, some public sector buyers consistently reject proposals where the purveyor expresses reservations about a third party's software or about unrealistic demands in the offering materials.

After the contract has been signed, the purveyors have also failed to live up to their part of the bargain by not indicating clearly enough that the *buyer's organization and staffing of the project is inadequate or that certain basic things, like risk assessments, are missing from the project.* In one of the projects covered by our investigation, all of the buyer's project participants (including the project management) were only connected to the development project on a half-time basis. Here, the purveyor ought to have called specific attention to the fact that this would tend to weaken the buyer's position and also render the requisite collaboration between the parts all the more difficult.

In one instance of the cases we have investigated, the purveyors have neglected to *promptly forewarn the buyer that the project's technological bases* – as seen in the light of the general development – were about to change in their basic character. It ought to have been the purveyor's job to furnish the buyer - on an ongoing basis - with up-to-date relevant knowledge that would make it possible to assess and to steer the technical risks of the project. In a project on developing a labor market information system it was the customer who continually had to ask the purveyor about the ongoing development and the upkeep of the control system (OS2) and the development tool (HPS). In the opinion of the work group, it ought to have been the purveyor who, on the basis of his/her own inclination, informed and counseled the customer about crucial technological developments and changes.

In several instances, the *purveyor has neglected to inform the buyer that the development of the system was delayed*. For example, in one project, the buyer knew long in advance that the purveyor would not be able to deliver the system at the appointed time. Lacking confidence in the ongoing collaboration, this question was never clarified until the purveyor had to eat humble pie – just before the deadline. This result in erosion of confidence in the purveyor's project control and force the buyer to employ contract control rather than effective project control.

We propose two scenarios for how future e-government projects might evolve if taken an activity driven and customer centric approach as advocated in the PPR-approach or a supply and organizational driven approach.

Table 10-1. Scenarios for the e-government application development: The customer and activity driven versus the supply and formal organizational driven approaches

Areas of recommendations	Customer and activity driven	Supply and formal organizational driven
Maturation of the organization	Customers demand and need for the application	Employees and management need for the application
	Customer get central role in development phase (prototype and beta)	Mgt get central role in development process
	Need for change in dealing with individual cases	Need for organizational readjustment/ reorganization
	Evaluation of the application only from the customer point of view	Organizational evaluation of the application
	Alignment with customers strategy and life pattern changes	Alignment with organizational strategy
Technology	Applications centered on activity improvement	Support activities in focus
	Core activities in focus	Organizational procedures benefits favored
	Customer-public sector interaction in focus	Intra- and interorganizational interaction
	Web interfaces to all applications	Intranet, extranet, internet interfaces feasible
Organization of the	Rapid development and prototyping	Focus on management,

development process	Customer training more important than staff training Direct customer representation in steering committee Minimizing of overhead costs	control, and milestones Staff training more in focus than customer training Indirect customer representation in steering committee Maximization of overhead costs
Interaction with purveyors and consultants	Customer competition Flexible projects with regards to changes in customer activity pattern Purveyor responsible for running and adjustment of system in implementation period Knowledge and experience transfer to customer with the application	Project competition Flexible projects Code of conduct Government transfer and accumulation of experience with application development

3.1   The maturation of the organization

From an institutional, or supply side, point of view managerial control and organizational strategic questions are in focus. This encompasses:
– Employees and management need for the application
– Management has the central role in development process
– Need for organizational readjustment/ reorganization
– Organizational evaluation of the application
– Alignment with organizational strategy
From the PPR-perspective, the central questions are
– Customers demand and need for the application
– Customer has the central role in development phase (prototype and beta)
– Need for change in dealing with individual cases
– Evaluation of the application only from the customer point of view
– Alignment with customers strategy and life pattern changes

What follows from the supply and formal organizational perspective is a firm anchoring of the project in the uppermost management. Here, there must be one person from the management direction who will assume chief responsibility for the project. Management's responsibility for the success of the IT project is thus rendered clear and unequivocal.

The assignment's commissioner, or project management, needs to develop an aggregate "prospectus", which will provide information about the overall circumstances surrounding the project, about which the project's interested parties have a right to know. As a minimum, this prospectus ought to include:

- A clear goal, which is measurable and integrated into the organization's total strategy.
- A cost/benefit analysis of the total project, so that whether or not there is sufficient documentation for the project's aggregate benefits is visible from the outset.
- A plan of action for how the organization can be ripened for purposes of developing and receiving the system. This plan ought to subsume both how the organization can achieve a common understanding of the project's requirements and which areas of competence need to be built up.
- There must be a special focus on the organization's capacity for establishing and driving a project organization.
- A risk-assessment of the project and guidelines for the continuing risk-control.

The supply and formal organizational perspective will seek to acquire experiences from similar public sector IT projects with respect to maturation of the organization, management, user involvement, risk-assessment, regulations concerning offerings and the project's success and experiences with selected collaborators.

The management must wait until the preliminary conditions are all in place before putting the project into action. Among other things, this involves the consideration that organization must have the necessary resources and areas of competence at its disposal for getting the assignment off the ground.

The necessary adaptation of the organization and its working procedures must transpire in parallel with the development of the system – and not only in the initial period when the system is to be put into use.

It has to be made clear to the members of the staff, from the very outset of the project, if there:

- are working processes that must be re-adjusted
- are going to be changes in the service level
- are going to be new products/services introduced
- are going to be changes in the size or the composition of the personnel
- are functions that will be centralized, decentralized or done away with entirely.

After implementation of the IT application, this perspective argues that the advantages of the new system materialize as quickly as possible. The more time that passes, the more difficult it becomes to realize the propounded success criteria and to assess whether or not the system has strengthened the organization's business-related goals. Thus, the management and the authorities empowered to make grants should ensure that the new system will contribute to the organization's attaining its goals.

3.2   Technology

From the supply and formal organizational point of view, the following issues are in focus with respect to the technology:
– Support activities in focus
– Organizational procedures benefits favored
– Intra- and interorganizational interaction
– Intranet, extranet, internet interfaces

By contract, the PPR-approach favors the following four areas of technology:
– Applications centered on activity improvement
– Core activities in focus
– Customer-public sector interaction in focus
– Web interfaces to all applications

The point of departure for the design of the system will from the formal organizational point of view include, whether standard software can be utilized or whether recycling elements of other public sector agencies' systems can help reducing the costs and decrease the time for the development of the software. Yet, the danger of putting the formal organization in front is that few or no ideas will be generated on activities other than the support activities and that intraorganizational benefits will be in favor. As a result building intra and extranet can outweigh internet and transparent systems.

3.3   Organization of the development project

The formal and supply oriented perspective will seek the following goals with respect to the organization of the software development process:
– Focus on management, control, and milestones
– Staff training more in focus than customer training
– Indirect customer representation in steering committee
– Maximization of overhead costs

By contrast, the PPR-approach will seek:
– Rapid development and prototyping
– Customer training more important than staff training
– Direct customer representation in steering committee
– Minimizing of overhead costs

From the PPR-perspective it is imperative that the aggregate IT project is split into partial projects with continuous deliveries. As a rule of thumb, every delivery in the project should be no longer than six months and every delivery involve not more than about thirty developers and an equal number of users. The partial projects ought to be autonomous, demarcated and serviceable parts of the total solution, which can be implemented in steps.

Although this need to split deliveries into small components and early prototyping also can be in line with formal and supplier perspective, the focus is on ongoing risk-assessments and to make sure that risks be eliminated or limited. If the IT project in question subsumes a number of different institutions, it is especially crucial to take the risk-assessment into account. Also, the formal organization perspective will be eager to establish a steering committee which will bear the responsibility for the overall strategic decisions, assignment of responsibility and roles for all the involved parties, and ongoing evaluation and quality control of project plans, prospectus, etc, by experienced project experts.

The project plan ought to establish the basis for a flexible contract which can serve to motivate both buyer and purveyor to cooperate – over the course of the entire project - on reaching the most optimal solutions and can ensure that this cooperation is based on project control more than juridical contract control:

– Room must be made for changes that might turn up along the way
– Clear principles for the cooperative processes must be set up, including the stipulation of who has the responsibility for changes, how the needs are going to be measured and what requirements are to be set up for the project control as well as the buyer's and the purveyor's staffing of the project.
– The contracts must operate not only with penalties, but also with positive incentives and bonus schemes.

Early on, the project management has to outline a communication plan that will ensure a thorough, continuous and open flow of information relating to the project, internally within the project organization, throughout the whole of the larger organization and outward to the media and the public eye.

Pilot studies with the new system must be made, which also ought to include tests of new procedures and tests about whether the personnel have been adequately introduced to - and have had a sufficient degree of instruction in - the new system. If it proves impossible to run pilot tests, mention of this ought to enter into the risk-assessment.

Systematic evaluations of the project ought to be carried out and the results must be made accessible to those planning new projects. This will make it easier for coming projects to compare their project plans with projects that have already been implemented.

Two the key differences between the two perspectives are user involvement and overhead costs. Whereas the formal organizational view will tend to form user groups of people from the public administration, the user groups will, from the PPR-perspective, be primarily from the customer segment.

In both cases, however, the role and the responsibility of the user groups must be made clear from the outset. It is crucial that the project management consistently assess and prioritize the users' needs in relation to both the technical design and the success criteria for the aggregate project. The instruction of the users must not include only the coming super-users and the instruction must be broader than the technical operation of the system. The new procedures, new services, new cooperative forms and the new intentions behind the changes must be part of the training.

Regarding overhead costs, there is an explicit call for minimizing overhead costs as part of the IT project from the PPR-perspective. Having taken a formal organizational point of view there is a danger that overhead costs remain unchanged or are even increased by transferring additional routines and tasks to other departments through interdepartmental IT projects.

3.4   Interaction with purveyors and consultants

With regards to interaction with purveyors and consultants, the formal and supply oriented perspective emphasizes:
– Project competition
– Flexible projects
– Codes of conduct
– Government transfer and accumulation of experience with application development

By contrast, the PPR approach emphasizes:
– Customer competition
– Flexible projects with regards to changes in customer activity pattern
– Purveyor responsible for running and adjustment of system in implementation period
– Knowledge and experience transfer to customer with the application

The difference between the two perspectives here are remarkable in particular with respect to the project competition versus the customer competition.

Experiences with utilizing project competitions in order to qualify the buyer's design of the IT project presupposes that the rules of this area can be administered in connection with large scale IT projects and that the government will be willing to award sufficiently large prizes so that it would be attractive to take part in the competition. Thus, the danger imposed by the higher cost of bidding is that there will be few companies that will bid and hence limit the competition.

From the PPR-perspective, the competition does not concern the IT projects per se but the customers using them. Thus, software developers and consultants need to demonstrate their capability to produce customer centric applications.

Also, the knowledge transfer mechanism differs in the sense that in the supply and formal organizational perspective, the construction and exchange of experiences involving public sector IT projects encompass experiences with the cooperation of the individual purveyors and consultants, with their areas of competence and within the quality of their work. This will constitute an important basis for the public sector's capacity to coordinate its purchases of IT and consultancy services and will pose clear demands to the purveyors with respect to the same.

Consequently, the possibilities for employing and holding on to a specially qualified project leader and key IT personnel in the service of the government ought to be seriously investigated. The practical allotment of roles between buyer and purveyor must be carefully documented. Over and above this, joint activities for the two parties ought to be scheduled, with an aim toward engendering a joint understanding of the project's goals. Such activities will have to be repeated after every large partial delivery. This can ensure the close and trustful cooperation between buyer and purveyor, which constitutes a prerequisite for a successful project elapse.

The crisis handling of the project ought to maintain a focus on the project's business goals and cost/benefit. It ought to ensure that both parts are working constructively to find the very best solutions even if such solutions may not be situated within the letter of the contract.

By contrast, the PPR-perspective emphasizes the transfer of capability to use the applications and to accumulate capabilities among the customers. Thus, does the proposed IT application require new capabilities from the end users, do they need these capabilities for other purposes, what should motivate the customers to spend time and energy to acquire the new competences? From the PPR-perspective, the purveyor of the system must assume responsibility for the running of the system during the initial period in order to rectify those errors and deficiencies that typically crop up in the first few months of any system's operation.

The perspectives share the call for more flexible contract models, which reflect the realities in modern IT projects, and which ought to be put into use. The contracts should supplement, to a greater extent, the necessary penalty provisions with a series of positive incentives. Yet there is a twist here in the sense that the PPR needs flexibility if the customers activity patterns change, whereas the supplier perspective needs flexibility if societal, legal, or intragovernmental concerns and priorities change.

From the supply and formal organizational perspective, it is of particular necessity that the IT branch associations and the consultancy concerns hammer out and maintain a code of conduct for the cooperation of large-scale IT projects. The relationship of responsibility and the expectations of the consultant's role and proper task must be made fully clear from the outset and must be reflected in the contract between the various parties. It is just as important to steer the consultancy assistance as it is to steer the other aspects of the aggregate developmental project. The consultants must document their qualifications and experiences specifically in relation to the task that is to be solved. The contract has to contain names of the key consultants who are going to be solving the assignment. Any subsequent deviations from the contract, in this respect, will have to be approved by the buyer, so that the consulting firm will not be advancing less qualified resources in the implementation of the project.

4.   CONCLUSIONS

This chapter has addressed practical issues concerning the development of applications for government. We formulated our recommendations in four groups: 1) maturation of the organization, 2) technology and frameworks for government IT projects, 3) organization of software development projects, and 4) interaction with purveyors and consultants. We stressed here the interaction with the purveyors and consultants although this is not suggesting that the three other set of recommendations are less important. Also, the obsession to perform contract regulation is stressed as a key area for change.

The two perspectives – or scenarios – can take future e-government applications in very different directions. The supply and formal organizational perspective has its strength in cashing in benefits from IT applications in the short run and the ongoing capacity to monitor and manage IT projects. In the e-procurement area case explored in Chapter 7 of this book there are elements of this perspective. The customer and activity driven approach (which is in some aspects more of a complement than substitute to the formal organizational perspective), is more risky and a potential source for cost increases since the formal control of the project is downplayed in favor of alignment with changing customer needs. Yet, there are clearly also elements in the PPR-perspective that could help reduce the costs, namely the reduction in applications that serve administrative purposes only, the explicit goal to reduce overhead costs, and rapid development and prototyping. Subsequently, we will most likely see the two approaches co exist and complement each other but in the long run we propose that the PPR approach will be more prevalent and dominant for the networked generation of future e-government applications.

Chapter 11

CONCLUSION

1. INTRODUCTION

To recap, this aim of this book "E-government and Public Sector Process Re-building: Dilettantes, Wheelbarrows, and Diamonds" has been to provide a *constructive input to rebuild and improve the activities and interaction with the citizens, companies, and the formally elected decision-makers.* The vehicle for the transition from formal government and in-house orientation is information systems encompassing a range of applications and technologies other than internet technologies only. Finally, we argue that the *dilettantes* in the public sector are in need of upgrading, rethinking, and refocusing of their use of IS.

Acknowledging the usefulness of digital wheel barrows, the PPR-approach proposes a complementary use of IS by adding an analytical mode of the use of IS. In the same line of argument, governments should start to acknowledge that most IT-applications are developed to be part of a set of activities which are intended for replacement whenever the diamonds are no longer serving their purpose. Just like the major part of the world market for diamonds are not flashy and shining *diamonds* that are only shown off on special occasions, but fabricated for use in industrialized settings.

The PPR-approach is controversial as it challenges three domains: i) the sphere of mainstream practice that presumes that building applications along the existing lines of government and processes is a valid and desired goal; ii) the bulk of governmental workers ask for and evaluate IS in the light of the benefits it brings them, and iii) the policies that have a solid belief in that by using IT in support activities and transactions the public sector will be transformed.

The three domains challenged are all part of the governmental approach to IT-approach that has grown and been cemented in all layers of government and by numerous developers and consultants as well. The triangle of government, developers, and consultants have been aiming for the easy gains with control, monitoring, and in-house benefits in focus for the IT-applications. Throughout this book we have argued that whilst the approach followed by government so far has been along the lines of how IT could help facilitate twenty, ten, and even five years ago, little has been achieved in terms of incorporating the new wave of computing technologies that are now being adopted by government, companies, and citizens.

The grand picture sketched in this book regarding how government approaches IT and its achievements in applying IT in customer and activity centric is far from being an idyllic Monet collection. Rather, the image that is evoked from the chapters is a profound transaction and formal organizational approach with government aiming to inter- and intraorganizational improvements. In doing this, government is successful in some implementation areas such as intranet but they are also caught by competing rationalities and conflicting agendas for the development of IT. Using Edvard Munch's cry-picture to illustrate our impression of the governmental use of IT is taking the negative parts too far. Yet, on a continuum from Monet to Munch, IT in government is closer to the later than the former at the spectra.

Using the PPR-approach as a guide for transforming this IT practice could help "*Moneting*" government although more research and practical experience clearly is needed to quantify and qualify the path and actions required for the migration of government. The extension, maturity, and revolutionary phases of the e-government migration fueled by the PPR-approach are essential to follow if the objectives of e-government are to materialize. By contrast, it will not be successful if the circular and internal improvements of intranets, e-procurement, and government-government services are setting the agenda for IS.

To demonstrate how the PPR-approach can work in practice, we have in this chapter formulated six actions. These actions will be described and discussed at length in the following section. We finish the chapter with an assessment of some of the soft and hard issues regarding the uptake of the PPR-method.

2. SIX ACTIONS TO START THE PROCESS OF REBUILDING

The PPR approach is concerned with information systems in non-trivial settings and is therefore likely to create some resistance / face major implementation challenges. As part of a EU Asia ICT project, we were asked to help specify an IS that could help the government to analyze and prioritize their resources better.

After various rounds of data gathering regarding the data flow, system architecture, etc., we found the true implementation hurdle: "If the system makes anybody unhappy, you will have to redesign the system...people will not support the system if it makes anybody unhappy. It needs to make people happy".

The PPR approach advocated here is not likely to succeed with such restrictions! The generation of IS implemented in government now is not going to be less challenging and less laborious. The cross-departmental, multi-functionality, and constant upgrading with backward integration modules will, without doubt, make people unhappy from time-to-time. We have formulated six actions (order, digitalize, terminate, customerize, competence-boost, revolutionize) but in most cases the label of "bullets" could be more prescriptive since the application of the PPR concepts is so challenging that one might need a firearm to pave the way for radical changes. The actions are summarized in Table 11.1 comprising the key words, actions, motivation, and impacts of each of the six actions.

Table 11-10. PPR-actions: motivation, examples, and impacts

Keyword	Action	Motivation	Impacts
Order	Bring order in the digital toolbox	Digital toolbox is full.	Awareness of customers, decision-makers, workers *digital orderliness* and ability to match needs with IT-application
		Disorder in toolbox Unable to find the tools Lacking knowledge on which tools to pick, or how to use them.	
		Tools and capabilities are rusty Data structure and repository follows governmental structure	Data *structure and repository* follow the customers' and decision-makers' need
Digitalize	Describe and/ or model your work related actions and processes. Argue which of	Avoidance of customer contact Widespread rhetoric	Force arguments against IT to come forward

	these actions cannot be digitalized	arguments against IT Support activities dominates IT use, rather than core	Customer alignment IT to be used in core activities
Terminate	Terminate all new IS applications that fail to benefit the customer, political decision-making and prioritizing	Transaction based IT-use In-house orientation 10% of IST oriented towards customers	Abandoning of Intranet Benefits for end-users being explicit 90% is oriented towards customers
Competence-boost	Make a mini-survey in your office of your frequent business partners and external citizens/ users about which IT-tool oriented courses, if any, they have been attending and when during the past five years	Outdated and sub-optimal skills Single-user and tasks upgrade	Network and activity upgrade Communities of enhanced practice IT-based upgrading outside work hours Incentives to skills upgrade Transfer of time to core activities
Organize	Transit the perception of the customers and decision-makers from physical presence to digital entity	perceive the customers and customers as physical entities with a digital entity with \n\n Formal organizational boundaries	perceive the customers and decision-makers as digital entities with a physical presence
Revolutionize	Please distribute the newly proposed IS in two groups: 1) functionalities that already are covered by existing IS and 2) IS that radical challenges the distribution of tasks and implementation of tasks	Incremental and ad hoc Following existing structures and routines	Radical and ongoing changes Activity focus

2.1 Action I: Bring order in the digital toolbox

Manifold routines might in theory be digitalized. Yet, in reality most routine processes are not digitalized. The reason why this mismatch occurs is similar to the reasons why the wonna-be-handyman Peter Jones always needs yet another tool, the newest tool, more tools before he can fix the house. Yet, if we back track the record of Peter Jones, we might start to wonder if it is indeed a lack of new tools that holds the lion's share of fault in the lopsided homemade garage, the children's unstable outdoor playhouse, or the perforated ceiling of the patio.

In most public offices the digital toolbox is to a large degree already full. The problem is often that the toolbox owner has disorder in his toolbox and he is unable to find the tools when he needs them. In addition, he may not know which tools to pick, or how to use them. Finally, when he finds the right tools, they may be rusty since they have not been used for ages and no attempts have been made to secure and maintain the tools. If there is disorder in governmental applications, document structure, and capability to match needs with IT applications there is little reason to believe that this would be any different among the customer group and decision-makers. Again we emphasize that there is nothing wrong in pursing orderliness in government but more importantly is orderliness among the customers.

The action line is grounded in the stacking of applications. When solving a problem too often the right and available applications are not used despite being available to the governmental employee. An example is use of the different elements in the Microsoft office suite where most users do not exceed the use of Word, Excel, Explorer, the mail client, and Powerpoint. Yet, building address books, inventory lists, case information etc. can often be done more completely and correctly in Access. Also, the use of applications such as chat programs and videoconferencing are often rejected due to previous negative experiences with the applications. Thus, the users disregard that applications and particular network technology and connection speed in the meantime have made these applications a lot more attractive to for example substitute and supplement physical meetings.

Whereas many governmental IT-departments are eager to upgrade the versions of their software, their eagerness is rarely accompanied by an eagerness among the users to explore the new features in version 7.02 as compared to version 7.01. Subsequently, there might be shareware and applications outside government that in some instances can substitute or complement governmental run software. An example is the groupware and virtual collaboration technologies that are available in shareware format.

Equal to this application upgrading and ability to find them, is the data- and document structure in government. Although there are manifold governmental workers who work in a structured manner, the PPR-approach realigns the document repositories towards the customers and will challenge the often individual structure on data. Thus, the issue is not whether the governmental can find the data when needed, but whether the customer/ decision-maker can find them when required. In the PPR-universe there is no other data apart from the ones required by customers and decision-makers.

Governmental workers will have to adopt the skills for search and logic in relation to data structure that the customers have – not the reverse.

2.2   Action II: Describe and/ or model your work related actions and processes. Argue which of these actions cannot be digitalized

"Why would I need more IT? What if more IT is not the solution, but the problem? If there is one thing I do not need more of, it is IT". "All I need is time to concentrate – I do not need more distractions" "Videoconferencing? No, we need face-to-face meetings to clear up matters. The internet is not really suitable for that".

All the quotes above are from public employees. They represent a picture of the public sector as a unity of workers that will use any means to prevent direct digital contact with the users and citizens. Clearly, there are plenty of (policy) reports that argue in favor of more computers and web-services in the public administration. The main challenge is that certain (most?) workers and professional associations' perception is that certain types of public services cannot be digitalized.

Process description techniques enable us to make the activities and processes visible and decompress them. The process modeling literature is full of examples that take up the challenge to model the most critical processes. We acknowledge that not all processes are routine in nature. Yet, the challenge is to focus on the parts. For example, few would argue that public supported childcare or eldercare can be digitalized. Yet, in a Danish municipality, video conferencing is now enabling a virtual contact between parents and children and the personnel.

The second benefit from action II is to engage the public servant/ sector in discussions on which processes cannot be digitalized. Most often, the public sector has the advantage of selecting the processes that can be digitalized. The disadvantage of the approach is that institutional forces and inertia achieve a pole position. By contrast, the second action bullet will prompt a query in the public sector to argue which mix of the existing structures, actors and tasks cannot be digitalized.

The third benefit from action II is to break new grounds for interactions and learning. For example, within the financial section sector, education is performed through the application of IT in what has been now labeled e-learning environments. Similar examples addressing the public sector's use of IT for enhancing their capabilities at the core of their job are scarce.

We recommend abandoning all training during the day-time for public servants and replacing it with after-hours training, predominately through digital media. This would help increase time spent on core-activities and help increase the overall IT-competence level. Clearly this shift should be accompanied by appropriate pay schemes for increased competencies. Assuming 10% of the work time is spent on training, transferring this to after work hours would free financial resources that can be used to increase salaries. This would link the increase closely to increases in productivity that occurs as a result of the increased training after work hours.

2.3 Action III: Terminate all new IS applications that fail to benefit the customer, political decision-making and prioritizing

Geographical information systems, legislative systems, etc. form another important body of IS that might play a role in actual policy processes, but may also "live their own life". In the third action bullet, we enforce the focus on the analysis of the end user. Employees, consultants and analysts asked to address the benefits of IS point to the impacts of IS on such areas as internal administrative efficiency, effectiveness and improvement of information access and quality. Indeed, there have been important positive impacts of IS within these areas during the 1980s and 1990s (chapter 3).

The main challenge in action III is to address the benefits of the new IS for the end user. The end user is not the public employee who uses the new application. Rather, it is the *customer* who is the end target of the processes of which IS is an increasingly important part. Also, IS plays a legitimate role regarding input to decision-making, prioritizing, and implementation of policies with the use of economic models and various business intelligence systems.

The action starts by distributing the existing IS into three target groups: 1) direct customer contact, 2) inter/intra governmental organizations, and 3) your own department/ office. Our hypothesis is that we will find a distribution where 10% of the IS is oriented towards customers, 20% towards intragovernmental or intergovernmental communications, and 70% towards internal communication within the office.

This situation needs to be changed so that customer orientation accounts for 90% and internal communication, intragovernmental and intergovernmental communications account for 10%. IT is likely this will be met by strong reactions such as: "Do you want us to drop existing, well-functioning applications just for the mere sake of re-orienting the applications?"

The residual from action bullet three addresses what you do not want to keep. As long as the IS application has benefits only for the citizens/ user of the public services and/ or the policy processes, no further action is needed.

Otherwise, the IS application needs to be terminated. One of the IS-applications that is at death row is intranet.

Abandoning the intranet is clearly a controversial action. We do not argue that intranet cannot serve rational objectives. Indeed sharing of data within government and the ability to transform data from one person to another in a digital format and keeping these in digital format once stored, is a key feature and advantage of using intranet, data bases, and various ERP-systems. The danger is that the focus is being attributed to maintaining the intranet, that more energy is spent on defining boundaries than delivering services, and that the orientation of the activities is being instrumentalized in self-assuring routines that hardly, if ever, are transparent or involve customers.

Thus, abandoning the intranet helps to get the picture straight that inter- and intragovernmental IT-applications should be implemented and used only where there are customers and decision-makers initiating and benefiting from the use.

2.4   Action IV: Make a mini-survey in your office of your frequent business partners and external citizens/ users about which IT-tool oriented courses, if any, they have been attending and when during the past five years.

In action IV, we address the update cycle of the IS-capability. The first step in the fifth action-bullet is to ask your colleagues, including the managers, the following question: "When did you last participate in a formal IT-course?"

It is likely that you will be met by a total silence broken by one who claims that the general public managers and employees do not need hands-on courses on IT – that is meant for the IT-professionals. It is not the manager's job to program, but to manage and decide. The rest of the group will argue that they have learnt to work with IT by themselves with some help from colleagues when they needed specific assistance. The last time they attended a formal IT-course was when DOS and the associated program generation (WordPerfect, Lotus Symphony/ 1-2-3) were introduced.

A test of this hypothesis is to ask one of your colleagues to mail you a random word document of ten pages or more. The document should be created either by themselves or a small team. After receiving the document, assess whether any style sheet functions or post-electronic typewriter functionalities have been used – beyond digital storage and retrieval of the data.

Clearly, a few had training in transforming to the Windows platform, but the majority learned it by doing. Our hypothesis is that most employees never acquired the fundamentals of the programs. The consequence is that the potential of the program is not exploited to the full extent or even partially. In most cases, any consideration of the technology networked organization of activities will most likely be very costly due to inadequate and wrong use of the IS.

The training could be supported by digital communities of practice or local physical communities, peers etc. Yet we are not too confident that such communities exist within the public sector. Public servants use of SMS, chat, videoconferencing etc. is not encouraging. On top, their ability to share trivial applications are not at a level where there supports the transition towards the PPR. To blame for most of this is the massive lack of awareness regarding the necessity for equipping the citizens of the network society with the technical capacity to get going. The public sector has been particularly hurt by the neglecting of skills. This is due to two reasons; generous IT-budget where consultants have been charging the public sector for services that in most cases each individual should be able to learn in less than two hours. The second reason is that the public sector (in the cases where IT budgets are few or restricted), manage to progress anyhow due to regulations, etc. Thus the push to learn the basic of the networked activity work is limited from both financial and legal fronts.

2.5 Action V: Transit from perceiving customers and decisions as physical entities to view them as digital entities

The fifth key action is to focus on decision-makers and customers by perceiving the customers and decision-makers as digital entities with a physical presence, rather than the reverse.

The web-interfaces are by and large built along existing patterns of physical interaction assuming a contact between person A that works in office A in Department A. The customer 1 lives at address 1 in municipality 1. The communication between A.A.A and 1.1.1 can be replaced by activity orientation where other employees can take over if A.A.A is not in or not responding fast enough. The bottle-necks of the public sector can be resolved this way. In the social security and educational sector, these problems are massive and call for immediate action.

Yet, the action is not about changes to communication flows only, but about changes to the communication patterns. The new generation of customers use applications such as SMS, chat, and virtual collaboration technologies that alter the way communication take place. In an experiment we did, we asked public managers to undertake a chat session addressing the up-take of Internet in their work activities. The most striking thing is that the managers started by defining what they should deliver and in what format. There quickly emerged a "leader" of the discussions, and throughout the session they had stick-to-the-point argumentation style. Tragically the session did not came up with any usable input that could not be found at any standard consultancy report on Internet.

This chat behavior is a direct contrast to the younger generations that will not stick to the point, They will not have a leader of the pack, but they will be creative and less concerned about the writing style and the output documentation. We believe that this will set the standard for communication between the coming users of the public sector services.

2.6   Action VI: Please distribute the newly proposed IS in two groups: 1) functionalities that already are covered by existing IS and 2) IS that radically challenges the distribution of tasks and implementation of tasks.

The key challenge of the last action is the consideration of changes, and improvement versus rebuilding. Largely, this is a revolutionary task more than it is a matter of marginal changes.

The big change from the 1990s thinking on BPR is that in the 2000s the PPR-approach has advocated revolution in activities and at actor level, rather than at organizational and impersonal level. Thus, although management has a role to play in directing and impeding the revolution process, the real shift is where the changes initiate, materialize, impact, and are evaluated.

Introduction of home offices, process improvement across organizational boundaries, and implementation of open source are examples that most likely will challenge the existing organization of work radically. There is a need for ongoing evaluations of the existing applications and the infrastructure, and their efficacy. Yet, simple software updates and hardware replacements are examples of initiatives that are not likely to challenge the organization of work. E-procurement, new accounting software packages, and a new Intranet platform are examples of initiatives that may fall within both categories.

3. OUTLOOK FOR THE UPTAKE OF THE PPR-APPROACH

The PPR-approach clashed with conventional thinking and the six actions formulated in this chapter will certainly be provocative to most employees, decision-makers, consultants, and IT-suppliers. This provocation will hopefully initiate a debate of the PPR-approach and the validity of the picture painted in this book on the uptake of e-government applications. This debate will be a necessity for the ongoing refinement of the PPR-approach and its role as the key concept for building future generations of e-government applications.

The actions can also be met by the more practitioner approach that will initiate a debate and assist in preparing how the actions can be taken one step further in implementation. This will be equally welcomed.

References

Adler, M. D. and E. A. Posner (1999). "Rethinking Cost-Benefit Analysis." *The Yale Law Journal 109*(2): 165-247.

Ahmed, A. S., H. Z. Henriksen, K. V. Andersen, et al. (2004). *E-Government: The Pile of Research 1998-2003*. Copenhagen, Department of Informatics, Copenhagen Business School. Accessed February 15 2004 at *http://www.inf.cbs.dk*.

Akrich, M. (1994). The Description of Technical Objects. *Shaping Technology / Building Society: Studies in Sociotechnical Change*. W. E. Bijker and J. Law. Cambridge Ma, The MIT Press: 205-224.

Aldrich, D. (1998). "Partners on the Net: Fdlp Partnering to Coordinate Remote Access to Internet-Based Government Information." *Government Information Quarterly 15*(1): 27-38.

Allen, B. A., L. Juillet, G. Paquet, et al. (2001). "E-Governance & Government on-Line in Canada: Partnerships, People & Prospects." *Government Information Quarterly 18*(2): 93-104.

Allison, G. T. (1984). Public and Private Management: Are They Fundamentally Alike in All Unimportant Respects? *New Directions in Public Administration*. B. Bozeman and J. Straussman. Palo Alto, CA, Mayfield Publishing.

Andersen, K. V., N. Bjørn-Andersen and J. Dedrick (2003). "Governance Initiatives Creating a Demand-Driven E-Commerce Approach: The Case of Denmark." *Information Society 19*(1): 95-105.

Andersen, K. V. and J. N. Danziger (1995). "Information Technology and the Political World: The Impacts of It on Capabilities, Interactions, Orientations and Values." *International Journal of Public Administration 18*(11): 1693-1724.

Andersen, K. V., C. Greve and J. Torfing (1996). "Reorganizing the Danish Welfare State 1982-93: A Decade of Conservative Rule." *Scandinavian Studies, 68*(2): 161-187.

Andersen, K. V., H. Z. Henriksen, A. S. Ahmed, et al. (2004). *Stray Dogs and Wild Cats Tracking Information Systems in Government?* 12th European Conference on Information Systems, Turku, Finland.

Andersen, K. V. and N. C. Juul (2002). *Integration Af Data I De Danske Kommuner*. København, Institut for Informatik ved Handelshøjskolen i København. Accessed March 15 2004 at *http://www.inf.cbs.dk*.

Andersen, K. V., N. C. Juul, H. Z. Henriksen, et al. (2000). *Business-to-Business E-Commerce: Enterprises Facing a Turbulent World*. Copenhagen, DJOEF-publishers.

Andersen, K. V., N. C. Juul, S. Korzen-Bohr, et al. (2003). *Fractional Institutional Endeavors to Push E-Procurement within Local Government*. International Conference of Electronic Commerce, Bled, Slovenia.

Andersen, K. V., N. C. Juul and M. H. Larsen (2001). *Counting Digital Procurement Impacts on Governmental Operations Using the Civo-Vids Methodology*. Proceedings of The European Conference on e-Government (ECEG 2001), Trinity College Dublin, Ireland.

Andersen, K. V. and P. K. Madsen (1992). "Expelled from the Garden of Eden: The Politics of Economic Modeling in Denmark." *Information and the Public Sector 2*(3): 233-257.

Andersen, K. V. and H. W. Nicolajsen (2001). *Digital Strategies for Organizational Change*. European Conference on Information Systems (ECIS), Bled, Slovenia.

Andersen, K. V. and Y. Sekiguchi (1997). *Computers in Japanese Local Government*. International Conference of Information Systems (ICIS), Atlanta.

Arcieri, F., G. Melideo, E. Nardelli, et al. (2002). "A Reference Architecture for the Certification of E-Services in a Digital Government Infrastructure." *Distributed and Parallel Databases 12*(2-3): 217-234.

Argyris, C., R. Putnam and D. Smith (1985). *Action Science: Concepts, Methods and Skills for Research and Intervention*. San Francisco, CA, Jossey-Bass.

Armstrong, A. (2002). "E-Government Work Force Planning: A Pilot Study." *The Journal of Government Financial Management 51*(2): 32-35.

Arterton, F. C. (1988). "Political Participation and Teledemocracy." *Political Science and Politics XXI*(3): 620-327.

Ashbaugh, S. and R. Miranda (2002). "Technology for Human Sources Management: Seven Questions and Answers." *Public Personnel Management 31*(1): 7-20.

Australian-New-South-Wales-Government (2003). *Electronic Procurement Implementation Strategy*. Accessed January 14 2004 at *http://www.cpsc.nsw.gov.au/e-procurement/*.

Bank, W. (2001). *World Bank Electronic Government Procurement (Egp) Forum*. Accessed January 23 2003 at *http://wbln0018.worldbank.org/OCS/egovforum.nsf/*.

Bartle, J. R. and R. L. Korosec (2003). "A Review of State Procurement and Contracting." *Journal of Public Procurement 3*(2): 192-214.

Becker, H. and C. Slaton (2000). *The Future of Teledemocracy*. Westport, Connecticut, Praeger.

Bellamy, C. (2002). "From Automation to Knowledge Management: Modernizing British Government with Icts." *International Review of Administrative Sciences 68*: 213-230.

Bellamy, C. (2002). "From Automation to Knowledge Management: Modernizing British Government with Icts." *International Review of Administrative Sciences 68*(2): 213-230.

Bellamy, C., I. Horrocks and J. Webb (1995). "Exchanging Information with the Public: From One-Stop Shops to Community Information Systems." *Local Government Studies* 21(1): 11-30.

Bellamy, C. and J. Taylor (1998). *Governing in the Information Age*. Buckingham, Open University Press.

Bennett, C. and C. Raab (1997). "The Adequacy of Privacy: The European Union Data Protection Directive and the North American Response." *Information Society* 13(3): 245-263.

Best, J. D. (1997). *The Digital Organization*. New York, John Wiley & Sons.

Bijker, W. E. (1994). The Social Construction of Fluorescent Lighting, or How an Aircraft Was Invented in Its Diffusion Stage. *Shaping Technology / Building Society: Studies in Sociotechnical Change*. W. E. Bijker and J. Law. Cambridge Ma, The MIT Press: 75-102.

Bjerknes, G. and T. Bratteteig (1995). "User Participation and Democracy: A Discussion of Scandinavian Research on System Development." *Scandinavian Journal of Information Systems* 7(2): 73-98.

Boh, W. F. (2003). *Knowledge Sharing Mechanisms in Project-Based Knowledge Work: Codification Versus Personalization*. International Conference on Information Systems (ICIS), Seattle, WA.

Bolman, L. G. and T. E. Deal (1997). *Reframing Organizations: Artistry, Choice, and Leadership*. San Francisco, CA, Jossey-Bass.

Borins, S. (2002). "On the Frontiers of Electronic Governance: A Report on the United States and Canada." *International Review of Administrative Sciences* 68(2): 199-211.

Box, R. C. (1999). "Running Government Like a Business - Implications for Public Administration Theory and Practice." *American Review of Public Administration* 29(1): 19-43.

Bozemann, B. (1989). *All Institutions Are Public: Bridging Public and Private Organizational Theories*. San Francisco, Jossey-Bass Publishers.

Brent, R. J. (1996). *Applied Cost-Benefit Analysis*. Cheltenham, Edward Elgar.

Bretschneider, S. (2003). "Information Technology, E-Government, and Institutional Change." *Public Administration Review* 63(6): 738-744.

Brown, M. M. (1996). "An Empirical Assessment of the Hurdles to Geographic Information System Success in Local Government." *State and Local Government Review* 28(3): 193-204.

Browning, G. and A. C. Powel (2002). *Electronic Democracy: Using the Internet to Transform American Politics*, Cyberage Books.

Brudney, J. L. and M. M. Brown (1992). "Do Geographic Information Systems Meet Public Managers' Expectations?" *State and Local Government Review* 4(2): 84-90.

Brunsson, N. (2000). *The Irrational Organization: Irrationality as a Basis for Organizational Action and Change*. Copenhagen, Copenhagen Business School Press.

Brynjolfsson, E. and B. Kahin, Eds. (2000). *Understanding the Digital Economy*. Boston, MA, MIT Press.

Burn, J. and G. Robins (2003). "Moving Towards E-Government: A Case Study of Organisational Change Processes." *Logistics Information Management* 16(1): 25-35.

Bødker, K., F. Kensing and J. Simonsen (2000). *Professionelle It-Forundersøgelser - Grundlaget for Bæredygtige It-Anvendelser. Hvordan Undgås It-Skandaler?* København, Samfundslitteratur.

Cablenet (2002). *E-Procurement Goes National - up to a Threshold.* Accessed January 14 2004 at
   http://www.kablenet.com/kd.nsf/Frontpage/B375A78E42F53B8180256B4400416E F0?OpenDocument.

Cadel, J. and D. Yeates (2001). *Project Management for Information Systems.* London, Prentice Hall, Financial Times Management.

Carbone, J. (2000). "Web, Outsourcing Revolutionize Buying." *Purchasing 129*(3): 50-62.

Carlitz, R. D. and R. W. Gunn (2002). "Online Rulemaking: A Step toward E-Governance." *Government Information Quarterly 19*(4): 389-405.

Castells, M. (2000). "Materials for an Exploratory Theory of the Network Society." *British Journal of Sociology 5*(1): 5-24.

Caudle, S. L. (1995). *Reengineering for Results: Update.* Washington, D.C, Alliance for Reinventing Government, National Academy of Public Administration Foundation.

Chadwick, A. and C. May (2003). "Interaction between States and Citizens in the Age of the Internet: "E-Government" in the United States, Britain, and the European Union." *Governance-an International Journal of Policy and Administration 16*(2): 271-300.

Chaffey, D. (2002). *E-Business and E-Commerce Management: Strategy, Implementation and Practice.* London, Prentice Hall, Financial Times.

Champy, J. (1995). *Reengineering Management. The Mandate for New Leadership.* New York, Harper Collins.

Champy, J. (2002). "Seven Steps to X-Engineering." *Executive Excellence 19*(6): 15-16.

Champy, J. (2002). *X-Engineering the Corporation: Reinvent Your Business in the Digital Age.* London, Hodder & Stroughton.

Chen, Y. C. and J. Gant (2001). "Transforming Local E-Government Services: The Use of Application Service Providers." *Government Information Quarterly 18*(4): 343-355.

Choi, S.-Y. and A. B. Whinston (2000). *The Internet Economy: Technology and Practice.* Austin, TX, SmartEcon Publishing.

Ciment, M. (2003). "A Personal History of the Nsf Digital Government Program." *Communications of the ACM 46*(1): 69-70.

Clarke, R. (1995). "Computer Matching by Government Agencies: The Failure of Cost/Benefit Analysis as a Control Mechanism." *Information Infrastructure & Policy 4*(1): 29-65.

Clement, A. (1994). "Computing at Work: Empowering Action by "Low-Level Users."" *Communications of the ACM 37*(1): 52-63.

Coase, R. H. (1937). "The Nature of the Firm." *Economica 16*: 386-405.

Coase, R. H. (1960). "The Problem of Social Cost." *Journal of Law and Economics 3*: 1-44.

Commission, E. (2002). *Eeurope 2002 - Accelerating E-Commerce.* Brussels, European Commission. Accessed January 14 2004 at *http://europa.eu.int.*

Congress., U. (2001). *E-Government Bill.* Accessed October 5 2002 at *http://www.senate.gov/%7Egov_affairs/leginfo.htm.*

Coombs, R. and R. Hull (1996). The Politics of It Strategy and Development in Organizations. *Information and Communication Technologies: Visions and Realities*. H. D. William. Oxford, Oxford University Press.

Council-for-Excellence-in-Government (2001). *E-Government: The Next American Revolution*. Washington, DC, Council of Excellence in Government.

Cresswell, A. M. and T. A. Pardo (2001). "Implications of Legal and Organizational Issues for Urban Digital Government Development." *Government Information Quarterly* 18(4): 269-278.

Croom, S. (2001). "Restructuring Supply Chains through Information Channel Innovation." *International Journal of Operations & Production Management* 21(4): 504.

CTG (2004). *E-Government - a Practical and Enduring Definition*. Albany, NY. Accessed January 13 2004 at *http://www.ctg.albany.edu/publications/newsletters/innovations_2003_winterspring ?chapter=9)*.

Currie, W. and R. Galliers, Eds. (1999). *Rethinking Management Information Systems: An Interdisciplinary Perspective*. Oxford, Oxford University Press.

Danish-Board-of-Technology (2001). *Experiences from National It-Projects: How Can It Be Done in a Better Way?* Copenhagen, Danish Board of Technology. Accessed March 15 2004 at *http://www.tekno.dk*.

Danziger, J. N. (1986). "Computing and the Political World." *Computers and the Social Sciences 2*: 183-200.

Danziger, J. N. and K. V. Andersen (2002). "Impacts of It on Politics and the Public Sector: Methodological, Epistemological, and Substantive Evidence from the "Golden Age" of Transformation." *International Journal of Public Administration 25*(5): 591-627.

Danziger, J. N. and K. L. Kraemer (1986). *People and Computers: The Impacts of Computers on End Users in Organizations*. New York, Columbia University Press.

Danziger, J. N., K. L. Kraemer and W. H. Dutton (1982). *Computers and Politics: High Technology in American Local Government*. New York, Columbia University Press.

Davenport, T. and J. E. Short (1990). "The New Industrial Engineering: Information Technology and Business Process Redesign." *Sloan Management Review. 31*(4): 11-27.

Davenport, T. H. (1993). *Process Innovation: Reengineering Work through Information Technology*. Boston, MA, Harvard Business School Press.

Davenport, T. H. and D. B. Stoddard (1994). "Reengineering: Business Change of Mythic Proportions." *MIS Quarterly 18*(2): 121-128.

Davidow, W. H. and M. S. Malone (1992). *The Virtual Corporation*. New York, Harper Collins.

De Haan, J. J. and K. v. Mol (1999). "Soft-Investments Appraisal Cost-Benefit Analysis of the Implementation of Work Groups as an Example." *International Journal of Operations & Production Management 19*(1): 38-55.

De Haan, J. J. and R. Peters (1989). Cost Benefit Analysis of the Introduction of the Computer Aided Production Technologies. *Management and New Production Systems*. K. Ferdows and C. Karlsson. Fontainebleau, INSEAD: 179-200.

De Haan, J. J. and N. Terra (1988). *Baten De Kosten? En Bedrijfseconomische Waardring Can Arbejdsplaatsverbetering*. Amsterdam, NIA.

Deb, G. K. (1999). "Electronic Governance - a Vehicle for the New World Order." *Electronics Information & Planning 27*(1): 29-33.

Demsey, J., R. E. Dvorak, E. Holen, et al. (1998). "A Hard and Soft Look at It Investments." *The McKinsey Quarterly*(1): 127-137.

Devadoss, P. R., S. L. Pan and J. C. Huang (2003). "Structurational Analysis of E-Government Initiatives: A Case Study of Sco." *Decision Support Systems 34*(3): 253-269.

DMITAR (1994). *Infosociety 2000*. Copenhagen, Danish Ministry of Information Technology and Research.

DMITAR (1997). *Information Technology in Danish Government*. Copenhagen, Danish Ministry of Information Technology and Research.

Donk, Snellen and Tops (1995). *Orwell in Athens. A Perspective on Informatization and Democracy*. Amsterdam, IOS Press.

Doty, P. and S. Erdelez (2002). "Information Micro-Practices in Texas Rural Courts: Methods and Issues for E-Government." *Government Information Quarterly 19*(4): 369-387.

Downs, A. (1967). *Inside Bureaucracy*. New York, Harper Collins Publisher.

Drucker, P. (1994). Introduction. *Techno Vision*. C. B. Wang. New York, McGraw-Hill.

Ducatel, K. (1994). "Transactional Telematics in the City." *Local Government Studies 20*(1): 60-77.

Dulio, D. A., D. L. Goff and J. A. Thurber (1999). "Untangled Web: Internet Use During the 1998 Election." *Political Science*: 53-59.

Dunkle, D. E., J. L. King, J. N. Perry, et al. (1994). "Personal Computers and the "Democratization" of Computing in Us City Governments." *Information and the Public Sector 3*(2): 115-133.

Dunlop, C. and R. Kling, Eds. (1991). *Computerization and Controversy: Value Conflicts and Social Choices*. San Diego, CA, Academic Press, Inc.

Dutton, W. H. and K. Guthrie (1991). "An Ecology of Games: The Political Construction of Santa Monica's Public Electronic Network." *Information and the Public Sector 1*(4): 279-301.

Dutton, W. H. and K. L. Kraemer (1985). *Modeling as Negotiating: The Political Dynamics of Computer Models in the Policy Process*. Norwood, NJ, Ablex.

Dutton, W. H. and M. Peltu, Eds. (1996). *Information and Communication Technologies*. Oxford, Oxford University Press.

Dyerson, R. and M. Roper (1991). "Managing Change in Britain: It Implementation in the Department of Social Security and the Inland Revenue." *Information and the Public Sector 1*(4): 303-328.

Earl, M., Ed. (1998). *Information Management: The Organizational Dimension*. Oxford, Oxford University Press.

Earl, M. J. (1999). *Management Strategies for Information Technology*. London, Prentice Hall.

Earl, M. J. (2004). Prototypes Are Not Pilots (and Vice Versa): Reflecting on a 25 Year Old Idea. *The Past and Future of Information Systems*. K. V. Andersen and M. T. Vendelø. Oxford, Elsevier: 7-12.

Easton, D. (1965). *A Systems Analysis of Political Life.* New York, John Wiley & Sons.

efokus (2003). *Baggrundsmateriale - Doip.* Accessed March 1 2004 at *http://www.efokus.dk.*

Engeström, Y., R. Engeström and T. Vähäaho (1999). When the Center Does Not Hold: The Importance of Knotworking. *Activity Theory and Social Practice: Cultural-Historical Approaches.* S. Chailkin, M. Hedegaard and U. J. Jensen. Aarhus, Aarhus University Press.

EPA (2003). *Greening Federal E-Procurement. Epa Region 1/2/3 Greening the Government Conference June 5, 2003.* Accessed at *http://www.newmoa.org/Newmoa/htdocs/prevention/greengovconf/presentations/el wood.pdf.*

EU (1993). *Directive 93/36 of June 14th, 1993.* Brussels, European Commission. Accessed March 15 2004 at *http://europa.eu.int.*

EU (2003). The Role of Egovernment for Europe's Future. Brussels, European Commission.

EU (2004). *Public Procurement in the European Union.* Brussels, European Commission. Accessed at *http://europa.eu.int/business/en/topics/publicproc/.*

Farbey, B., F. Land and D. Targett (1999). "The Moving Staircase: Problems of Appraisal and Evaluation in a Turbulent Environment." *Information Technology and People* *12*(3): 238-49.

Farnham, D. and S. Horton, Eds. (1996). *Managing the New Public Services.* London, MacMillan Ltd.

Faucheux, C. (1997). "How Virtual Organizing Is Transforming Management Science." *Communications of the ACM 40*(9): 50-55.

Ferlie, E., A. Pettigrew, L. Ashburner, et al. (1996). *The New Public Management in Action.* Oxford, Oxford University Press.

Fischer, R. J. (1994). "An Overview of Performance Management." *Public Management* *76*(9): 82-88.

Fitzgerald, B. and D. Howcroft (1998). "Towards Dissolution of the Is Research Debate: From Polarisation to Polarity." *Journal of Information Technology 13*(4): 313-326.

Fitzgerald, B. and T. Kenny (2003). *Open Source Software in the Trenches: Lessons from a Large-Scale Oss Implementation.* International Conference on Information Systems (ICIS), Seattle, WA.

Fletcher, P. D. (2003). "The Government Paperwork Elimination Act: Operating Instructions for an Electronic Government." *International Journal of Public Administration* *25*(5): 723-736.

Frenkel, K. A. (1988). "Computers and Elections." *Communications of the ACM 31*(10): 1176-1183.

Gallie, W. B. (1956). "Essentially Contested Concepts." *Proceedings of the Aristotelian Society 51*: 167-198.

Garson, G. D. (1992). "Implementing Computer Modeling in State Government: A Human Resource Information System Focus." *State and Local Government Review 24*(2): 77-83.

Gibbs, J., K. L. Kraemer and J. Dedrick (2003). "Environment and Policy Factors Shaping Global E-Commerce Diffusion: A Cross-Country Comparison." *Information Society* *19*(1): 5-18.

Giddens, A. (1990). *The Consequences of Modernity.* Cambridge, Polity Press.

Giesbers, J. (2001). *Baan Experiences*. 14th Bled Electronic Commerce Conference, Slovenia.

Goerdeler, A. (2003). Electronic Public Procurement in Germany. *Business Briefing: Global Purchasing & Supply Chain Strategies*.

Golubchik, L., W. C. Cheng, C. F. Chou, et al. (2003). "Bistro - a Scalable and Secure Data Transfer Service for Digital Government Applications." *Communications of the Acm 46*(1): 50-51.

Grantham, C. E. (1999). *The Future of Work: The Promise of the New Digital Work Society*, McGraw-Hill Professional Publishing.

Gregor, S. and R. B. Johnston (2001). *Theory of Interorganizational Systems: Industry Structure and Processes of Change*. Proceedings of the 34th Hawaii International Conference on Systems Sciences (HICSS).

Greiner, L. E. and V. E. Schein (1989). *Power and Organization Development: Mobilizing Power to Implement Change*. Reading, MA, Addison-Wesley.

Grossman, L. K. (1995). *The Electronic Republic: Reshaping Democracy in the Information Age*. New York, Viking.

Grupe, F. H. (1995). "Commercializing Public Information: A Critical Issue for Governmental Is Professionals." *Information and Management 28*(4): 229-241.

Grönlund, Å. (2000). *Managing Electronic Services: A Public Sector Perspective*. London, Springer.

Grönlund, Å. (2003). "Emerging Electronic Infrastructures - Exploring Democratic Components." *Social Science Computer Review 21*(1): 55-72.

Grönlund, Å. (2004). State of the Art in E-Gov Research - a Survey. *First Scandinavian Workshop on E-Government*. Örebro, Örebro University.

Gurbaxani, V. and S. Whang (1991). "The Impact of Information Systems on Organizations and Markets." *Communications of the ACM 34*(1): 59-73.

Ham, C. and M. Hill (1993). *The Policy Process in the Modern Capitalist State*. New York, Wheatsheaf Books.

Hamilton, S. and N. Chervany (1981). "Evaluating Information Systems Effectiveness: Comparing Evaluation Approaches." *MIS Quarterly 5*(3): 55-69.

Hammer, M. (1990). "Reengineering Work. Don't Automate, Obliterate." *Harvard Business Review 90*: 104-112.

Hammer, M. (1996). *Beyond Reengineering*. London, Harper Collins.

Hammer, M. and J. Champy (1993). *Reengineering the Corporation: A Manifesto for Business Revolution*. New York, HarperCollins Publishers.

Hammer, M. and S. A. Stanton (1995). *The Reengineering Revolution*. New York, Harper Collins.

Hanseth, O. and K. Braa (1999). Hunting for the Treasure at the End of the Rainbow: Standardizing Corporate It Infrastructure. *New Information Technologies in Organizational Processes*. O. K. Ngwenyama, L. Introna, M. Myers and J. I. DeGross. Amsterdam, Kluwer Academic Publishers: 121-140.

Haque, M. S. (2002). "E-Governance." *International Review of Administrative Sciences 68*: 231-250.

Hax, A. and D. L. Wilde II (1999). "A Delta Model: Adaptive Management for a Changing World." *Sloan Management Review 40*(2): 11-28.

Hedberg, B., G. Dahlgren, J. Hansson, et al. (1997). *Virtual Organizations and Beyond: Discover Imaginary Systems*. New York, John Wiley & Sons.

Hedberg, B., G. Dahlgren, J. Hansson, et al. (1998). *Virtual Organizations and Beyond: Discover Imaginary Systems*. New York, Wiley Series in Practical Strategy.

Heeks, R., Ed. (1999). *Reinventing Government in the Information Age: International Practice in It-Enabled Public Sector Reform*. London, Routledge.

Henry, J. W. and R. W. Stone (1994). "Computer Self-Efficacy and Outcome Expectancy: The Effects on the End-User's Job Satisfaction." *Computer Personnel 16*(4): 15-34.

Heptinstal, D. (2001). "The Mutual Benefits of Involvement." *Working with Older People 5*: 24-26.

Hepworth, M. E. (1992). "The Municipal Information Economy?" *Local Government Studies 18*(3): 148-157.

Hertzum, M. (1995). "Computer Support for Document Management in the Danish Central Government." *Information Infrastructure & Policy 4*(2): 107-129.

Hirschman, A. O. (1970). *Exit, Voice, and Loyality: Responses to Decline in Firms, Organizations, and States*. Cambridge, MA, Harvard University Press.

Hoff, J. (1992). "Evaluation of Information Technology in Private and Public Sector Contexts." *Informatization and the Public Sector. 2*(4): 307-328.

Hoff, J. (2002). "Demokratiforestillinger Og Magt I Informationssamfundet." *GRUS*(66): 34-55.

Hoff, J., I. Horrocks and P. Tops, Eds. (1999). *Democratic Governance and New Technology*. London, Routledge.

Hoff, J. and K. Stormgaard (1991). "Information Technology between Citizen and Administration." *Information and the Public Sector 1*(3): 213-235.

Holmes, D., Ed. (1997). *Virtual Politics: Identity and Community in Cyberspace*. London, Sage Publications.

Holmes, D. (2001). *E-Gov: E-Business Strategies for Government*. London, Nicholas Brealey Publishing.

Honig, B. and J. Lampel (2000). "Interorganizational Entrepreneurship in a Global Arena." *International Journal of Organizational Analysis 8*(4): 343-363.

Hovy, E. (2003). "Using an Ontology to Simplify Data Access." *Communications of the ACM 46*(1): 47-.

Hutton, G. (1996). *Business Process Reengineering: A Public Sector View*. New York, John Wiley & Sons.

IAB (1999). Integrated Service Delivery: Governments Using Technology to Serve the Citizen International, Federal, State, and Local Government Experiences. Washington, D.C., USA., Intergovernmental Advisory Board.

Ingelstam, L. and I. Palmlund (1991). "Computers and People in the Welfare State: Information Technology and Social Security in Sweden." *Informatization and the Public Sector. 1*(2): 5-20.

Intel (2003). *Moore's Law*. Accessed January 31 2004 at *http://www.intel.com/research/silicon/mooreslaw.htm*.

Ireland, G. o. (2003). *Public Sector Procurement Opportunities*. Accessed January 10 2003 at *http://www.etenders.gov.ie*.

ITU (2001). *Yearbook of Statistics 1991-2000*. Genève, International Telecommunication Union.

Jaeger, P. T. (2002). "Constitutional Principles and E-Government: An Opinion About Possible Effects of Federalism and the Separation of Powers on E-Government Policies." *Government Information Quarterly 19*(4): 357-368.

Jensen, C. B. (2000). Press Release. Holstebro, Association of Procurement Managers.

Jones, D. S. (2002). "Procurement Practices in the Singapore Civil Service: Balancing Control and Delegation." *Journal of Public Procurement 2*(1): 29-53.

Juan, F. M. M. (2002). "Expert Meeting on the Context of the Study on Trans Border Public Procurement." *Presentation*.

Kaneda, T. (1994). "Informatization Experience of Japanese City Governments During the 1980s: The Period When the Widespread Use of Personal Computers Forced City Governments to Change Their Information Processing." *Informatization and the Public Sector. 3*(2): 149-161.

Kaplan, S. and M. Sawhney (2000). "E-Hubs: The New B2b Marketplaces." *Harvard Business Review*(May-June): 97-103.

Kheng, C. B. and S. Al-Hawamdeh (2002). "The Adoption of Electronic Procurement in Singapore." *Electronic Commerce Research, 2*(1): 61-73.

King, J. L. (1983). "Centralized Versus Decentralized Computing: Organizational Considerations and Management Options." *Computing Surveys 15*(4): 319-349.

King, J. L., V. Gurbaxani, K. L. Kraemer, et al. (1994). "Institutional Factors in Information Technology Innovation." *Information Systems Research 5*: 139-169.

King, J. L. and K. L. Kraemer (1984). " Evolution and Organizational Information Systems:An Assessment of Nolan's Stage Model." *Communications of the ACM 27*(5): 466-475.

King, W. R. (2002). "It Capabilities, Business Processes, and Impact on the Bottom Line." *Information Systems Management 19*(2): 85-87.

Kjerstad, E. and S. Vagstad (2000). "Procurement Auctions with Entry of Bidders." *International Journal of Industry Organization 18*(8): 1243-1257.

Klausen, K. C. (2000). *Leadership and Management: Roles and Styles among Local Government Ceos*. IPMN conference at the MGSM, Macquire University, Sydney, Australia.

Kling, R. (1996). *Computerization and Controversy: Value Conflicts and Social Choices*. San Diego, Academic Press.

Kling, R. and R. Lamb (1999). *It and Organizational Change in Digital Economies: A Socio-Technical Perspective*. Washington, DC, Department of Commerce.

KMD (2001). *Valgresultater*. Accessed December 16 2001 at *http://www.kmdvalg.dk*.

Knudsen, L. K., T. Larsen and N. J. M. Pedersen (2002). *Den Offentlige Sektor (the Public Sector)*. Copenhagen, Copenhagen Business School Press.

Kock, N. (2000). "Benefits for Virtual Organizations from Distributed Groups." *Communications of the ACM 43*(11): 107-112.

Koga, T. (2003). "Access to Government Information in Japan: A Long Way toward Electronic Government?" *Government Information Quarterly 20*(1): 47-62.

Koh, C. E. and V. R. Prybutok (2003). "The Three Ring Model and Development of an Instrument for Measuring Dimensions of E-Government Functions." *Journal of Computer Information Systems 43*(3): 34-39.

KPMG (2000). Analyse Af Statslige Indkøb [Procurement in Central Government]. Copenhagen, Ministry of Research and Information Technology.

Kraemer, K. L., K. V. Andersen and J. L. Perry (1995). "Information Technology and Transitions in the Public Service: A Comparison of Scandinavia and the United States." *International Journal of Public Administration 17*(10): 1871-1905.

Kraemer, K. L., J. N. Danziger, D. E. Dunkle, et al. (1993). "The Usefulness of Computer-Based Information to Public Manager." *MIS Quarterly 17*(2): 129-148.

Kraemer, K. L., W. Mitchell, M. Weiner, et al. (1974). *Integrated Municipal Information Systems*. New York, Praeger.

Kraljic, P. (1983). "Purchasing Must Become Supply Management." *Harvard Business Review 61*(5): 109-117.

Kraut, R., S. Dumais and S. Koch (1989). "Computerization, Productivity, and Quality of Work-Life." *Communications of the ACM 32*(2): 220-238.

Lai, V. S. and J. L. Guynes (1997). "An Assessment of the Influence of Organizational Characteristics on Information Technology Adoption Decision: A Discriminative Approach." *IEEE Transactions on Engineering Management 44*: 146-157.

Lamb, R. (2002). *Intranet Boundaries: Social Actors and Systems Integration*. 15th Bled Electronic Commerce Conference, Bled, Slovenia.

Lamb, R. and E. Davidson (2002). *Social Scientists: Managing Identity in Socio-Technical Networks*. Thirty-fifth Annual Hawaii International Conference on Systems Sciences, Kona-Kailua, Hawaii.

Lamb, R. and R. Kling (2003). "Reconceptualizing Users as Social Actors in Information Systems Research." *MIS Quarterly 27*(2): 197-235.

Lambrinoudakis, C., S. Gritzalis, F. Dridi, et al. (2003). "Security Requirements for E-Government Services: A Methodological Approach for Developing a Common Pki-Based Security Policy." *Computer Communications 26*(16): 1873-1883.

Landman, T. (2002). *Map-Making and Analysis of the Main International Initiatives on Developing Indicators on Democracy and Good Governance*. Paris, OECD. Accessed December 7 2003 at *http://www.oecd.org/dataoecd/0/28/20755719.pdf*.

Lane, J.-E. (2000). *New Public Management: An Introduction*. London, Routledge.

Laswell, H. (1936). *Who Gets What, When, How*. New York, Whittlesey House.

Laudon, K. L. and J. P. Laudon (2000). *Management Information Systems: Organization and Technology in the Networked Enterprise*. Upper Saddle River, NJ, Prentice Hall.

Layne, K. and J. W. Lee (2001). "Developing Fully Functional E-Government: A Four Stage Model." *Government Information Quarterly 18*(2): 122-136.

Leavitt, H. (1970). Applied Organizational Change in Industry: Structural, Technological and Human Approaches. *Management and Motivation*. V. H. Vroom and E. L. Deci. Middlesex, Pinguin.

Lee, M. and L. F. Cunningham (2001). "A Cost/Benefit Approach to Understanding Service Loyalty." *The Journal of Services Marketing. 15*(2): 113-133.

Leizerov, S. (2000). "Privacy Advocacy Groups Versus Intel: A Case Study of How Social Movements Are Tactically Using the Internet to Fight Corporations." *Social Science Computer Review 18*(4): 461-483.

Lenk, K. (2002). "Electronic Service Delivery: A Driver of Public Sector Modernisation." *Information Polity 7*(2-3): 87-96.

Liao, S. H., C. H. Cheng, W. B. Liao, et al. (2003). "A Web-Based Architecture for Implementing Electronic Procurement in Military Organisations." *Technovation 23*(6): 521-532.

Lipnack, J. and J. Stamps (1997). *Virtual Teams: Reaching across Space, Time, and Organizations with Technology.* New York, John Wiley & Sons, Inc.

Lowry, P. B., C. C. Albrecht, J. F. Nunamaker, et al. (2003). "Evolutionary Development and Research on Internet-Based Collaborative Writing Tools and Processes to Enhance Ewriting in an Egovernment Setting." *Decision Support Systems 34*(3): 229-252.

Lucas, H. C. (1996). *The T-Form Organization: Using Technology to Design Organizations for the 21st Century.* San Francisco, CA, Jossey-Bass Publishers.

Luling, D. (2001). "Taking It Online: Anyway, Anyplace, Anytime...Tennessee Anytime." *The Journal of Government Financial Management 50*(2): 42.

MacIntosh, R. (2003). "Bpr: Alive and Well in the Public Sector." *International Journal of Operations & Production Management 23*(3): 327-344.

Maira, A. and P. Scott-Morgan (1997). *The Accelerating Organization: Embracing the Human Face of Change.* New York, McGraw-Hill.

Malone, T. W., J. Yates and R. I. Benjamin (1987). "Electronic Markets and Electronic Hierarchies." *Communications of the ACM*: 484-497.

Mann, C., L., S. E. Eckert and S. C. Knight (2000). *Global Electronic Commerce: A Policy Primer.* Washington, DC, Institute for International Economics.

Marche, S. and J. D. McNiven (2003). "E-Government and E-Governance: The Future Isn't What It Used to Be." *Canadian Journal of Administrative Sciences-Revue Canadienne Des Sciences De L Administration 20*(1): 74-86.

Marcus, L. (1983). "Power, Politics, and Mis Implementation." *Communications of the ACM 26*(6): 430-444.

Markus, L. and D. Robey (1988). "Information Technology and Organizational Change: Causal Structure in Theory and Research." *Management Science 34*(5): 583-598.

Masetti, B. and R. W. Zmud (1996). "Measuring the Extent of Edi Usage in Complex Organizations: Strategies and Illustrative Examples." *MIS Quarterly 20*(3): 331-345.

McAdam, R. a. D., J. (1999). "Business Process Reengineering in the Public Sector: A Study of Staff Perceptions and Critical Success Factors." *Business Process Management Journal 5*(1): 33-52.

McCue, C. P. and J. T. Pitzer (2000). "Centralized Vs. Decentralized Purchasing: Current Trends in Governmental Procurement Practices." *Journal of Public Budgeting, Accounting, and Financial Management 12*(3): 400-421.

McDonald, J. F. (2001). "Cost-Benefit Analysis of Local Land Use Allocation Decisions." *Journal of Regional Science 41*(2): 277-299.

McFarlan, F. W. (1991). Information Technology Changes the Way You Compete. *Strategy: Seeking and Securing Competitive Advantage.* C. A. Montgomery and M. E. Porter. Boston, MA, Harvard Business Review Book: 77-88.

McHenry, W. K. (2003). "Using Knowledge Management to Reform the Russian Criminal Procedural Codex." *Decision Support Systems 34*(3): 339-357.

McNeal, R. S., C. J. Tolbert, K. Mossberger, et al. (2003). "Innovating in Digital Government in the American States." *Social Science Quarterly 84*(1): 52-70.

Micheletti, M. (2000). "End of Big Government: Is It Happening in the Nordic Countries?" *Governance-an International Journal of Policy and Administration 13*(2): 265-278.

Miewald, R. D. and K. J. Mueller (1987). "The Use of Information Technology in Oversight by State Legislatures." *State and Local Government Review Winter*: 22-28.

Millard, J. (2003). "The (R)E-Balancing of Government." *UPGRADE IV*(2): 48-51.

Mintzberg, H. (1979). *The Structuring of Organizations.* Englewood Cliffs, NJ, Prentice Hall.

Mintzberg, H. (1998). *Mintzberg on Management: Inside Our Strange World of Organizations.* New York, The Free Press.

Mishan, E. J. (1971). *Cost-Benefit Analysis.* London, Allen and Unwin.

Mitchell, K. (2000). "Instituting E-Procurement in the Public Sector." *Public Management 82*(11): 21-25.

Moreton, R. and M. Chester (1996). *Transforming the Business: The It Contribution.* London, McGraw Hill.

Mowshowitz, A. (1997). "Virtual Organization." *Communications of the ACM 40*(9): 30-37.

Myers, M., G. Paré and C. Urquhart (2000). *Three Perspectives: If Markus' 1983 Classic Study, "Power, Politics, and Implementation" Were Being Reviewed Today.* International Conference on Information Systems, Brisbane.

Negroponte, N. (1995). *Being Digital.* London, Hodder and Stoughton.

NIGP (1996). National Association of State Purchasing Officials/National Association of State Information Resource Executives Joint Force on Information Technology and Procurement Reform.

Nolan, R. L. (1979). "Managing the Crises in Data Processing." *Harvard Business Review 52*(7): 115-126.

Nolan, R. L. and C. Gibson (1974). "Managing the Four Stages of Edp Growth." *Harvard Business Review 52*(1): 76-88.

Nolan, T. V., K. A. Jarema and J. Austin (1999). "An Objective Review of the Journal of Organizational Behavior Management: 1987-1997." *Journal of Organizational Behaviour Management 19*(3): 83-114.

Norris, D. F. (1989). "High Tech in City Hall: Uses and Effects of Microcomputers in United States Local Governments." *Social Science Computer Review 7*(2): 137-146.

Norris, D. F. (1992). "Gender, Job, and Effects of Microcomputers in Public Organizations." *State and Local Government Review 24*(2): 65-70.

North, D. C. (1981). *Structure and Change in Economic History.* New York, Norton.

Northrop, A., D. E. Dunkle, K. L. Kraemer, et al. (1994). "Computers, Police, and the Fight against Crime." *Information and the Public Sector 3*(1): 21-45.

Northrop, A., K. L. Kraemer, D. E. Dunkle, et al. (1990). "Payoffs from Computerization: Lessons over Time." *Public Administration Review 50*(5): 505-514.

Notess, G. R. (2000). *Finding Online Government Publications.* Accessed March 2 2004 at *http://notess.com/write/archive/200006ww.html.*

Noy, E. (1999). "There Are Profits in Your Management Control Systems." *Management Auditing Journal 14*(7): 363-367.

OECD (1995). *Governance in Transition: Public Management Reforms in Oecd Countries.* Paris, OECD. Accessed March 15 2004 at *http://www.oecd.org.*

OECD (2000). *Oecd Information Technology Outlook - Icts, E-Commerce and the Information Economy.* Paris, OECD. Accessed March 15 2004 at *http://www.oecd.org.*

OECD (2003). *The E-Government Imperative.* Paris, OECD. Accessed March 15 2004 at *http://www.oecd.org.*

O'Looney, J. (1997). *Beyond Maps: Gis and Decision Making in Local Government.* Washington, DC, ICMA.

Olson, M. (1965). *The Logic of Collective Action, Public Goods and the Theory of Groups.* Boston, MA, Harvard University Press.

Oravec, J. A. (1996). *Virtual Individuals, Virtual Groups.* New York, Cambridge University Press.

Orlikowski, W. J. and C. S. Iacono (2000). The Truth Is Not out There: An Enacted View of the "Digital Economy". *Understanding the Digital Economy.* E. Brynjolfsson and B. Kahin. Boston, MA, MIT Press.

Orlikowsky, W. J. (1996). "Improvising Organizational Transformation over Time: A Situated Change Perspective." *Information Systems Research 7*(1): 63-92.

Osborne, D. and T. Gaebler (1992). *Reinventing Government:: How the Entrepreneurial Spirit Is Transforming the Public Sector.* New York, The Penguin Group.

O'Sullvan, L. and J. M. Geringer (1993). "Harnessing the Power of Your Value Chain." *Long Range Planning 26*(2): 59-68.

Overman, E. S. and D. T. Loraine (1994). "Information for Control: Another Management Proverb?" *Public Administration Review 54*(2): 193-196.

Parker, B. (2003). "Maori Access to Information Technology." *Electronic Library 21*(5): 456-460.

Pedersen, M. K., M. H. Larsen and C. Berntsen (2002). *Contested Hegemony: The Demise of Industrial Economics in Information Systems Analyses?* 25th IRIS Conference, Kulhuse.

Peled, A. (2001). "Centralization or Diffusion? Two Tales of Online Government." *Administration & Society 32*(6): 686-709.

Pfeffer, J. (1997). *Managing with Power: Politics and Influence in Organizations.* Harvard, HA, Harvard Business School Press.

Piccoli, G. and B. Ives (2000). *Virtual Teams: Managerial Behavior Control's Impact on Team Effectiveness.* International Conference on Information Systems, Brisbane, Australia.

PLS-Rambøll-Management (2000). *It I Praksis.* Copenhagen, PLS Rambøll Management. Accessed May 10 2003 at *http://www.pls.dk.*

PLS-Rambøll-Management (2001). *It I Praksis.* Copenhagen, PLS Rambøll Management. Accessed May 10 2003 at *http://www.pls.dk.*

PLS-Rambøll-Management (2002). *It I Praksis*. Copenhagen, PLS Rambøll Management. Accessed May 10 2003 at *http://www.pls.dk*.

Polanyi, M. (1958). *Personal Knowledge*. London, Routledge.

Porter, M. E. (1985). *Competitive Advantages*. New York, Free Press.

Porter, M. E. (2001). "Strategy and the Internet." *Harvard Business Review*(March): 61-78.

Potter, A. (2002). "Accessibility of Alabama Government Web Sites." *Journal of Government Information 29*(5): 303-317.

Remenyi, D. (2002). *The Value Scorecard: Beyond the Business Case*. European Conference on Information Technology Evaluation (ECITE), Paris.

Remenyi, D. and A. Money (1995). *The Effective Measurement and Management of It Costs and Benefits*. Lounghborough, Butterworth-Heinemann.

Rodan, G. (1998). "The Internet and Political Control in Singapore." *Political Science Quarterly 113*(1): 63-89.

Salem, J. A. (2003). "Public and Private Sector Interests in E-Government: A Look at the Doe's Pubscience." *Government Information Quarterly 20*(1): 13-27.

Saltman, R. G. (1988). "Accuracy, Integrity and Security in Computerized Vote-Tallying." *Communications of the ACM 31*(10): 1184-1191.

Saunders, M. (1997). *Strategic Purchasing and Supply Chain Management*. London, Pitman Publishing.

Scacchi, W. (2001). "Redesigning Contracted Service Procurement for Internet-Based Electronic Commerce: A Case Study." *Information Technology and Management 2*(3): 3131-3334.

Scheepers, A. W. A. (1994). "Informatization in Street-Level Bureaucracies: Bureaucratic Competence and Discretion in Dutch Municipal Social Services Departments." *Information and the Public Sector 3*(1): 47-61.

Schuler, D. (1994). "Building a New Participatory Medium." *Communications of the ACM 37*(1): 39-51.

Sekiguchi, Y. and K. V. Andersen (1999). "Information Systems in Japanese Government." *Information Infrastructure and Policy 6*(3): 109-26.

Senior, B. (2002). *Organisational Change*. London, Prentice Hall, Financial Times Management.

Sepic, R. and K. Kase (2002). "The National Biological Information Infrastructure as an E-Government Tool." *Government Information Quarterly 19*(4): 407-424.

Serafeimidis, V. and S. Smithsson (2000). "Information Systems Evaluation in Practice." *Journal of Information Technology 15*(2): 93-105.

Shapiro, C. and H. R. Varian (1999). *Information Rules: A Strategic Guide to the Network Economy*. Boston, MA, Harvard Business School Press.

Shi, W. (2002). "The Contribution of Organizational Factors in the Success of Electronic Governnment Commerce." *International Journal of Public Administration 25*(5): 629-657.

Silcock, R. (2001). "What Is E-Government?" *Parliamentary Affairs 54*(1): 88-101.

Sinclair, T. P. (2001). "Implementation Theory and Practice: Uncovering Policy and Administration Linkages in the 1990s." *International Journal of Public Administration 24*(1): 77-94.

Singh, D. T. M. (2003). An E-Procurement Model and B2b Exchanges: An Australian Example. *Seeking Success in E-Business: A Multidisciplinary Approach.* K. V. Andersen, S. Elliot, P. Swatman, E. Trauth and N. Bjørn-Andersen. Amsterdam, Kluwer.

Smith, M. R. and L. Marx, Eds. (1994). *Does Technology Drive History? The Dilemma of Technological Determinism.* Cambridge, MA, MIT Press.

Smith, M. S., J. Bailey and E. Brynjolfsson (1999). Understanding Digital Markets: Review and Assessment. *Understanding the Digital Economy.* E. Brynjolfsson and B. Kahin, MIT Press.

Snellen, I. (2002). "Electronic Governance: Implications for Citizens, Politicians and Public Servants." *International Review of Administrative Sciences 68*(2): 183-198.

Snellen, I. T. M. (1994). "Automation of Policy Implementation." *Information and the Public Sector 3*(2): 135-148.

Snellen, I. T. M. and W. v. d. Donk (1998). *Public Administration in an Information Age: A Handbook.* Amsterdam, IOS Press.

Solomon, M. (2002). "Project Portfolio Management." *Computerworld 36*(12): 52.

SOS (2000). *Elder Care in Sweden.* Stockholm, The Swdish National Board of Health and Welfare. Accessed December 7 2003 at *http://www.sos.se/SOS/PUBL/REFERENG/0015004E.htm.*

Stabell, C. B. and O. D. Fjeldstad (1998). "Configuring Value for Competitive Advantage: On Chains, Shops and Networks." *Strategic Management Journal 19*: 413-437.

Stamoulis, D., D. Gouscos, P. Georgiadis, et al. (2001). "Revisiting Public Information Management for Effective E-Government Services." *Information Management & Computer Security 9*(4): 146.

Standishgroup (1994). *The Chaos Report.* Accessed March 15 2004 at *http://www.standishgroup.com/.*

Statistics-Denmark (2002). *Danske Kommuners Brug Af It 2002*, Statistics Denmark. Accessed May 29 2003 at *http://www.dst.dk/it.*

Statistics-Denmark (2003). *Befolkningens Brug Af Internet 2. Halvår 2003.* Copenhagen, Statistics Denmark. Accessed March 15 2004 at *http://www.dst.dk/it.*

Statistics-Denmark (2003). *Danske Kommuners Brug Af It 2003.* Copenhagen, Statistics-Denmark. Accessed May 29 2003 at *http://www.dst.dk/it.*

Stepney, P. (2000). *E-Governance: Weber's Revenge?* Political Studies Association - UK 50th Conference, London.

Steyaert, J. (2000). "Local Governments Online and the Role of the Resident: Government Shop Versus Electronic Community." *Social Science Computer Review 18*(1): 3-16.

Strejcek, G. and M. Theil (2003). "Technology Push, Legislation Pull? E-Government in the European Union." *Decision Support Systems 34*(3): 305-313.

Talero, E. (2001). *Overview of Electronic Government Procurement.* Washington, The World Bank Group. Accessed March 15 2004 at *http://www.worldbank.org/html/fpd/infrastructure/infraforum/presentations/e-procurement.pdf.*

Tan, C. W. and S. L. Pan (2003). "Managing E-Transformation in the Public Sector: An E-Government Study of the Inland Revenue Authority of Singapore (Iras)." *European Journal of Information Systems. 12*(4): 269-281.

Tapscott, D., Ed. (1999). *Creating Value in the Network Economy*. Harvard Business Review Book Series. Boston, MA, Harvard Business School Press.

Teo, Hock-Hai, Tan, et al. (1997). "Organizational Transformation Using Electronic Data Interchange: The Case of Tradenet in Singapore." *Journal of Management Information Systems 13*(4): 139-166.

Thai, K. V. and R. Grimm (2000). "Government Procurement: Past and Current Developments." *Journal of Public Budgeting, Accounting & Financial Management 12*(2): 231 - 247.

The-White-House (2001). *A Blueprint for New Beginnings: A Responsible Budget for America's Priorities*. Washington, The White House. Accessed March 15 2004 at *http://www.whitehouse.gov/news/usbudget/blueprint/budtoc.html*.

Thompson, C. S. (2002). "Enlisting on-Line Residents: Expanding the Boundaries of E-Government in a Japanese Rural Township." *Government Information Quarterly 19*(2): 173-188.

Thong, J. Y. L., C.-S. Yap and K.-L. Seah (2000). "Business Process Reengineering in the Public Sector: The Case of the Housing Development Board in Singapore." *Journal of Management Information Systems 17*(1): 245-271.

Tigre, P. B. (2003). "Brazil in the Age of Electronic Commerce." *The Information Society 19*(1): 33-44.

Tillman, B. (2003). "More Information Could Mean Less Privacy." *Information Management Journal 37*(2): 20.

Timmers, P. (2000). *Electronic Commerce: Strategies and Models for Business-to-Business Trading*. New York, Wiley.

UN (2003). World Public Sector Report: E-Government at the Crossroads. New York, United Nations.

Vagstad, S. (2000). "Centralized Vs. Decentralized Procurement: Does Dispersed Information Call for Decentralized Decision-Making?" *International Journal of Industry Organization 18*(6): 949-963.

Varshney, U. and R. J. Vetter (2000). "Emerging Mobile and Wireless Networks." *Communications of the ACM 43*(6): 73-81.

Watson, R. T. and B. Mundy (2001). "A Strategic Perspective of Electronic Democracy." *Communications of the ACM 44*(1): 27-30.

Weber, M. (1958). From Max Weber: Essays in Sociology. H. Gerth and C. W. Mills. New York, Oxford University Press.

Weick, K. E. (1969). *The Social Psychology of Organizing*. Reading, MA, Addison-Wesley.

Weick, K. E. (1989). "Theory Construction as Disciplined Imagination." *Academy of Management Review 14*(4): 516-531.

Weick, K. E. (1990). Technology as Equivoque: Sensemaking in New Technologies. *Technology and Organizations*. P. S. Goodman and L. S. Sproull. San Francisco, Jossey-Bass: 1-44.

Weick, K. E. (1995). *Sensemaking in Organizations*. Thousand Oaks, CA, Sage Publications.

Weikart, L. and P. J. Carlson (1998). "Implementing Computer Systems in the Face of Fiscal Scarcity: A Model for Technologically Frustrated Managers." *Public Productivity & Management Review 21*(3): 284-292.

Weizenbaum, J. (1976). *Computer Power and Human Reason*. Cambridge, MA, MIT Press.

Whetten, D. A. (1989). "What Constitutes a Theoretical Contribution?" *Academy of Management Review 14*(4): 490-495.

Whitson, T. L. and L. Davis (2001). "Best Practices in Electronic Government: Comprehensive Electronic Information Dissemination for Science and Technology." *Government Information Quarterly 18*(2): 79-91.

Wigand, R. T. (1995). "Electronic Markets and Virtual Value Chains on the Information Superhighway." *Sloan Management Review*: 2-72.

Wikipedia (2003). *Free Radical.* Accessed January 2 2004 at *http://en.wikipedia.org.*

Wildawsky, A. (1964). *The Politics of the Budgetary Process.* Boston, Little, Brown & Company.

Willcocks, L., Ed. (1994). *Information Management: The Evaluation of Information Systems Investments.* London, Chapman & Hall.

Willcocks, L. P., D. F. Feeny and G. Islei (1997). *Managing It as a Strategic Resource.* London, The McGraw-Hill Companies.

Williams, R. and D. Edge (1996). "The Social Shaping of Technology." *Research Policy 25*: 865-899.

Williamson, O. E. (1975). *Markets and Hierarchies.* New York, Free Press.

Wong, P. K. (2003). "Global and National Factors Affecting E-Commerce Diffusion in Singapore." *The Information Society 19*(1): 19-32.

World-Bank (2003). *E-Government Definition.* Washington, The World Bank. Accessed at *http://www1.worldbank.org/publicsector/egov/definition.htm.*

Yedla, S. and J. K. Parikh (2001). "Economic Evaluation of a Landfill System with Gas Recovery for Municipal Solid Waste Management: A Case Study." *Journal of Environment & Pollution 15*(4): 433-447.

Zeffane, R. (1994). "The Influence of Computer Usage on Employees and Managers' Satisfaction: Findings from the Australian Telecommunications." *Human Systems Management 13*(4): 269-282.

Zuboff, S. (1988). *In the Age of the Smart Machine.* New York, Basic Books.

Zuurmond, A. (1994). "From Bureaucracy to Infocracy: A Tale of Two Cities." *Information Infrastructure & Policy 3*(3/4): 189-204.